Leopold Wagner

Modern Political Orations

Leopold Wagner

Modern Political Orations

ISBN/EAN: 9783337133320

Printed in Europe, USA, Canada, Australia, Japan

Cover: Foto ©Suzi / pixelio.de

More available books at **www.hansebooks.com**

MODERN POLITICAL ORATIONS

CONTENTS.

———o———

	PAGE
LORD BROUGHAM ON NEGRO EMANCIPATION	1
T. B. MACAULAY ON THE PEOPLE'S CHARTER	24
W. J. FOX ON THE CORN LAWS	35
DANIEL O'CONNELL ON REPEAL OF THE UNION	41
R. L. SHEIL ON THE JEWISH DISABILITIES BILL	51
ALEXANDER COCKBURN ON THE GREEK DIFFICULTY	60
SIR BULWER LYTTON ON THE CRIMEAN WAR	77
THE EARL OF ELLENBOROUGH ON THE POLISH INSURRECTION	94
JOHN BRIGHT ON THE SUSPENSION OF THE HABEAS CORPUS ACT	101
THE RIGHT HON. ROBERT LOWE ON PARLIAMENTARY REFORM	113
THE RIGHT HON. GATHORNE HARDY ON THE IRISH CHURCH	140
EARL RUSSELL ON THE BALLOT	158
ISAAC BUTT ON HOME RULE	164
A. M. SULLIVAN ON THE IRISH NATIONAL DEMANDS	172
THE EARL OF BEACONSFIELD ON THE BERLIN CONGRESS	180
JOSEPH COWEN ON THE FOREIGN POLICY OF ENGLAND	190
THE RIGHT HON. W. E. GLADSTONE ON THE BEACONSFIELD MINISTRY	224

Contents.

	PAGE
CHARLES BRADLAUGH AT THE BAR OF THE HOUSE OF COMMONS	242
JUSTIN M'CARTHY IN DEFENCE OF HIS COLLEAGUES	249
LORD RANDOLPH CHURCHILL ON THE EGYPTIAN CRISIS	261
THE RIGHT HON. JOSEPH CHAMBERLAIN ON LIBERAL AIMS	267
CHAS. S. PARNELL ON THE COERCION BILL	283
THE RIGHT HON. JOHN MORLEY ON HOME RULE	292
RICHARD COBDEN ON THE CORN LAWS	311

APPENDIX.

I. "THE TIMES" ON "PARNELLISM AND CRIME"	329
II. ORIGINAL SOURCES OF THE SPEECHES	343

LORD BROUGHAM ON NEGRO EMANCIPATION.

House of Lords, February 20th, 1838.

[When the House assembled on this date, Lord Brougham, in a speech of singular power and earnestness, introduced this motion :—" That an humble address be presented to Her Majesty, earnestly beseeching Her Majesty to take immediate steps for negotiating with the Governments of Spain and Portugal, and obtaining the concurrence of the Governments of France and the United States in such negotiations, with a view to declare the trade in slaves piracy, wherever the same is carried on ; and making those who carry it on liable to all the pains and consequences of piracy." Anticipating a Mass Meeting in Exeter Hall, he also spoke at great length in favour of the abolition of Negro Apprenticeship.]

I do not think, my Lords, that ever but once before in the whole course of my public life I have risen to address either House of Parliament with the anxiety under which I labour at this moment. The occasion to which alone I can liken the present was when I stood up in the Commons to expose the treatment of that persecuted missionary, whose case gave birth to the memorable debate upon the condition of our negro brethren in the Colonies—a debate happily so fruitful of results to the whole of this great cause. But there is this difference between the two occasions to sustain my spirits now, that, whereas at the former period the horizon was all wrapt in gloom, through which not a ray of light pierced to cheer us, we have now emerged into a comparatively bright atmosphere, and are pursuing our journey full of hope. For this we have mainly to thank that important discussion, and those eminent men who bore in it so conspicuous a part. And now I feel a greater gratification in being the means of enabling your Lordships, by sharing in this great and glorious work, nay, by leading the way towards its final accomplishment, to increase the esteem in which you are held by your fellow-citizens; or if, by any differences of opinion on recent measures you may unhappily have lost any portion of the public favour, I know of no path more short, more sure, or more smooth, by which you may regain it. But I will not rest my right to your co-operation upon any such grounds as these. I claim your help by a higher title. I rely upon the justice of my cause—I rely upon the power of your consciences—I rely upon your duty to God and to man—I rely upon your consistency with yourselves—and, appealing to your own measure of 1833, if you be the same men in 1838, I call upon you to finish your own work, and give at length a full effect to the wise and Christian principles which then guided your steps.

I rush at once into the midst of this great argument—I drag before you once more, but I trust for the last time, the African Slave Trade which I lately denounced here, and have so often elsewhere. On this we are all agreed. Whatever difference of opinion may exist on the question of Slavery, on the Slave Traffic there can be none. I am now furnished with a precedent which may serve for an example to guide us. On Slavery, we have always held that the Colonial Legislature could not be trusted; that, to use Mr Canning's expression, you must beware of allowing the masters of slaves to make laws upon Slavery. But upon the detestable Traffic in Slaves, I can show you the proceeding of a Colonial Assembly, which we should ourselves do well to adopt after their example. These masters of slaves, not to be trusted on that subject, have acted well and wisely on this. The Legislature of Jamaica, owners of slaves, and representing all other slave owners, feel that they also represent the poor negroes themselves; and they approach the throne, expressing themselves thankful—tardily thankful, no doubt—that the traffic has been for thirty years put down in our own Colonies, and beseeching the Sovereign to consummate the great work by the only effectual means—of having it declared piracy by the law of nations, as it is robbery and piracy and murder by the law of God! This Address is precisely that which I desire your Lordships to present to the same Gracious Sovereign. After showing how heavily the Foreign Slave Trade presses upon their interests, they take higher ground in this remarkable passage—

> "Nor can we forego the higher position, as a question of humanity; representing all classes of the Island, we consider ourselves entitled to offer to your Majesty our respectful remonstrance against the continuance of this condemned traffic in human beings. As a community, composed of the descendants of Africa as well as Britain, we are anxious to advance the character of the country, and we therefore entreat your Majesty to exert your interest with foreign Powers to cause this trade at once to be declared piracy, as the only effectual means of putting it down, and thereby to grace the commencement of your auspicious reign."

My Lords, I will not stop to remind the lawgivers of Jamaica why it is that the Slave Traffic is a crime of so black a dye. I will not remind them that if Slavery were no more the Trade in Slaves must cease; that if the West Indies were like England, peopled with free men and cultivated only by free hands, where no man can hold his fellow-creature in bondage, and the labourer cannot be tormented by his masters; if the cart-whip having happily been destroyed, the doors of the prison-house were also flung open, and chains and bolts and collars were unknown, and no toil endured but by the workmen's consent, nor any effort extorted by dread of punishment; the traffic which we justly call not a trade but a crime, would no longer inflict the miseries with which it now loads its victims, who, instead of being conveyed to a place of torture and misery, would be carried into a land of liberty and enjoyment. Nor will I now pause to consider the wishes of some Colonies, in part, I am grieved to say, granted by the Government, that the means should be afforded them of bringing over what they call labourers from other parts of the globe, to share in the sufferings of slavery, hardly mitigated under the name of Apprenticeship. That you should ever join your voices with them on this matter is a thing so out of the question, that I will not detain you with any other remark upon it. But so neither have I any occasion to go at present into the subject of the Slave Trade altogether, after the statements which I lately made in this place upon the pernicious effects of our head money, the frightful extent of the negro traffic, and the horrible atrocities which mark its course still more awfully now than before. In order to support my claim upon your Lordships for the measure which alone can extirpate such enormities, I need but refer you to these statements. Since I presented them here, they have been made public, indeed, promulgated all over the kingdom, and they have met with no contradiction, nor excited the least complaint in any quarter, except that many have said the case was understated; and that in one place, and only in one, I have been charged with exaggeration. I have read with astonishment, and I repel with scorn the insinuation, that I had acted the part of an advocate, and that some of my statements were coloured to serve a cause. How dares any man so to accuse me? How dares any one, skulking under a fictitious name, to launch his slanderous imputations from his covert? I come forward in my own person. I make the charge in the face of day. I drag the criminal to trial. I openly call down justice on his head. I defy his attacks. I challenge investigation. How dares any concealed adversary to charge me as an advocate speaking from a brief, and misrepresenting the facts to serve a purpose?

But the absurdity of this charge even outstrips its malice. I stated that the negroes were thrown overboard in pairs during a chase, to lighten the ship and enable her to escape— thrown overboard in fetters, that they might sink, and not be witnesses against the murderers. The answer is, that this man, if man he be, had been on board slave ships, and never seen such cruelties. I stated that the fetters were not locked, but rivetted in the forge. The answer is, that the writer had been on board of slave ships, and seen fetters which were locked, and not rivetted. How dares any man deny a statement made upon authority, referred to by name, on such a trumpery story as this? As well might he argue that a murder, sworn to by fifty or a hundred credible witnesses, had never been committed, because someone came forward and said he had not seen it done. Did I not give the particulars? Did I not avouch my authority? Did I not name the gallant officer from whose official report, printed and published, my account was taken? Did I not give the respected name of Commodore Hayes, one of the best-esteemed officers in Her Majesty's Service? I, indeed, understated the case in many particulars. But, my Lords, if I have not been chargeable with exaggeration—if all who took part in the former debate, whether in or out of office, agreed in acquitting me of that—so neither shall I be charged for the future with understating the atrocities of the case. What I then withheld I will now tell—and not keeping back my authority now any more than I did before, I appeal to my noble friend near me (Lord Sligo) for the truth of the appalling story, himself a planter and an owner of slaves. I ask him if he did not know a vessel brought in with a cargo of 180 or 200 wretched beings, jammed into a space three feet and a half in height. [LORD SLIGO.—Two and a half.] There, my Lords, I am understating again. Into that space of two feet and a half between the decks, that number of miserable creatures were jammed, like inanimate lumber, certainly in a way in which no Christian man would crowd dumb animals. My noble friend will say whether or not that vessel, whose slaves had never been released, or even washed, or in any way cleansed, since it left the African coast, presented an intolerable nuisance to all the senses—a nuisance unfit for any description. Nor is this all. I will be chargeable with understatements no more! The ophthalmia had broken out among the poor creatures thus kept in unspeakable torment; and as often as anyone was seized, instead of affording him any medical or other assistance, he was instantly cast overboard, and sunk in his chains, with the view of stopping the infection. I will understate things no more! I said before that as many as 700 slaves were carried across the sea in one ship; there I stopped, for to those who know what a slave ship is, this suffices to harrow up every feeling of the soul. But another vessel brought away, first and last, in one voyage, 980 miserable, unoffending, simple beings; and of this number, without any chase or accident, or violence, or any acts of wholesale murder such as those we have been contemplating, 600 perished on the voyage, through the hardships and sufferings inseparably connected with this execrable traffic. Of 2,300 or 2,400 carried away by our other ships, no less than 1,500 perished in like manner, having fallen a sacrifice to the pestilential hold.

How this enormous crime of these foreign nations is to be rooted out, I know full well. You must no longer treat it as a mere contraband trade—no longer call murder smuggling, or treat pirates as offenders against the revenue laws. As long as our slave traders were so dealt with, they made this calculation—"If we escape three times in four, our profits are so large that the seizure and confiscation can well be afforded; nay, if we are taken as often as we escape, the ships netting £20,000, £30,000, even as much as £50,000 and £60,000 a voyage, we can well afford to lose £1,500 or £2,000 when the adventure fails." So they ran the risk, and on a calculation of profit and loss were fully justified. But I had in 1811 the singular happiness of laying the axe to the root of this detestable system. I stopped all these calculations by making the trade felony, and punishing it as such; for well I knew that they who would run the risk of capture, when all they could suffer by it was a diminution of their profits, would be slow to put their heads in the noose of the halter which their crimes so richly deserved. The measure passed through all its stages in both Houses without one dissenting voice; and I will venture to assert that ever since, although English capital, I have too much reason to think, finds its way into the Foreign Slave Trade, no Englishman is concerned directly with it in any part of the world. Trust me, the like course must be taken if we would put an end to the same crimes in other countries; piracy and murder must be called by their right names, and visited with their appropriate penalties. That the Spanish and Portuguese traders now make the same calculations which I have been describing, is a certain fact. I will name one— Captain Inza, of the ship *Socorra*, who, on being captured, had the effrontery to boast that he had made fourteen slave voyages, and that this was the first time he had been taken. Well might he resolve to run so slight a risk for such vast gains; but had the fate of a felon pirate awaited him, not all the gains which might tempt his sordid nature would have prevailed upon him to encounter that hazard. I formerly recounted instances of murder done by wholesale in the course of the chase of our cruisers. I might have told a more piteous tale, and I will no longer be accused of understating this part of the case either. Two vessels were pursued. One after another, negroes were seen to be thrown overboard to the number of a hundred and fifty, of all ages—the elder and stronger ones loaded with their fetters to prevent them from swimming or floating, the weaker were left unchained to sink or expire; and this horrible spectacle was presented to the eyes of our cruisers' men; they saw, unable to lend any help, the water covered with these hapless creatures, the men sinking in their chains; the women and—piteous sight!—the infants and children struggling out their little strength in the water till they, too, were swallowed up and disappeared.

I now approach a subject, not, indeed, more full of horrors, or of greater moment, but on which the attention of the people has for some time past been fixed with an almost universal anxiety, and for your decision upon which they are now looking with the most intense interest, let me add, with the liveliest hopes. I need not add that I mean the great question of the condition into which the slaves of our Colonies were transferred as preparatory to their complete liberation — a subject upon which your table has been loaded with so many petitions from millions of your fellow-countrymen. It is right that I should first remind your Lordships of the anxious apprehensions which were entertained in 1833, when the Act was passed, because a comparison of those fears with the results of the measure will form a most important ingredient of the argument which I am about to urge for the immediate liberation of the apprentices. I well remember how uneasy all were looking forward to the 1st of August, 1834, when the state of slavery was to cease, and I myself shared in those feelings of alarm when I contemplated the possible event of the vast but yet untried experiment. My fears proceeded first from the character of the masters. I knew the nature of man, fond of power, jealous of any interference with its exercise, uneasy at its being questioned, offended at its being regulated and constrained, averse, above all, to have it wrested from its hands, especially after it has been long enjoyed, and its possession can hardly be severed from his nature. But I also was aware of another and a worser part of human nature. I knew that whoso has abused power, clings to it with a yet more convulsive grasp. I dreaded the nature of man, prone to hate whom he has injured; because I knew that law of human weakness which makes the oppressor hate his victim, makes him who has injured never forgive, fills the wrongdoer with vengeance against those whose right it is to vindicate those injuries on his own head. I knew that this abominable law of our evil nature was not confined to different races, contrasted hues, and strange features, but prevailed also between white man and white—for I never yet knew anyone hate me but those whom I had served, and those who had done me some grievous injustice. Why then should I expect other feelings to burn within the planter's bosom, and govern his conduct towards the unhappy beings who had suffered so much and so long at his hands? But, on the part of the slaves, I was not without some anxiety when I considered the corrupting effects of that degrading system under which they had for ages groaned, and recognised the truth of the saying in the first and the earliest of profane poets, that "the day which makes a man a slave robs him of half his value." I might well think that the West Indian slave offered no exception to this maxim, that the habit of compulsory labour might have incapacitated him from voluntary exertion; that overmuch toil might have made all work his aversion; that never having been accustomed to provide for his own wants, while all his supplies were furnished by others, he might prove unwilling or unfit to work for himself, the ordinary inducements to industry never having operated on his mind. In a word, it seemed unlikely that long disuse of freedom might have rendered him too familiar with his chains to set a right value on liberty, or that, if he panted to be free, the sudden transition from the one state to the other, the instantaneous enjoyment of the object of his desires, might prove too strong for his uncultured understanding; might overset his principles, and render him dangerous to the public peace. Hence it was that I entertained some apprehensions of the event, and yielded reluctantly to the plan proposed of preparing the negroes for the enjoyment of perfect freedom by passing them through the intermediate state of Indentured Apprenticeship.

Let us now see the results of their sudden though partial liberation, and how far those fears have been realised; for upon this must entirely depend the solution of the present question—Whether or not it is safe now to complete the Emancipation which, if it only be safe, we have not the shadow of right any longer to withhold. Well, then, let us see. The 1st of August came, the object of so much anxiety and so many predictions—that day so joyously expected by the poor slaves, so sorely dreaded by their hard taskmasters; and surely, if there ever was a picture interesting, even fascinating, to look upon, if there ever was a passage to a people's history that redounded to their eternal honour, if ever triumphant answer was given to all the scandalous calumnies for ages heaped upon an oppressed race, as if to justify the wrongs done them, that picture, and that passage, and that answer were exhibited in the uniform history of that auspicious day all over the islands of the Western Sea. Instead of the horizon being lit up with the lurid fires of rebellion, kindled by a sense of natural though lawless revenge, and the just resistance to intolerable oppression, the whole of that wide-spread scene was mildly illuminated with joy, contentment, peace, and goodwill towards men. No civilised nation, no people of the most refined character, could have displayed, after gaining a sudden and signal victory, more forbearance, more delicacy, in the enjoyment of their triumph, than these poor untutored slaves did upon the great consummation of all their wishes which they had just attained. Not a gesture or a look was seen to scare the eye—not a sound or a breath from the negro's lips was heard to grate on the ear of the planter. All was joy, congratulation, and hope. Everywhere were to be seen groups of these harmless folks assembled to talk over their good fortunes, to communicate their mutual feelings of happiness, to speculate on their future prospects. Finding that they were now free in name, they hoped soon to taste the reality of liberty. Feeling their fetters loosened, they looked forward to the day which should see them fall off, and the degrading marks which they left be effaced from their limbs. But all this was accompanied with not a whisper that could give offence to the master by reminding him of the change. This delicate, calm, tranquil joy was alone to be marked on that day over all the chain of the Antilles. Amusements there were none to be seen on that day—not even their simple pastimes by which they had been wont to beguile the hard hours of bondage, and which reminded that innocent people of the happy land of their forefathers, whence they had been torn by the hands of Christian and civilised men. The day was kept sacred as the festival of their liberation, for the negroes are an eminently pious race. Every church was crowded from early dawn with devout and earnest worshippers. Five or six times in the course of that memorable Friday were all those churches filled and emptied in succession by multitudes, who came, not to give mouth-worship or eye-worship, but to render humble and hearty thanks to God for their freedom at length bestowed. In countries where the bounty of nature provokes the passions, where the fuel of intemperance is scattered with a profuse hand, I speak the fact when I tell that not one negro was seen in a state of intoxication. Three hundred and forty thousand slaves in Jamaica were at once set free on that day, and the peaceful festivity of those simple men was disturbed only on a single estate, in one parish, by the irregular conduct of three or four persons, who were immediately kept in order, and tranquillity was in one hour restored.

But the termination of slavery was to be an end of all labour; no man would work unless compelled; much less would anyone work for hire. The cart-whip was to resound no more, and no more could exertion be obtained from the indolent African. I set the past against these predictions. I have never been in the West Indies; I was one of those whom, under the name of reasoners, and theorists, and visionaries, all planters pitied for incurable ignorance on Colonial affairs; one of those who were forbidden to meddle with matters of which they could only judge who had the practical knowledge of experienced men on the spot obtained. Therefore I now appeal to the fact—and I also appeal to one who has been to the West Indies, is himself a planter, and was an eye-witness of the things upon which I call for his confirmatory testimony. It is to my noble friend (Lord Sligo) that I appeal. He knows, for he saw, that ever since slavery ceased, there has been no want of inclination to work in any part of Jamaica, and that labour for hire is now to be had without the least difficulty by all who can afford to pay wages, the apprentices cheerfully working for those who will pay them during the hours not appropriated to their masters. My noble friend made an inquisition as to the state of this important matter in a large part of his government; and I have his authority for stating that, in nine estates out of ten, labourers for hire were to be had without the least difficulty. Yet this was the people of whom we were told, with a confidence that set all contradiction at defiance, with an insulting pity for the ignorance of us who had no local experience, that without the lash there could be no work done, and that, when it ceased to vex him, the African would sink into sleep. The prediction is found to have been ridiculously false; the negro peasantry is as industrious as our own, and wages furnish more effectual stimulus than the scourge. Oh, but, said the men of Colonial experience—the true practical men—this may do for some kinds of produce. Cotton may be planted, coffee may be picked, indigo may be manufactured—all these kinds of work the negro may probably be got to do; but, at least, the cane will cease to grow, the cane-piece can no longer be hoed, nor the plant be hewn down, nor the juice boiled, and sugar will utterly cease out of the land. Now let the man of experience stand forward—the practical man, the inhabitant of the Colonies—I require that he now come forth with his prediction, and I meet him with the fact; let him but appear, and I answer for him, we shall hear him prophesy no more. Put to silence by the past, which even these confident men have not the courage to deny, they will at length abandon this untenable ground. Twice as much sugar by the hour were found, on my noble friend's inquiry, to be made since the apprenticeship, as under the slave system, and of a far better quality; and one planter on a vast scale has said that. with twenty free labourers he could do the work of a hundred slaves. But linger not on the islands where the gift of freedom has been but half bestowed. Look at Antigua and Bermuda, where the wisdom and the virtue have been displayed of at once giving Complete Emancipation. To Montserrat the same appeal might have been made, but for the folly of the Upper House, which threw out the Bill passed in the Assembly by the representatives of the planters. But in Antigua and in Bermuda, where for the last three years and a half there has not even been an apprentice—where all have been at once made as free as the peasantry of this country—the produce has increased, not diminished, and increased notwithstanding the accidents of bad seasons, droughts, and fires.

My Lords, I have proved my case, and may now call for judgment. I have demonstrated every part of the proposition, which alone it is necessary that I should maintain, to prove the title of the apprentice to instant freedom from his taskmasters, because I have demonstrated that the liberation of the slave has been absolutely, universally safe—attended with not even inconvenience—nay, productive of ample benefits to his master. I have shown that the apprentice works without compulsion, and that the reward of wages are a better incentive than the punishment of the lash. I have proved that labour for hire may anywhere be obtained as it is wanted, and can be purchased. All the apprentices working extra hours for hire, and all the free negroes, wherever their emancipation has been complete, worked harder by much for the masters who have wherewithal to pay them, than the slave can toil for his owner, or the apprentice for his master. Whether we look to the noble-minded Colonies which have at once freed their slaves, or to those who still retain them in a middle and half-free condition, I have shown that the industry of the negro is undeniable, and that it is constant and productive in proportion as he is the director of its application and the master of its recompense. But I have gone a great deal further—I have demonstrated by a reference to the same experience, the same unquestioned facts—that a more quiet, peaceful, inoffensive, innocent race is not to be found on the face of this earth than the Africans—not while dwelling in their own happy country, and enjoying freedom in a natural state under their own palm trees and by their native streams—but after they have been torn away from it, enslaved, and their nature perverted in your Christian land, barbarised by the policy of civilised states; their whole character disfigured, if it were possible to disfigure it, all their feelings corrupted, if you could have corrupted them. Every effort has been made to spoil the poor African, every source of wicked ingenuity exhausted to deprave his nature, all the incentives of misconduct placed around him by the fiend-like artifice of Christian civilised men, and his excellent nature has triumphed over all your arts; your unnatural culture has failed to make it bear the poisonous fruit that might well have been expected from such abominable husbandry, though enslaved and tormented, degraded and debased, as far as human industry could effect its purpose of making him bloodthirsty and savage, his gentle spirit has prevailed, and preserved, in spite of all your prophecies, aye, and of all your efforts, unbroken tranquillity over the whole Charaibean chain!

Have I not proved my case? I show you that the whole grounds of the arrangement of 1833, the very pretext for withholding Complete Emancipation—alleged incapacity for labour and risk of insurrection—utterly fail. I rely on your own records; I refer to that record which cannot be averred against. I plead the record of your own Statute. On what ground does its preamble rest the necessity of the intermediate or apprentice state, all admitting that nothing but necessity would justify it?—

"Whereas it is expedient that provision should be made, promoting the industry and securing the good conduct of the manumitted slaves."

Those are the avowed reasons for the measure, those its only defence. All men confessed that were it not for the apprehension of liberated slaves not working voluntarily, and not behaving peaceably, of slavery being found to have unfitted them for industry, and of a sudden transition to perfect freedom being fraught with danger to the peace of society, you had no right to make them indentured apprentices, and must at once get them wholly free. But the fear prevailed, which, by the event, I have now a right to call a delusion; and the apprenticeship was reluctantly agreed to. The delusion went further. The planter succeeded in persuading us that he would be a vast loser by the change, and we gave him twenty millions sterling money to indemnify him for the supposed loss. The fear is found to be utterly baseless, the loss is a phantom of the brain, a shape conjured up by the interested parties to frighten our weak minds, and the only reality in this mockery is the payment of that enormous sum to the crafty and fortunate magician for his incantations. The spell is dissolved, the charm is over, the unsubstantial fabric of calculating alarm, reared by the Colonial body with our help, has been crushed to atoms, and its fragments scattered to the world. And now, I ask, suppose it had been ascertained in 1833, when you made the Apprenticeship law, that those alarms were absolutely groundless, the mere phantom of a sick brain, or contrivance of a sordid ingenuity, would a single voice have been raised in favour of the intermediate state? Would the words Indentured Apprenticeship ever have been pronounced? Would the man have been found endued with the courage to call for keeping the negro in chains one hour after he had been acknowledged entitled to his freedom?

My Lords, I cannot better prove the absolute necessity of putting an immediate end to the state of apprenticeship than by showing what the victims of it are daily fated to endure. The punishments inflicted are of monstrous severity. The law is wickedly harsh; its execution is committed to hands that exasperate that cruelty. For the vague, undefined, undefinable offence of insolence, thirty-nine lashes; the same number for carrying a knife in the pocket; for cutting the shoot of a cane-plant, fifty lashes, or three months' imprisonment in that most loathsome of all dungeons, a West Indian gaol. There seems to have prevailed at all times, among the law-givers of the slave colonies, a feeling of which I grieve to say those of the Mother country have partaken; that there is something in the nature of a slave, something in the disposition of the African race, something in the habits of those hapless victims of our crimes, our cruelties, and frauds, which requires a peculiar harshness of treatment from their rulers, and makes what in other men's cases we call justice and mercy cruelty to Society, and injustice to the law in theirs, inducing us to visit with the extremity of rigour in the African what if done by our own tribes would be slightly visited, or not at all, as though there were in the negro nature something so obdurate that no punishment with which they can be punished would be too severe. Prodigious, portentous injustice! As if we had a right to blame any but ourselves for whatever there may be of harsh or cunning in our slaves; as if we were entitled to visit upon him that disposition, were it obdurate—those habits, were they insubordinate—those propensities were they dishonest (all of which I deny them to be, and every day's experience justifies my denial); but were those charges as true as they are foully slanderous, and absolutely false, is it for us to treat our victims harshly for failings or for faults with which our treatment of him has corrupted and perverted his nature, instead of taking to ourselves the blame, punishing ourselves at least with self-abasement, and atoning with deepest shame for having implanted vice in a pure soil? If some capricious despot were, in the career of ordinary tyranny, to tax his pampered fancy to produce something more monstrous, more unnatural than himself; were he to graft the thorn upon the vine, or place the dove among vultures to be reared, much as we might marvel at this freak of a perverted appetite, we should marvel still more if we saw tyranny, even its own measure of proverbial unreasonableness, and complain because the grape was not gathered from the thorn, or because the dove so trained had a thirst for blood. Yet this is the unnatural caprice, this the injustice, the gross, the foul, the outrageous, the monstrous, the incredible injustice of which we are daily and hourly guilty towards the whole of the ill-fated African race!

My Lords, we fill up the measure of this injustice by executing laws wickedly conceived, in a yet more atrocious spirit of cruelty. Our whole punishments smell of blood. Let the treadmill stop, from the weary limbs and exhausted frames of the sufferers no longer having the power to press it down the requisite number of turns in a minute—the lash instantly resounds through the mansion of woe! Let the stone spread out to be broken, not crumble fast enough beneath the arms already scarred, flayed, and wealed by the whip—again the scourge tears afresh the half-healed flesh! My Lords, I have had my attention directed within the last two hours to the new mass of papers laid on our table from the West Indies. The bulk I am averse to break, but a sample I have culled from its hateful contents. Eleven females were punished by severe flogging, and then put on the treadmill, where they were compelled to ply until exhausted nature could do no more. When faint, and about to fall off, they were suspended by the arms in such a manner that has been described to me by a most respectable eye-witness of similar scenes, but not so suspended as that the mechanism could revolve clear of their person; for the wheel at each turn bruised and galled their legs, till their sufferings had reached the pitch when life can no longer even glimmer in the socket of the weary frame. In the course of a few days these wretched beings languished, to use the language of our law —that law which is so constantly and systematically violated— and "languishing, died." Ask you if crimes like these, murderous in their legal nature, as well as frightful in their aspect, passed unnoticed; if inquiry was neglected to be made respecting those deaths in a prison? No such thing! The forms of justice were on this head peremptory even in the West Indies, and those forms, the handmaids of justice, were present, though their sacred mistress was far away. The coroner duly attended, his jury were regularly empannelled; eleven inquisitions were made in order, and eleven verdicts returned. Murder? Manslaughter? Misdemeanour? Misconduct? No! but "Died by the visitation of God!" Died by the visitation of God! A lie!—a perjury!—a blasphemy! The visitation of God! Yes; for it is among the most awful of these visitations by which the inscrutable purposes of His will are mysteriously accomplished, that He sometimes arms the wicked with power to oppress the guiltless; and if there be any visitation more dreadful than another—any which more tries the faith and vexes the reason of erring mortals—it is when Heaven showers down upon the earth the plague—not of scorpions, or pestilence, or famine, or war—but of unjust judges or perjured jurors—wretches who pervert the law to wreak their personal vengeance or compass their sordid ends, and forswear themselves on the gospels of God, to the end that injustice may prevail, and the innocent be destroyed—

> "Sed non immensum Spatiis confecimus æquor
> Et jam tempus equis formantia soluere colla."

I hasten to a close. There remains little to add. It is, my Lords, with a view to prevent such enormities as I have feebly pictured before you, to correct the administration of justice, to secure the comforts of the negroes, to restrain the cruelty of the tormentors, to amend the discipline of the prisons, to arm the governors with local authority over the police; it is with those views that I have formed the first five of the resolutions now upon your table, intending they should take effect during the very short interval of a few months which must elapse before the sixth shall give complete liberty to the slave. I entirely concur in the observation of Mr Burke, repeated and more happily expressed by Mr Canning, that the masters of slaves are not to be trusted with making laws upon slavery; that nothing they do is ever found effectual; and that if by some miracle they even chance to enact a wholesome regulation, it is always found to want what Mr Burke calls "the executory principle"; it fails to execute itself. But experience has shown that when the law-givers of the Colonies find you are firmly determined to do your duty, they anticipate you by doing theirs. Thus, when you announced the Bill for amending the Emancipation Act, they outstripped you in Jamaica, and passed theirs before you could reach them. Let then your resolutions only show you to be in good earnest now, and I have no doubt a corresponding disposition will be evinced on the other side of the Atlantic. These improvements are, however, only to be regarded as temporary expedients—as mere palliatives of an enormous mischief, for which the only efficient remedy is that Complete Emancipation which I have demonstrated by the unerring and incontrovertible evidence of facts, as well as the clearest deductions of reason, to be safe and practicable, and therefore proved to be our imperative duty at once to proclaim.

From the instant that glad sound is wafted across the ocean, what a blessed change begins; what an enchanting prospect unfolds itself! The African, placed on the same footing with other men, becomes in reality our fellow-citizen—to our feelings, as well as in his own nature, our equal, our brother. No difference of origin or colour can now prevail to keep the two castes apart. The negro, master of his own labour, only induced to lend his assistance if you make it his interest to help you; yet that aid being absolutely necessary to preserve your existence, becomes an essential portion of the community, nay, the very portion upon which the whole must lean for support. This ensures him all his rights; this makes it not only no longer possible to keep him in thraldom, but places him in a complete and intimate union with the whole mass of Colonial society. Where the driver and the gaoler once bore sway, the lash resounds no more, nor does the clank of the chain any more fall upon the troubled ear; the fetter has ceased to gall the vexed limb, and the very mark disappears which for a while it had left. All races and colours run together the same glorious race of improvement. Peace unbroken, harmony uninterrupted, calm unruffled, reigns in mansion and in field, in the busy street and the fertile valley, where nature, with the lavish hand she extends under the tropical sun, pours forth all her bounty profusely, because received in the lap of cheerful industry, not extorted by hands cramped with bonds. Delightful pictures of general prosperity and social progress in all the arts of civility and refinement!

But another form is near!—and I may not shut my eyes to that less auspicious vision! I do not deny that danger exists—I admit it to be not far distant from our path. I descry it, but not in the quarter to which West Indian eyes for ever turn. The planter, as usual, looks in the wrong direction. Averting his eyes from the real risk, he is ready to pay the price of his blindness, and rush upon his ruin. His interest tells him he is in jeopardy, but it is a false interest, and misleads him as to the nature of the risk he runs. They who always dreaded Emancipation, who were alarmed at the prospect of negro indolence, who stood aghast at the vision of negro rebellion, should the chains cease to rattle, or the lash to resound through the air, gathering no wisdom from the past, still persist in affrighting themselves and scaring you with imaginary apprehensions from the transition to entire freedom out of the present intermediate state. But that intermediate state is the very source of all their real danger; and I disguise not its magnitude from myself. You have gone too far if you stop here and go no further; you are in imminent hazard if, having loosened the fetters, you do not strike them off; if, leaving them ineffectual to restrain, you let them remain to fall, and to irritate, and to goad. Beware of that state yet more unnatural than slavery itself—liberty bestowed by halves—the power of resistance given—the inducement to submission withheld. You have let the slave taste of the cup of freedom; while intoxicated with the draught, beware how you dash the cup away from his lips! You have produced the progeny of liberty — see the prodigious hazard of swathing the limbs of the gigantic infant; you know not the might that may animate it. Have a care, I beseech you, have a care how you rouse the strength that slumbers in the sable peasant's arm! The children of Africa under the tropical sun of the West, with the prospect of a free negro republic in sight, will not suffer themselves to be tormented when they no longer can be controlled. The fire in St Domingo is raging to windward, its sparks are borne on the breeze, and all the Charaibean Sea is studded with the materials of explosion. Every tribe, every shade of the negro race will combine, from the fiery Koromantin to the peaceful Oboe, and the ghastly shape of the Colonial destruction meets the astonished eye—

> "If shape it may be called, that shape has none
> Distinguishable in member, joint, or limb;
> Or substance may be called that shadow seems;
> For each seems either. Black it stood as night,
> Fierce as ten furies, terrible as Hell!"

I turn from the horrid vision, that my eye may rest once more on the prospect of enduring empire and peace founded upon freedom. I regard the freedom of the negro as accomplished and sure. Why? Because it is his right, because he has shown himself fit for it, because a pretext or a shadow of a pretext can no longer be devised for withholding that right from its possessor. I know that all men at this day take a part in the question, and they will no longer bear to be imposed upon now they are well informed. My reliance is firm and unflinching upon the great change which I have witnessed—the education of the people unfettered by party or by sect—witnessed from the beginning of its progress, I may say from the hour of its birth. Yes! It was not for a humble man like me to assist at royal births with the illustrious Prince who condescended to grace the pageant of this opening Session, or the great Captain and Statesman in whose presence I am now proud to speak. But with that illustrious Prince, and with the father of the Queen, I assisted at that other birth, more auspicious still. With them, and with the head of the house of Russell, incomparably more illustrious in my eyes, I watched over its cradle—I marked its growth—I rejoiced in its strength—I witnessed its maturity—I have been spared to see it ascend the very height of supreme power, directing the Councils of State, accelerating every great improvement, uniting itself with every good work, propping all useful institutions, extirpating abuses in all our institutions, passing the bounds of our European dominion, and in the New World as in the Old, proclaiming that freedom is the birthright of man; that distinction of colour gives no title to oppression; that the chains now loosened must be struck off, and even the marks they have left effaced—proclaiming this by the same eternal law of our nature which makes nations the masters of their own destiny, and which in Europe has caused every tyrant's throne to quake! But they need feel no alarm at the progress of light who defend a limited monarchy and support popular institutions, who place their chiefest pride not in ruling over slaves, be they white or be they black, not in protecting the oppressor, but in wearing a constitutional crown, in holding the sword of justice with a hand of mercy, in being the first citizen of a country whose air is too pure for slavery to breathe, and on whose shores, if the captive's foot but touch, his fetters of themselves fall off. To the resistless progress of this great principle I look with a confidence which nothing can shake. It makes all improvement certain; it makes all change safe which it produces, for none can be brought about, unless all has been prepared in a cautious and salutary spirit.

So now the fulness of time is come for at length discharging our duty to the African captive. I have demonstrated to you that everything is ordered—every previous step taken—all safe, by experience shown to be safe, for the long-desired consummation. The time has come, the trial has been made, the hour is striking; you have no longer a pretext for hesitation, or faltering, or delay. The slave has shown, by four years' blameless behaviour and devotion to the pursuits of peaceful industry, that he is as fit for his freedom as any English peasant, aye, or any Lord whom I now address. I demand his rights; I demand his liberty without stint. In the name of justice and of law, in the name of reason, in the name of God, who has given you no right to work injustice, I demand that your brother be no longer trampled upon as your slave! I make my appeal to the Commons, who represent the free people of England, and I require at their hands the performance of that condition for which they paid so enormous a price—that condition which all their constituents are in breathless anxiety to see fulfilled! I appeal to this House! Hereditary judges of the first tribunal in the world, to you I appeal for justice! Patrons of all the arts that humanise mankind, under your protection I place humanity herself! To the merciful Sovereign of a free people, I call aloud for mercy to the hundreds of thousands for whom half a million of her Christian sisters have cried out; I ask that their cry may not have risen in vain. But, first, I turn my eye to the Throne of all justice, and devoutly humbling myself before Him who is of purer eyes than to behold such vast iniquities, I implore that the curse hovering over the head of the unjust and the oppressor be averted from us, that your hearts may be turned to mercy, and that over all the earth His will may at length be done!

T. B. MACAULAY[1] ON THE PEOPLE'S CHARTER.

House of Commons, May 3rd, 1842.

[On this date Mr Thomas Duncombe, the member for Finsbury, moved that the petitioners of the document entitled "The People's Charter," presented by him on the previous day, be allowed to be heard at the Bar of the House. Mr Macaulay vigorously opposed the motion, which was rejected by 287 votes to 49.]

Sir,—I am particularly desirous of saying a few words upon this question, because upon a former evening, when a discussion took place upon a motion of the hon. member for Rochdale (Mr W. S. Crawford), I was prevented from being in my place by accidental circumstances. I know that the absence of some of the members of the late Government on that occasion was considered and spoken of as exhibiting in their minds an inattention to this subject, or a want of sympathy for the interests of the humbler classes of the people of this country. For myself, I can answer that I was compelled to absent myself on account of temporary indisposition. A noble friend of mine, to whose absence particular allusion was made, was prevented from attending the House by purely accidental circumstances; and no member of the late Administration, I am persuaded, was withheld by any unworthy motives from stating his opinions on this subject. In the observations which I shall now make to the House, I shall attempt to imitate, as far as I can, the very proper temper of the speech of the right hon. baronet,

---

[1] Afterwards Baron Macaulay.

the Secretary of State for the Home Department (Sir James Graham); but if I should be betrayed into the use of any expressions not entirely consistent with a calm view of the question, the House will attribute it to the warmth with which I view the subject generally, and no one who is acquainted with my feelings will attribute it to any want of kindness or of good will towards those who have signed the petition which has been presented to the House.

With regard to the motion which has been made, I cannot conscientiously vote for it. The hon. member for Finsbury (Mr T. Duncombe) has shaped the motion with considerable skill, so as to give me a very fair plea to vote for it, if I wished to evade the discharge of my duty, so that I might say to my Conservative constituents: "I never supported Universal Suffrage on those extreme points for which these petitioners call;" or to a large assembly of Chartists: "When your case was before the Commons, on that occasion I voted with you." But I think that in a case so important, I should not discharge my duty if I had recourse to any such evasion, and I feel myself compelled to meet the motion with a direct negative. And it seems to me that if we depart from our ordinary rule of not hearing persons at the bar of this House under circumstances of this nature, it must be understood, by our adopting such a course, if not that we are decidedly favourable to the motion which is made, at least that we have not fully made up our minds to resist what the petitioners ask. For my own part, my mind is made up in opposition to their prayer, and, being so, I conceive that the House might complain of me, and that the petitioners might also complain of me, if I were to give an untrue impression of my views by voting in favour of this motion; and I think that if I took such a course, and in three or four years hence I gave a distinct negative to every one, or to the most important clauses of the Charter, there would be much reason to complain of my disingenuousness. An accusation founded upon such grounds, I shall, if I can, prevent their bringing against me.

In discussing this question I do not intend, as the right hon. member for Westminster (Mr J. T. Leader) has suggested, to deal with the contents of the petition with any degree of harshness. To the terms of it I can scarcely allude, but to the essence of it I must refer; and I cannot but see that what the petitioners demand is that we should immediately, without alteration, deduction, or addition, pass the Charter into a law; and when the hon. member for Finsbury calls on the House to hear persons in support of the prayer of the petition at the bar, I say that if he can contend that the object of that inquiry will be to investigate causes of the public distress, by all means let the motion be carried; I will not oppose it. But when I see that the petitioners send to this House, demanding that a particular law shall be passed, without addition, deduction, or modification, and that immediately, and that they demand that persons shall be heard at the bar of the House in favour of that law, I say that to allege that the only object of the inquiry is to ascertain the causes of public distress is a paltering with the question to which the House will pay no attention. There are parts of the Charter to which I am favourable, for which I have voted, which I would always support; and in truth, of all the six points of the Charter, there is only one to which I entertain extreme and unmitigated hostility. I have voted for the ballot. With regard to the proposition that there should be no property qualification required for members of this House, I cordially agree, for I think that where there is a qualification of property required for the constituent body, a qualification for the representative is altogether superfluous. And it is absurd, that while the members for Edinburgh and Glasgow are required to have no property qualification, the hon. member for Marylebone or Finsbury must possess such a qualification. I say that if the principle is to be adopted at all, let it be of universal application; if it be not so, let it be abandoned. It is no part of the Constitution of the kingdom that such a qualification should be required; nor is it a part of the consequences of the Revolution; but, after all, it was introduced by a bad Parliament, now held in no high esteem, and for the purpose of defeating the Revolution, and excluding the Protestant succession to the Crown. With regard to the other points of the Charter, I cannot support the proposition for annual Parliaments, but I should be willing to meet the wishes of the petitioners by limiting their duration to a shorter period than that for which they may now endure. But I do not go the length of the Charter, because there is one point which is its essence, which is so important that if you withhold it nothing can produce the smallest effect in taking away the agitation which prevails, but which, if you grant, it matters not what else you grant, and that is universal suffrage, or suffrage without any qualification of property at all. Considering that as by far the most important part of the Charter, and having a most decided opinion that such a change would be utterly fatal to the country, I feel it my duty to say that I cannot hold out the least hope that I shall ever, under any circumstances, support that change.

The reasons for this opinion I will state as shortly as I can. And, in the first place, I beg to say that I entertain this view upon no ground of finality; indeed, the remarks which I have already made preclude such a supposition, but I do admit my belief that violent and frequent changes in the government of a country are not desirable. Every great change, I think, should be judged on its own merits. I am bound by no tie to oppose any legislative reform which I really believe will conduce to the public benefit; but I think that that which has been brought forward as an undoubted and conclusive argument against a change of this sort, that it is perfectly inconsistent with the continuance of the monarchy or of the House of Lords, has been much overstated. And this I say, though I profess myself a most faithful subject to Her Majesty, and by no means anxious to destroy the connection which exists between the monarchy, the aristocracy, and the Constitution, I cannot consider either the monarchy or the aristocracy as the end of government, but only as its means. I know instances of governments with neither a hereditary monarchy or aristocracy, yet flourishing and successful, and therefore I conceive this argument to have been overstated. But I believe that universal suffrage would be fatal to all purposes for which government exists, and for which aristocracies and all other things exist, and that it is utterly incompatible with the very existence of civilisation. I conceive that civilisation rests on the security of property; but I think that it is not necessary for me, in a discussion of this kind, to go through the arguments, and through the vast experience which necessarily leads to this result; but I will assert that while property is insecure it is not in the power of the finest soil, or of the moral or intellectual constitution of any country, to prevent the country sinking into barbarism; while, on the other hand, while property is secure, it is not possible to prevent a country from advancing in prosperity. Whatever progress this country has made, in spite of all the misgovernment which can possibly be imputed to it, it cannot but be seen how irresistible is the power of the great principle of security of property. Whatever may have been the state of war in which we were engaged, men were still found labouring to supply the deficiencies of the State; and if it be the fact that all classes have the deepest interest in the security of property, I conceive that this principle follows, that we never can, without absolute danger, entrust the supreme government of the country to any class which would to a moral certainty be induced to commit great systematic inroads against the security of property.

I assume that this will be the result of this motion, and I ask whether the Government, being placed at the head of the majority of the people of this country, without any pecuniary qualification, they would continue to maintain the principle of the security of property? I think not. And if I am called upon to give a reason for this belief—not meaning to refer to the words of the petition with any harsh view—I will look to the petition to support what I have said. The petition must be considered as a sort of declaration of the intentions of the body who, if the Charter is to become law, is to become the sovereign body of the State—as a declaration of the intentions of those who would, in that event, return the majority of the representatives of the people to this House. If I am so to consider it, it is impossible for me to look at these words without the greatest anxiety—

"Your petitioners complain that they are enormously taxed to pay the interest of what is called the National Debt—a debt amounting at present to £800,000,000, being only a portion of the enormous amount expended in cruel and expensive wars for the suppression of all liberty, by men not authorised by the people, and who, consequently, had no right to tax posterity for the outrages committed by them upon mankind."

If I am really to understand that as an indication of the opinion of the petitioners, it is an expression of an opinion that a national bankruptcy would be just and politic. If I am not so to understand it, I am utterly at a loss to know what it means. I conceive for my own part that it is impossible to make any distinction between the right of the fundholder to his dividends, and the right of the landholder to the rent for his land, and I say that the author of this petition makes no such distinction, but treats all alike. The petitioners then speak of monopolies, and they say—

"Your petitioners deeply deplore the existence of any kind of monopoly in this nation; and whilst they unequivocally condemn the levying of any tax upon the necessaries of life, and upon those articles principally required by the labouring classes, they are also sensible that the abolition of any one monopoly will never unshackle labour from its misery until the people possess that power under which all monopoly and oppression must cease. Your petitioners respectfully mention the existing monopolies of the suffrage, of paper money, of machinery, of land, of the public press, of religion, of the means of travelling and transit, and of a host of other evils too numerous to mention, all arising from class legislation."

Now, I ask whether this is not a declaration of the opinion of the petitioners that landed property should cease to exist? The monopoly of machinery, however, is also alluded to, and I suppose that will not be taken to refer to the monopoly of machinery alone, but the monopoly of property in general—a view which is confirmed when we further look to the complaint of the monopoly of the means of transit. Can it be anything but a confiscation of property—of the funds and of land—which is contemplated? And is it not further proposed that there should be a further confiscation of the railways also? I verily believe that that is the effect of the petition. What is the monopoly of machinery and land which is to be remedied? I believe that it is hardly necessary for me to go into any further explanation; but if I understand this petition rightly, I believe it to contain a declaration that the remedies for the evils of which it complains, and under which this country suffers, are to be found in a great and sweeping confiscation of property; and I am firmly convinced that the effect of any such measure would be, not merely to overturn those institutions which now exist, and to ruin those who are rich, but to make the poor poorer, and the amount of the misery of the country even greater than it is now represented to be.

I am far from bringing any charge against the great body of those who have signed this petition—as far as I am from approving of the conduct of those who, in procuring the petition to be signed, have put the sentiments which it embodies into a bad and pernicious form. I ask, however, are we to go out of the ordinary course of Parliamentary proceedings for the purpose of giving it reception? I believe that nothing is more natural than that the feelings of the people should be such as they are described to be. Even we ourselves, with all our advantages of education, when we are tried by the temporary pressure of circumstances, are too ready to catch at anything which may hold out the hope of relief—to incur a greater evil in future, which may afford the means of present indulgence; and I cannot but see that a man, having a wife at home to whom he is attached growing thinner every day, children whose wants become every day more pressing, whose mind is principally employed in mechanical toil, may have been driven to entertain such views as are here expressed, partly from his own position, and partly from the culpable neglect of the Government to supply him with the means and the power of forming a better judgment. Let us grant that education would remedy these things; shall we not wait until it has done so before we agree to such a motion as this? Shall we, before such a change is wanted, give them the power and the means of ruining, not only the rich, but themselves? I have no more unkind feeling towards these petitioners than I have towards the sick man who calls for a draught of cold water, although he is satisfied that it would be death to him; nor than I have for the poor Indians whom I have seen collected round the granaries in India at a time of scarcity, praying that the doors might be thrown open and the grain distributed. But I would not in the one case give the draught of water, nor would I in the other give up the key of the granary; because I know that by doing so I shall only make a scarcity a famine, and by giving such relief enormously increase the evil. No one can say that such a spoliation of property as these petitioners point at would be a relief to the evils of which they complain; and I believe that no one will deny that it would be a great addition to the mischief which is proposed to be removed. But if such would be the result, why should such power be conferred upon the petitioners? That they should ask for it is not blamable; but on what principle is it that we, knowing that their views are entirely delusive, should put into their hands the irresistible power of doing all this evil to us and to themselves?

The only argument which can be brought forward in favour of the proposition is, as it appears to me, that this course which is demanded to be left open to the petitioners will not be taken; that although the power is given, they will not, and do not, intend to execute it. But surely this would be an extraordinary way of treating the prayer of the petition, and it would be somewhat singular to call upon the House to suppose that those who are seeking for a great concession put the object of their demand in a much higher manner than that which presented itself to their own minds. How is it possible that, according to the principles of human nature, if you give them this power, it will not be used to its fullest extent? There has been a constant and systematic attempt for years to represent the Government as being able to do, and so bound to attempt, that which no Government ever attempted; and instead of the Government being represented, as is the truth, as being supported by the people, it has been treated as if the Government supported the people; it has been treated as if the Government possessed some mine of wealth—some extraordinary means for supplying the wants of the people; as if they could give them bread from the clouds—water from the rocks—to increase the bread and the fishes five thousand-fold. Is it possible to believe that the moment you give them absolute, supreme, irresistible power they will forget all this? We propose to give them supreme power. In every constituent body throughout the empire, capital and accumulated property is to be placed absolutely at the foot of labour. How is it possible to doubt what the result will be? Suppose such men as the hon. members for Bath and Rochdale being returned to sit in the House, who would, I believe, oppose such measures of extreme change as would involve a national bankruptcy. What should be the effect if their first answer to their constituents should be, "Justice and the public good demand that this thirty millions a year should be paid"? Then, with regard to land, supposing it should be determined that there should be no partition of land—and it is hardly possible to conceive that there are men to be found who would destroy all the means of creating and increasing wages, and of creating and increasing the trade and commerce of this country, which gives employment to so many—is it possible that the three millions of people who have petitioned the House should insist on the prayer of their petition?

I do not wish to say all that forces itself on my mind with regard to what might be the result of our granting this Charter. Let us, if we can, picture to ourselves the consequences of such a spoliation as it is proposed should take place. Would it end with one spoliation? How could it? That distress which is the motive now for calling on the House to interfere, would be only doubled and trebled by the Act; the measure of distress would become greater after that spoliation, and the bulwarks against fresh acts of the same character would have been removed. The Government would rest upon spoliation—all the property which any man possessed would be supported by it; and is it possible to suppose that a new state of things would exist wherein everything that was done would be right? What must be the effect of such a sweeping confiscation of property? No experience enables me to guess at it. All I can say is, that it seems to me to be something more horrid than can be imagined. A great community of human beings, a vast people, would be called into existence in a new position; there would be a depression, if not an utter stoppage, of trade, and of all those vast engagements of the country by which our people were supported; and how is it possible to doubt that famine and pestilence would come before long to wind up the effects of such a system? The best thing which I can expect, and which I think every one must see as the result, is, that in some of the desperate struggles which must take place in such a state of things, some strong military despot must arise, and give some sort of protection—some security to the property which may remain. But if you flatter yourselves that after such an occurrence you would ever see again those institutions under which you have lived, you deceive yourselves; you would never see them again, and you would never deserve to see them. By all neighbouring nations you would be viewed with utter contempt, and that glory and prosperity which has een so envied would be sneered at, and your fate would thus be told: "England," it would be said, "had her institutions, imperfect though they were, but which contained within themselves the means of remedying all imperfections. Those institutions were wantonly thrown away for no purpose whatever, but because she was asked to do so by persons who sought her ruin; her ruin was the consequence, and she deserves it." Believing this, I will oppose with every faculty which I possess the proposition for Universal Suffrage.

The only question is, whether this motion should be agreed to. Now, if there is any gentleman who is disposed to grant Universal Suffrage with a full view of all its consequences, I think that he acts perfectly conscientiously in voting for this motion; but I must say that it was with some surprise that I heard the hon. baronet the member for Leicester (Sir J. Easthope) agreeing with me as he does in the principles which I advocate, say, notwithstanding, that he is disposed to vote simply for the motion for permitting these petitioners to come to our bar to speak in defence of their petition. [Sir J. Easthope.—To expound their opinions.] I conceive their opinions are quite sufficiently expounded. They are of such an extent that I cannot, I must confess, pretend to speak of them with much respect. I shall give on this occasion a perfectly conscientious vote against hearing the petitioners at the bar; and it is my firm conviction that in doing so I am not only doing that which is best with respect to the State, but that I am really giving to the petitioners themselves much less reason for complaining than those who vote for their being heard now, but who will afterwards vote against their demand.

W. J. FOX ON THE CORN LAWS.

Drury Lane Theatre, March 29th, 1843.

[This was the first of the great meetings convened at Drury Lane Theatre by the Manchester Anti-Corn Law League. The vast edifice was crowded to its utmost capacity.]

Mr Chairman and Gentlemen,—On the subject of the Corn Laws it is, I believe, impossible to find a new argument. Everything that can be said is but an illustration of old ones. Of the truth of this remark I will myself be an instance in the few remarks I will have to make on the subject. It is not to be wondered at, however, that it is impossible to say anything new on the subject of the Corn Laws, for there are no new arguments against oppression and robbery of the poor and helpless. And yet, how is it, notwithstanding it is so well known that nothing new can be said on the Corn Laws, that such multitudes as I now see before me—and these of such respectability—throng these meetings? How is it that such an excitement has arisen, and is increasing, on the subject throughout the country? To solve this problem we must look further and deeper into things than is necessary for the mere flourishings of rhetoric. This state of things indicates that there is going on a great national movement—a movement which has been originated by wrong, which has progressed amidst difficulties, until it now shows the power of opinion in the enforced pliability of the Government. But the fact is, that the repeal of the Corn Laws is no longer a question to be settled by argument. Had it been to be settled in this way, the great work would have been achieved long ago. All the principles of the Corn Law repealers are admitted; yet these laws still remain in the Statute Book. The question originated with speculative theorists in political economy, who put forth their occasional views in magazines or in newspapers; it has grown up into this enormous, this general, this triumphant agitation; and yet the question is not carried. Why? Because we have to deal with sinister interests, not with the convictions of the understanding. The supporters of the Corn Laws are very fond of complaining of the long speeches made by the Leaguers against them when they know they have nothing novel to say. Now, I should be very glad to effect a compromise with those objectors. I should be very ready to say to them, "If you will spare our pockets, we will spare your intellects. If you will allow the people's mouths to be filled, we will abstain from filling your ears with their remonstrances. If you will untax our bread, we will no longer tax your patience."

It is true that the subject is an exhausted one; but why is it exhausted? It is because the advocates of Free Trade have not shrunk from grappling with any and every view of the question that can be presented to them. Whatever argument has been used, they have met with some resistless fact, completely destroying its effect, and to that extent exhausting the subject. They have met the question in every light. Take it as a foreign question, and they urge that it promotes war, not peace; that even, if it does not raise hostile armies against this country, it raises up hostile armies against our commerce. Take it as a home question, and it leads directly and at once to the inquiry, whether England is to continue to be the home of Englishmen? The Corn Laws are making England but a dilapidated home for Englishmen, and already have upholders of these laws arrived at that point when they would rather export our people than import their food. The Saxon laws bred their serfs as slaves, and they sold them out of the country as slaves. But they fed them! They gave the food to enhance the price of the people; we are now prepared to give away the people in order to enhance the price of the food. Looking at it further as a home question, I wonder that even in a financial point of view the Minister does not see how ill these laws operate. Surely the annual payment out of the country of £40,000,000 for the benefit of one class must materially diminish the tax-paying power of the whole people.

If we look at it as a statistical question, why, the League has collected every information that figures can afford; until the arguments that spring from them grow as thick as the rank grass or the leaves on the graves of those victims of the provision laws, who ought still to be living by the fruits of their honest industry. Sometimes the question is looked at as a question of charity; there, too, the League is not behind with its view of the subject. Even the bread that is given in charity must first pay the tax imposed by these laws; and if, by a royal begging letter, some hundreds of thousands of pounds are collected for the poor of Paisley, why, the rapacity of this dominant class must needs step in and take some £30,000 of the money thus bestowed in charity. That Book which we profess to revere tells us to pray for our daily bread; therefore it cannot possibly teach men to tax our daily bread. There is one precept in that Book with the fulfilment of which these laws directly interfere; there the young man is told to sell all he has and give it to the poor. That precept it is impossible to obey in our day. The Corn Laws have rendered it impossible. It must be altered, and in future it will stand: "Sell all thou hast, and divide the proceeds between the richest and the poorest, between the pauper and the landlord."

Or look at it as a class question. What class is it that is interested in the maintenance of these laws? It cannot be the farmer, because the rent screw is turned upon him for every extra shilling a quarter he makes on his corn. It cannot be the labouring classes, for look at the wages of eight shillings a week for a family of seven or eight persons. It is not the commercial class, for the present system keeps them out of a foreign as well as a home market. It cannot be the literary class, for who would care to provide food for the mind, when the food for the body is so heavily taxed? Then, in fact, it cannot be any class but that very small one, composed of some 10,000 or 20,000 (not more) of nominal owners of the soil. I speak not of that much larger class of real holders of landed property, whose interests are identified with the welfare of their country, because in proportion as the towns increase in wealth, and the people in comfort, so does their property increase in value. I speak not of these, but of the merely titular possessors of mortgaged property—men who seek only the means of meeting present exigencies, and who care not that they will leave the remainder of their estates to be discussed by their impoverished posterity. And is it for the sake of such a class as this that a great people is to be stopped in their onward march? Suppose they do realise the cash which seems to be the object of all their legislation, can they shake off the condition that invariably attaches to its acquirement? While they receive their share of the Bread Tax, can they avoid also receiving their share of the odium, of the deep responsibility that attends it, the responsibility of having perilled the safety of the country, of having struck at the root of its prosperity, of having turned the industrious out of employment, earning not the blessings, but the curses of those whom their laws have driven to the state in which they are ready to perish, of exposing themselves to the reprobation of all good men, and to the unfailing retribution of providential justice?

One great argument used in favour of these laws is that they make England independent of all the world. A much more proper way to take it is that they make all the world independent of England. They isolate Great Britain from the family of nations, and they are the destruction of that intercourse, and that interchange of kindness which it seems to be the plan of Providence in thus dividing mankind into nations to promote. The question now is no longer one of argument, as I have already said; it is a question of will. The will of the landlords, it is, arrayed against everlasting justice. Man toils for his bread by the sweat of his brow—it is just that he should receive that bread untaxed, for the artificial enhancement of his neighbour's profit; but those who tax will tax anything. They have laid a tax upon the light—they would, if they could, lay a tax upon the eyes for gazing upon the beauty of the heavens; they would lay a tax upon Cassiopeia's chariot, and on Orion's belt, they would impose a fixed duty on the shining of the Pleiades, and place the Greater and the Lesser Bear on a sliding scale. But it seems that we are to be debarred from agitating for a repeal of these laws because Sir Robert Peel has introduced his measure of last Session. That bantling of now exactly a year and a day old is too young, the right hon. baronet thinks, to be put to death. He asks for a trial. As if the other schemes had not been tried! What are we to try? Is it the principle of the measure? Why, Sir Robert Peel has himself given up the principle in agreeing to the arrangement for the importation of American corn through Canada. That is virtually a fixed duty of 10/ or 12/, and a surrender of the very principle which Sir Robert Peel has come into office pledged to maintain. It is a fixed duty, only by a circumbendibus.

We are asked to give this measure a trial. Why, if we do, what will be the result? We know well enough already what the real operation of the plan will be; and in the meantime the work of ruin will still be going on. There will be more foreign tariffs, more shut-up mills, more discharges of workmen, more distress and misery among the industrial classes; and all these evils are to be incurred for the sake of imposing a tax on bread—the boldest step any Government can take—and certainly imposing on the proposers of it not only a ministerial, but a very deep and heavy personal and individual responsibility. But if Sir Robert Peel has his experiment, the Leaguers have theirs also, and they have come here to this place to try it. The agitation of the question of repeal of the Corn Laws has marched up from Manchester to the metropolis—it has spread far and wide, and now we shall see who will hold out the longest, the people or the Minister. That individual and the people are both the subjects, the slaves of that class which lords over all, and commands and masters the ministers and the legislature, the navy, aye, and the Church; that class which even commands the Crown. The people of this country, with all their untiring industry, their ingenuity, and amiable dispositions, are the mere appendages of the dirty acres which are inherited by that class. The very disgrace, the unspeakable degradation of the Corn Laws, is intolerable, to say nothing of the sufferings which they are calculated to inflict. We are therefore glad to welcome the League amongst us; the people, being part and parcel of the League, are determined to aid and support it; we shall devote ourselves to it, not merely by attending their weekly meetings in this theatre or elsewhere, but we will solemnly and soberly pledge ourselves to it as a religious sentiment. We shall swear by Him who liveth for ever and ever that this egregious folly of the Corn Laws, this foul wrong, this atrocious iniquity, shall be utterly and for ever abolished.

DANIEL O'CONNELL ON REPEAL OF THE UNION.

Hill of Tara, August 15th, 1843.

[Of all mass meetings ever heard of, this was unquestionably the greatest. It was computed by reliable witnesses, not at all favourable to the cause which O'Connell espoused, that no fewer than a quarter of a million persons must have been present. They came from all parts of the country round, under the guidance of their parish priests.]

Fellow-Irishmen,—It would be the extreme of affectation in me to suggest that I have not some claim to be the leader of this majestic meeting. It would be worse than affectation; it would be drivelling folly, if I were not to feel the awful responsibility to my country and my Creator which the part I have taken in this mighty movement imposes on me. Yes; I feel the tremendous nature of that responsibility. Ireland is roused from one end to the other. Her multitudinous population has but one expression and one wish, and that is for the extinction of the Union and the restoration of her nationality. (*A cry of* "No compromise!") Who talks of compromise? I have come here, not for the purpose of making a schoolboy's attempt at declamatory eloquence, not to exaggerate the historical importance of the spot on which we now stand, or to endeavour to revive in your recollection any of those poetic imaginings respecting it which have been as familiar as household words. But this it is impossible to conceal or deny, that Tara is surrounded by historical reminiscences which give it an importance worthy of being considered by everyone who approaches it for political purposes, and an elevation in the public mind which no other part of Ireland possesses. We are standing upon Tara of the Kings; the spot where the monarchs of Ireland were elected, and where the chieftains of Ireland bound themselves, by the most solemn pledges of honour, to protect their native land against the Dane and every stranger. This was emphatically the spot from which emanated every social power and legal authority by which the force of the entire country was concentrated for the purposes of national defence.

On this spot I have a most important duty to perform. I here protest, in the name of my country and in the name of my God, against the unfounded and unjust Union. My proposition to Ireland is that the Union is not binding on her people. It is void in conscience and in principle, and as a matter of constitutional law I attest these facts. Yes, I attest by everything that is sacred, without being profane, the truth of my assertions. There is no real union between the two countries, and my proposition is that there was no authority given to anyone to pass the Act of Union. Neither the English nor the Irish Legislature was competent to pass that Act, and I arraign it on these grounds. One authority alone could make that Act binding, and that was the voice of the people of Ireland. The Irish Parliament was elected to make laws and not to make legislatures; and, therefore, it had no right to assume the authority to pass the Act of Union. The Irish Parliament was elected by the Irish people as their trustees; the people were their masters, and the members were their servants, and had no right to transfer the property to any other power on earth. If the Irish Parliament had transferred its power of legislation to the French Chamber, would any man assert that the Act was valid? Would any man be mad enough to assert it; would any man be insane enough to assert it, and would the insanity of the assertion be mitigated by sending any number of members to the French Chamber? Everybody must admit that it would not. What care I for France?—and I care as little for England as for France, for both countries are foreign to me.

The very highest authority in England has proclaimed us to be aliens in blood, in religion, and in language. (*Groans.*) Do not groan him for having proved himself honest on one occasion by declaring my opinion. But to show the invalidity of the Union I could quote the authority of Locke on "Parliament." I will, however, only detain you by quoting the declaration of Lord Plunket in the Irish Parliament, who told them that they had no authority to transfer the legislation of the country to other hands. As well, said he, might a maniac imagine that the blow by which he destroys his wretched body annihilates his immortal soul, as you to imagine that you can annihilate the soul of Ireland—her constitutional rights.

I need not detain you by quoting authorities to show the invalidity of the Union. I am here the representative of the Irish nation, and in the name of that moral, temperate, virtuous, and religious people, I proclaim the Union a nullity. Saurin, who had been the representative of the Tory party for twenty years, distinctly declared that the Act of Union was invalid. He said that the Irish House of Commons had no right, had no power, to pass the Union, and that the people of Ireland would be justified, the first opportunity that presented itself, in effecting its repeal. So they are. The authorities of the country were charged with the enactment, the alteration, or the administration of its laws. These were their powers; but they had no authority to alter or overthrow the Constitution. I therefore proclaim the nullity of the Union. In the face of Europe I proclaim its nullity. In the face of France, especially, and of Spain, I proclaim its nullity; and I proclaim its nullity in the face of the liberated States of America. I go farther, and proclaim its nullity on the grounds of the iniquitous means by which it was carried. It was effected by the most flagrant fraud. A rebellion was provoked by the Government of the day, in order that they might have a pretext for crushing the liberties of Ireland. There was this addition to the fraud, that at the time of the Union Ireland had no legal protection. The Habeas Corpus Act was suspended, and the lives and liberties of the people were at the mercy of courts-martial. You remember the shrieks of those who suffered under martial law. One day from Trim the troops were marched out and made desolate the country around them. No man was safe during the entire time the Union was under discussion. The next fraud was that the Irish people were not allowed to meet to remonstrate against it. Two county meetings, convened by the High Sheriffs of these counties, pursuant to requisitions presented to them, were dispersed at the point of the bayonet. In King's County the High Sheriff called the people together in the Court-house, and Colonel Connor of the North Cork Militia, supported by artillery and a troop of horse, entered the Court-house at the head of 200 of his regiment and turned out the Sheriff, Magistrates, Grand Jurors, and freeholders assembled to petition against the enactment of the Union. (A VOICE.— "We'll engage they won't do it now!") In Tipperary a similar scene took place. A meeting convened by the High Sheriff was dispersed at the point of the bayonet. Thus public sentiment was stifled; and if there was a compact, as is alleged, it is void on account of the fraud and force by which it was carried. But the voice of Ireland, though forcibly suppressed at public meetings, was not altogether dumb. Petitions were presented against the Union to which were attached no less than 770,000 signatures. And there were not 3,000 signatures for the Union, notwithstanding all the Government could do.

My next impeachment against the Union is the gross corruption with which it was carried. No less than £1,275,000 was spent upon the rotten boroughs, and £2,000,000 was given in direct bribery. There was not one office that was not made instrumental to the carrying of the measure. Six to seven judges were raised to the Bench for the votes they gave in its support; and no less than twelve bishops were elevated to the Episcopal Bench for having taken the side of the Union; for corruption then spared nothing to effect its purpose—corruption was never carried so far; and if this is to be binding on the Irish nation, there is no use in honesty at all. Yet in spite of all the means employed, the enemies of Ireland did not succeed at once. There was a majority of eleven against the Union the first time. But before the proposition was brought forward a second time, members who could not be influenced to vote for the measure were bribed to vacate their seats, to which a number of English and Scotch officers, brought over for the purpose, were elected, and by their votes the Union was carried. In the name of the great Irish nation I proclaim it a nullity. At the time of the Union the national debt of Ireland was only £20,000,000. The debt of England was £440,000,000. England took upon herself one-half the Irish debt, but she placed upon Ireland one-half of the £440,000,000. England since that period has doubled her debt, and admitting a proportionate increase as against Ireland, the Irish debt would not now be more than £40,000,000; and you may believe me when I say it in the name of the great Irish people, that we will never pay one shilling more. In fact, we owe but £30,000, as is clearly demonstrated in a book lately published by a near and dear relative of mine, Mr John O'Connell, the member for Kilkenny. I am proud that a son of mine will be able, when the Repeal is carried, to meet any of England's financiers, and to prove to them the gross injustice inflicted upon Ireland.

My next impeachment of the Union is its destructive and deleterious effect upon the industry and prosperity of the country. The county of Meath was once studded with noble residences. What is it now? Even on the spot where what is called the great Duke of Wellington was born, instead of a splendid castle or noble residence, the briar and the bramble attest the treachery that produced them. You remember the once prosperous linen-weavers of Meath. There is scarcely a penny paid to them now. In short, the Union struck down the manufactures of Ireland. The Commissioners of the Poor Law prove that 120,000 persons in Ireland are in a state of destitution during the greater part of each year. How is it that in one of the most fertile countries in the world this should occur? The Irish never broke any of their bargains nor their treaties, and England never kept one that was made on her part. There is now a union of the legislatures, but I deny that there is a union of the nations, and I again proclaim the Act a nullity. England has given to her people a municipal reform extensive and satisfactory, while to Ireland she gives a municipal reform crippled and worthless. But the Union is more a nullity on ecclesiastical grounds; for why should the great majority of the people of Ireland pay for the support of a religion which they do not believe to be true? The Union was carried by the most abominable corruption and bribery, by financial robbery on an extensive scale, which makes it the more heinous and oppressive; and the result is that Ireland is saddled with an unjust debt, her commerce is taken from her, her trade is destroyed, and a large number of her people thus reduced to misery and distress.

Yes, the people of Ireland are cruelly oppressed, and are we tamely to stand by and allow our dearest interests to be trampled upon? are we not to ask for redress? Yes, we will ask for that which alone will give us redress—a Parliament of our own. And you will have it too, if you are quiet and orderly, and join with me in my present struggle. (*Loud cheers.*) Your cheers will be conveyed to England. Yes, the majority of this mighty multitude will be taken there. Old Wellington began by threatening us, and talked of civil war, but he says nothing about it now. He is getting inlet holes made in stone barracks. Now, only think of an old general doing such a thing, as, if there were anything going on, the people would attack stone walls! I have heard that a great deal of brandy and biscuits have been sent to the barracks, and I sincerely hope the poor soldiers will get some of them. Your honest brothers, the soldiers, who have been sent to Ireland, are as orderly and as brave men as any in Ireland. I am sure that not one of you has a single complaint to make against them. If any of you have, say so. (*Loud cries of* "No, no!") They are the bravest men in the world, and therefore I do not disparage them at all when I state this fact, that if they are sent to make war against the people, I have enough women to beat them. There is no mockery or delusion in what I say. At the last fight for Ireland, when we were betrayed by a reliance on English honour, which we would never again confide in—for I would as soon confide in the honour of a certain black gentleman who has got two horns and hoofs—but, as I was saying, at the last battle for Ireland, when, after two days' hard fighting, the Irish were driven back by the fresh troops brought up by the English to the bridge of Limerick, at that point when the Irish soldiers retired fainting it was that the women of Limerick threw themselves in the way, and drove the enemy back fifteen, twenty, or thirty paces. Several of the poor women were killed in the struggle, and their shrieks of agony being heard by their countrymen, they again rallied and determined to die in their defence, and, doubly valiant in the defence of the women, they together routed the Saxons. Yes, I repeat, I have enough women to beat all the army of Ireland. It is idle for any minister or statesman to suppose for a moment that he can put down such a struggle as this for liberty. The only thing I fear is the conduct of some ruffians who are called Ribbonmen. I know there are such blackguards, for I have traced them from Manchester. They are most dangerous characters, and it will be the duty of every Repealer, whether he knows or by any means can discover one of them, immediately to hand him over to justice and the law. The Ribbonmen only by their proceedings can injure the great and religious cause in which I am now engaged, and in which I have the people of Ireland at my back.

This is a holy festival in the Catholic Church—the day upon which the Mother of our Saviour ascended to meet her Son, and reign with Him for ever. On such a day I will not tell a falsehood. I hope I am under her protection while addressing you, and I hope that Ireland will receive the benefit of her prayers. Our Church has prayed against Espartero and his priest-terrorising, church-plundering marauders, and he has since fallen from power—nobody knows how, for he makes no effort to retain it. He seems to have been bewildered by the Divine curse, for without one rational effort the tyrant of Spain has faded before the prayers of Christianity. I hope that there is a blessing in this day, and, fully aware of its solemnity, I assure you that I am afraid of nothing but Ribbonism, which alone can disturb the present movement. I have proclaimed from this spot that the Act of Union is a nullity, but in seeking for Repeal I do not want you to disobey the law. I have only to refer to the words of the Tories' friend, Saurin, to prove that the Union is illegal. I advise you to obey the law until you have the word of your beloved Queen to tell you that you shall have a Parliament of your own. (*Cheers, and loud cries of* "So we will!") The Queen—God bless her!—will yet tell you that you shall have a legislature of your own—three cheers for the Queen! (*Immense cheering.*)

On the 2nd of January last I called this the Repeal year, and I was laughed at for doing so. Are they laughing now? No; it is now my turn to laugh; and I will now say that in twelve months more we will have our Parliament again on College Green. The Queen has the undoubted prerogative at any time to order her Ministers to issue writs, which, being signed by the Lord Chancellor, the Irish Parliament would at once be convened without the necessity of applying to the English Legislature to repeal what they appear to consider a valid Act of Union. And if dirty Sugden would not sign the writ, an Irish Chancellor would soon be found who would do so. And if we have our Parliament again in Dublin, is there, I would ask, a coward amongst you who would not rather die than allow it to be taken away by an Act of Union? (*Loud cries of* "No one would ever submit to it!" "We'd rather die!" etc.) To the last man? (*Cries of* "To the last man!") Let every man who would not allow the Act of Union to pass hold up his hand. (*An immense forest of hands was shown.*) When the Irish Parliament is again assembled, I will defy any power on earth to take it from us again. Are you all ready to obey me in the course of conduct which I have pointed out to you? (*Cries of* "Yes, yes!") When I dismiss you to-day, will you not disperse and go peaceably to your homes—("Yes, yes, we will!") —every man, woman, and child?—in the same tranquil manner as you have assembled? ("Yes, yes!") But if I want you again to-morrow, will you not come to Tara Hill? ("Yes, yes!") Remember, I will lead you into no peril. If danger should arise, it will be in consequence of some persons attacking us, for we are determined not to attack any person; and if danger does exist, you will not find me in the rear rank. When we get our Parliament, all our grievances will be put an end to; our trade will be restored, the landlord will be placed on a firm footing, and the tenants who are now so sadly oppressed will be placed in their proper position. "Law, Peace, and Order" is the motto of the Repeal banner, and I trust you will all rally round it. (*Cries of* "We are all Repealers!") I have to inform you that all the magistrates who have recently been deprived of the Commission of the Peace have been appointed by the Repeal Association to settle any disputes which may arise amongst the Repealers in their respective localities. On next Monday persons will be appointed to settle disputes without expense, and I call on every man who is the friend of Ireland to have his disputes settled by arbitrators without expense, and to avoid going to the Petty Sessions.

I believe I am now in a position to announce to you that in twelve months more we will not be without having an Hurrah! for the Parliament on College Green. (*Immense cheering.*) Your shouts are almost enough to call to life those who rest in the grave. I can almost fancy the spirits of the mighty dead hovering over you, and the ancient kings and chiefs of Ireland, from the clouds, listening to the shouts sent up from Tara for Irish liberty. Oh! Ireland is a lovely land, blessed with the bounteous gifts of Nature, and where is the coward who would not die for her? (*Cries of* "Not one!") Your cheers will penetrate to the extremity of civilisation. Our movement is the admiration of the world, for no other country can show so much force with so much propriety of conduct. No other country can show a people assembled for the highest national purposes that can actuate man; can show hundreds of thousands able in strength to carry any battle that ever was fought, and yet separating with the tranquillity of schoolboys. You have stood by me long—stand by me a little longer, and Ireland will be again a nation.

R. L. SHEIL ON THE JEWISH DISABILITIES BILL.

HOUSE OF COMMONS, FEBRUARY 7TH, 1848.

[FROM the time of Mr Robert Grant's motion for the admission of Jews to Parliament, April 5th, 1830, when Mr Macaulay made his maiden speech in the House, Bills to this end were repeatedly brought in, and occasionally passed by the Commons, but always thrown out by the Lords. The election of Baron Rothschild for the City of London, in 1847, added a new zest to Jewish Emancipation. It was not, however, until 1858 that the Jewish Disabilities were entirely removed.]

SIR,—If the hon. the learned and exceedingly able gentleman who has just sat down (Mr Walpole) had been a member of the House of Commons when the member for Tamworth brought forward the measure of Emancipation, the speech which he has this night pronounced against the Jews would have been fully as apposite upon that great historical occasion. With all his habits of fine forensic discrimination, I do not think that he can distinguish between the objections urged against the Catholic and against the Jew. He has, for example, strenuously insisted that, in the writ by which the sheriff is commanded to hold an election, a reference is made to the maintenance of the Anglican Church. That objection is nearly as strong when applied to the Unitarian, the Baptist, the Independent, and above all, to the professors of the religion to which it is my good fortune to belong. That men subject to all the duties should be deemed unworthy of the rights of Englishmen, appears to me to be a remarkable anomaly. The enjoyment of rights ought not to be dissociated from the liabilities to duties. A British subject ought in every regard to be considered a British citizen; and inasmuch as the professors of the most ancient religion in the world, which, as far as it goes, we not only admit to be true, but hold to be the foundation of our own, are bound to the performance of every duty which attaches to a British subject, to a full fruition of every right which belongs to a British citizen, they have, I think, an irrefragable title. A Jew born in England cannot transfer his allegiance from his Sovereign and his country; if he were to enter the service of a foreign Power engaged in hostilities with England, and were taken in arms, he would be accounted a traitor. Is a Jew an Englishman for no other purposes than those of condemnation? I am not aware of a single obligation to which other Englishmen are liable from which a Jew is exempt; and if his religion confers on him no sort of immunity, it ought not to affect him with any kind of disqualification.

It has been said, in the course of these discussions, that a Jew is not subject to penalties, but to privations. But what is privation but a synonym for penalty? Privation of life, privation of liberty, privation of property, privation of country, privation of right, privation of privilege—these are degrees widely distant indeed, but still degrees in the graduated scale of persecution. The Parliamentary disability that affects the Jew has been designated in the course of these debates by the mollified expressions to which men who impart euphemism to severity are in the habit of resorting; but most assuredly an exclusion from the House of Commons ought, in the House of Commons itself, to be regarded as a most grievous detriment. With the dignity, and the greatness, and the power of this, the first assembly in the world, the hardship of exclusion is commensurate. Some of the most prominent opponents of this measure are among the last by whom a seat in Parliament ought to be held in little account. On this branch of the case—the hardship of an exclusion from this House—I can speak as a witness as well as an advocate. I belong to that great and powerful community which was a few years ago subject to the same disqualification that affects the Jew; and I felt that disqualification to be most degrading. Of myself I will not speak, because I can speak of the most illustrious person by whom that community was adorned. I have sat under the gallery of the House of Commons, by the side of Mr O'Connell, during a great discussion on which the destiny of Ireland was dependent. I was with him when Plunket convinced, and Brougham surprised, and Canning charmed, and Peel instructed, and Russell exalted and improved. How have I seen him repine at his exclusion from the field of high intellectual encounter in those lists in which so many competitors for glory were engaged, and into which, with an injurious tardiness, he was afterwards admitted! How have I seen him chafe the chain which bound him down, but which, with an effort of gigantic prowess, he burst at last to pieces! He was at the head of millions of an organised and indissoluble people. The Jew comes here with no other arguments than those which reason and truth supply; but reason and truth are of counsel with him; and in this assembly, which I believe to represent, not only the high intelligence, but the highmindedness of England, reason will not long be baffled, and truth, in fulfilment of its great aphorism, will at last prevail.

I will assume that the exclusion from this House is a great privation, and I proceed to consider whether it be not a great wrong. Nothing but necessity could afford its justification; and of this plea we should be taught, by a phrase which has almost grown proverbial, to beware. Cardinal Caraffa relied upon necessity when he founded that celebrated tribunal whose practices are denounced by you, but upon whose maxims have a care lest you should unconsciously proceed. The sophistications of intolerance are refuted by their inconsistencies. If a Jew can choose, wherefore should he not be chosen? If a Jew can vote for a Christian, why should not a Christian vote for a Jew? Again, the Jew is admissible to the highest municipal employments; a Jew can be High Sheriff—in other words, he can empannel the jury by which the first Christian Commoner in England may be tried for his life. But if necessity is to be pleaded as a justification for the exclusion of the Jew, it must be founded on some great peril which would arise from his admission. What is it you fear? What is the origin of this Hebrewphobia? Do you tremble for the Church? The Church has something perhaps to fear from eight millions of Catholics, and from three millions of Methodists, and more than a million of Scotch seceders. The Church may have something to fear from the assault of sectaries from without, and still more to fear from a sort of spurious Popery, and the machinations of mitred mutiny from within; but from the Synagogue — the neutral, impartial, apathetic, and unproselytising Synagogue—the Church has nothing to apprehend. But it is said that the House will become unchristianised. The Christianity of the Parliament depends on the Christianity of the country; and the Christianity of the country is fixed in the faith, and inseparably intertwined with the affections of the people. It is as stable as England herself, and as long as Parliament shall endure, while the Constitution shall stand, until the great mirror of the nation's mind shall have been shattered to pieces, the religious feelings of the country will be faithfully reflected here. This is a security far better than can be supplied by a test which presents a barrier to an honest Jew, but which a scornful sceptic can so readily and so disdainfully overleap.

Reference has been made in the course of these discussions to the author of " The Decline and Fall of the Roman Empire." A name still more illustrious might have been cited. Was not the famous St John—was not Bolingbroke, the fatally accomplished, the admiration of the admirable, to whom genius paid an almost idolatrous homage, and by whom a sort of fascination was exercised over all those who had the misfortune to approach him—was not the unhappy sceptic, by whom far more mischief to religion and morality must have been done than could be effected by half a hundred of the men by whom the Old Testament is exclusively received, a member of this House? Was he stopped by the test that arrests the Jew; or did he not trample upon it and ascend through this House to a sort of masterdom in England, and become the confidential and favourite adviser of his Sovereign? He was not only an avowed and ostentatious infidel, but he was swayed by a distempered and almost insane solicitude for the dissemination of his disastrous disbelief. Is it not then preposterous that a man by whom all revealed religion is repudiated, who doubts the immortality of the soul, doubts a future state of rewards and punishments, doubts in a superintending Providence, believes in nothing, fears nothing, and hopes for nothing, without any incentive to virtue, and without any restraint upon depravity excepting such as a sense of conventional honour or the promptings of a natural goodness may have given him—is it not, I say, preposterous, and almost monstrous, that such a man, for whom a crown of deadly nightshade should be woven, should be enabled, by playing the imposture of a moment and uttering a valueless formula at the table of the House, to climb to the pinnacle of power; and that you should slap the doors of this House with indignity upon a conscientious man who adheres to the faith in which he was born and bred; who believes in the great facts that constitute the foundation of Christianity; who believes in the perpetual existence of the nobler portion of our being; who believes in future retribution and in recompense to come; who believes that the world is taken care of by its almighty and everlasting Author; who believes in the mercy of God, and practises humanity to man; who fulfils the ten great injunctions in which all morality is comprised; whose ear was never deaf to the supplications of the suffering; whose hand is as open as day to charity; and whose life presents an exemplification of the precepts of the Gospel far more faithful than that of many a man by whom, in the name of the Gospel, his dishonouring and unchristian disabilities are most wantonly, most injuriously, and most opprobriously maintained? But where in the Scripture—in what chapter, in what text, in what single phrase—will you find an authority for resorting to the infliction of temporal penalty, or of temporal privation of any kind, as a means of propagating heavenly truth? You may find an authority, indeed, in the writings of jurists and of divines, and in the stern theology of those austere and haughty churchmen by whom the Pharisaical succession, far better than the Apostolical, is personally and demonstratively proved. But you will not find it in the New Testament; you will not find it in Matthew, nor in Mark, nor in Luke, nor in John, nor in the epistles of the meek and humble men to whom the teaching of all nations was given in charge; above all, you will not find in it anything that was ever said, or anything that was ever done, or anything that was ever suffered, by the Divine Author of the Christian religion, who spoke the Sermon on the Mountain, who said that the merciful should be blessed, and who, instead of ratifying the anathema which the people of Jerusalem had invoked upon themselves, prayed for forgiveness for those who knew not what they did, in consummating the Sacrifice that was offered up for the transgressions of the world.

It was not by persecution, but despite of it—despite of imprisonment, and exile, and spoliation, and shame, and death, despite the dungeon, the wheel, the bed of steel, and the couch of fire—that the Christian religion made its irresistible and superhuman way. And is it not repugnant to common reason, as well as to the elementary principles of Christianity itself, to hold that it is to be maintained by means diametrically the reverse of those by which it was propagated and diffused? But, alas! for our frail and fragile nature, no sooner had the professors of Christianity become the co-partners of secular authority than the severities were resorted to which their persecuted predecessors had endured. The Jew was selected as an object of special and peculiar infliction. The history o. that most unhappy people is, for century after century, a trail of chains and a track of blood. Men of mercy occasionally arose to interpose in their behalf. St Bernard—the great St Bernard, the last of the Latin Fathers—with a most pathetic eloquence took their part. But the light that gleamed from the ancient turrets of the Abbey of Clairvaux was transitory and evanescent. New centuries of persecution followed; the Reformation did nothing for the Jew. The infallibility of Geneva was sterner than the infallibility of Rome. But all of us—Calvinists, Protestants, Catholics—all of us who have torn the seamless garment into pieces, have sinned most fearfully in this terrible regard.

It is, however, some consolation to know that in Roman Catholic countries expiation of this guilt has commenced. In France and in Belgium all civil distinction between the Protestant and the Jew is at an end. To this Protestant country a great example will not have been vainly given. There did exist in England a vast mass of prejudice upon this question, which is, however, rapidly giving way. London, the point of Imperial centralisation, has made a noble manifestation of its will. London has advisedly, deliberately, and with benevolence aforethought, selected the most prominent member of the Jewish community as its representative, and united him with the first Minister of the Crown. Is the Parliament prepared to fling back the Jew upon the people, in order that the people should fling back the Jew upon the Parliament? That will be a dismal game, in the deprecation of whose folly and whose evils the Christian and the statesman should concur. But not only are the disabilities which it is the object of this measure to repeal at variance with genuine Christianity, but I do not hesitate to assert that they operate as impediments to the conversion of the Jews, and are productive of consequences directly the reverse of those for which they were originally designed. Those disabilities are not sufficiently onerous to be compulsory, but they are sufficiently vexatious to make conversion a synonym for apostacy, and to affix a stigma to an interested conformity with the religion of the State. We have relieved the Jew from the ponderous mass of fetters that bound him by the neck and by the feet; but the lines which we have left, apparently light, are strong enough to attach him to his creed, and make it a point of honour that he should not desert it.

There exists in this country a most laudable anxiety for the conversion of the Jews. Meetings are held, and money is largely subscribed for the purpose; but all these creditable endeavours will be ineffectual unless we make a restitution of his birthright to every Englishman who professes the Jewish religion. I know that there are those who think that there is no such thing as an English, or a French, or a Spanish Jew. A Jew is but a Jew; his nationality, it is said, is engrossed by the hand of recollection and of hope, and the house of Jacob must remain for ever in a state of isolation among the strange people by whom it is encompassed. In answer to these sophistries I appeal to human nature. It is not wonderful that when the Jew was oppressed, and pillaged, and branded in a captivity worse than Babylonian, he should have felt upon the banks of the Thames, or of the Seine, or the Danube, as his forefathers felt by the waters of the Euphrates, and that the psalm of exile should have found an echo in his heart. This is not strange; it would have been strange if it had been otherwise; but justice—even partial justice—has already operated a salutary change.

In the same measure in which we have relaxed the laws against the Jews, that patriot instinct by which we are taught to love the land of our birth has been revived. British feeling has already taken root in the heart of the Jew, and for its perfect development nothing but perfect justice is required. To the fallacies of fanaticism give no heed. Emancipate the Jew—from the Statute-book of England be the last remnant of intolerance erased for ever; abolish all civil discriminations between the Christian and the Jew, fill his whole heart with the consciousness of country. Do this, and we dare be sworn that he will think, and feel, and fear, and hope as you do; his sorrow and his exultation will be the same; at the tidings of English glory his heart will beat with a kindred palpitation, and whenever there shall be need, in the defence of his Sovereign and of his country, his best blood, at your bidding, will be poured out with the same heroic prodigality as your own.

ALEXANDER COCKBURN[1] ON THE GREEK DIFFICULTY.

HOUSE OF COMMONS, JUNE 28TH, 1850.

[WHAT was known about this time as the celebrated "Don Pacifico Case" originated as follows:—Don Pacifico, a Jew, of Portuguese extraction, was a native of Gibraltar, and therefore a British subject. He resided at Athens, where it was a time-honoured custom to burn an effigy of Judas Iscariot at Easter. The police prevented this celebration in 1847, whereupon the mob, attributing the action to the influence of the Jews, wrecked their resentment upon Don Pacifico, whose house stood close to the spot annually chosen for the burning of Judas. His claim against the Greek Government, side by side with that of Mr Finlay, being ignored, the British Government took upon itself to redress the wrongs of its subjects.]

I THINK, Sir, as I was personally and pointedly alluded to in the course of the debate last night by the right hon. the Member for the University of Oxford (Mr Gladstone), that the House will not consider me presumptuous if I trespass for a short time upon its patience. I am anxious, Sir, in the first place, if the House will indulge me for a moment, to set myself right with the right hon. gentleman. He was pleased, in the course of his observations in the House last night, to say that I had "sneered" at him. Now, I beg to assure the right hon. gentleman and the House that nothing on earth was further from my wishes or intentions than to show him the slightest disrespect or discourtesy. The right hon. gentleman,

---

[1] Afterwards Lord Chief-Justice of England.

with his accustomed talent, threw down the gauntlet on the floor of this House, and challenged a reply from any hon. member to the facts which he stated, or to the principles of law which he then enunciated. I felt, Sir, at the time, as truly and as fully convinced as I ever was of anything in my life, that the right hon. gentleman's facts were totally inaccurate, and that his law was utterly intolerable. I ventured, therefore, to accept the challenge which he so threw out, and I meant by my cheer on that occasion—a mode which I believe to be a perfectly parliamentary one of expressing that sentiment—to say that I was ready and anxious to accept the challenge of the right hon. gentleman, and I am now prepared to answer him, although I am fully conscious of the vast difference of ability and disparity of power which exists between us; for the right hon. gentleman, from his position, his high character, and above all, his great abilities, is entitled to be treated with the utmost respect by every member of this House.

Having thus put myself right with the right hon. gentleman, I must take the liberty of saying this, that in all my experience I never heard such a series of misrepresentations and mis-statements as those which were made by the right hon. gentleman; and I will undertake to prove this assertion, step by step, and position by position, if the House will grant me its indulgence and forbearance. I feel, however, the great difficulty in which I am placed in entering upon this debate. If I go into the details of the case for the purpose of showing the fallacies, both in the statements and arguments of the right hon. gentlemen, I shall be told, by and by, because I have the misfortune of belonging to a legal profession, that it was a *nisi prius* mode of conducting my argument. I think, however, that the manner in which the discussion of this subject has been conducted, both in this House and in another place, has given us abundant evidence that it is not those only who practise in Westminster Hall who are possessed of the power of arguing in *nisi prius* fashion. For of all the pettifogging proceedings which I have ever known during my experience, this is the worst. It was so commenced elsewhere, and in the same spirit it has been conducted here. If hon. gentlemen choose to introduce this subject to Parliament, and make a grave accusation against Her Majesty's Government, and then conduct it, not upon the great principles of natural honour, but by raising questions of minute details and technicalities, by grossly perverting facts and distorting evidence, and by an utter misrepresentation of what were the true principles that ought to govern this case, let them not be astonished if those who belong to the legal profession, whose habits are to criticise and investigate with logical strictness every species of evidence, to minutely analyse facts as well as study the broad principles of municipal and national law, stung to the quick by the manifest injustice of this proceeding, should rush into the discussion; and above all, let not the charge come from them, that the men having these acquirements are treating the subject in a *nisi prius* spirit.

I am now speaking for the interest of my profession; and I must say that I never heard an observation more ungracious, or made in worse taste, than that which fell from the right hon. baronet the member for Ripon (Sir F. Graham), following, as it did, on the admirable speech of my hon. and learned friend, the member for Oxford (Mr William Page Wood), than which, a more masterly analysis of facts, and a more convincing speech in point of argument and of law, I never heard. It certainly never was surpassed in this House or in any other place. It altogether demolished the whole case against the Government in all that respected Greece. And yet, the right hon. baronet, because he found he was unable to grapple with the arguments of my hon. and learned friend, nor even tried to do so, said: "Oh, it is not fair to deal with this great question upon such narrow ground, or with reference to the case of Greece alone—it is all founded upon blue-books, a pack of rubbish; mere *nisi prius*. Let us come to that which is the great issue to be decided by the House, the foreign policy of the Government." Now, that certainly strikes me as being a very odd position for the right hon. baronet to take, when it is considered that the verdict which has been passed by the other House of Parliament against Her Majesty's Government, and in consequence of which verdict they are requested to resign, proceeded entirely, not upon the question of the general policy of the Government, but exclusively and distinctly upon the line pursued by them in respect of Greece. The right hon. baronet then went into the whole of the foreign policy of the country, leaving out of view the whole of the Greek case. The right hon. baronet was followed by the right hon. gentleman for South Wiltshire (Mr Sidney Herbert), and he followed exactly in the same track, threw the Greek question overboard, and took his stand upon the foreign policy of the Government. Then came the right hon. gentleman the member for the University of Oxford, whom I suppose, we are now to consider as the representative of Lord Stanley in this House : " Gladstone *vice* Disraeli," am I to say, resigned or superseded ?

There are, therefore, two questions before the House. The right hon. baronet, the member for Ripon, and the right hon. member for South Wiltshire, boldly come forward and take up the question of the whole foreign policy of the Government; while the right hon. gentleman the member for the University of Oxford, arguing his case upon the *nisi prius* style, takes his stand upon the Greek question only. Which of these two different positions is the House to consider? Is it the right hon. baronet the member for Ripon, or that of the right hon. gentleman the member for the University of Oxford? It is a matter of perfect indifference to me. I am prepared to go into both. But I must say this, that I do not think, if you sever your cases for the prosecution, if the hon. gentlemen will allow me to use so technical a phrase, and shift the ground of your accusation from one point to the other, I claim as a right that we may be fairly heard upon both. And do not tell us when we meet you on the

Greek case, that it is all mere *nisi prius*, but allow us to show you what the facts are, and what the nature of your arguments, and I will undertake to say that we will demolish your whole case, nor leave you a leg to stand upon.

Her Majesty's Government have, it appears, interfered in the affairs of Greece for the purpose of redressing certain wrongs sustained by the subjects of this Empire; and the point in dispute is whether they were justified in the course which they took upon that occasion. Now, as it is impossible to dispute that in this instance the subjects of Her Majesty have sustained wrong—a fact which no one has attempted to deny—they were most unquestionably entitled to redress from the Government of the country in which they happened to be at the time they sustained such wrong; but if the laws of that country where the wrongs were perpetrated afforded no means of redress, they became unquestionably entitled to redress from the Government of that country; and if the Government would not redress those wrongs, it was not only the right, but the bounden duty of the Government of this country to interfere on behalf of its subjects, and to obtain redress for the wrongs which they had suffered. I take it to be a fundamental principle in the policy of nations that it is the right and duty of a State to protect its subjects against injuries sustained at the hands of other States, or subjects of such States. This has been the principle upon which nations have acted in all ages. The noble Lord who addressed the House the other night (Lord Palmerston) referred to the great principle that the Roman State never allowed a Roman citizen to be injured. But what said the right hon. member for the University of Oxford to that? He said that it was because Rome exercised a universal dominion over the world; because it considered a Roman citizen as superior to the subjects of all other States, and by its universal supremacy and power was enabled to tyrannise over other countries, and obtain redress for the wrongs sustained by its citizens even in cases where they were not entitled to such redress. I dissent from that position altogether. I say that it was not after the

Roman Empire had become established, and had obtained its supremacy over the whole world, that that position was first taken up by the Roman State. It was a principle upon which it acted from the very earliest ages of the Empire, and therefore it was that the great orator was entitled triumphantly to exclaim, with all the noble pride and triumph of a Roman, " *Quot bella majores nostri suscepti erint, quot cives Romani injuria affecti sunt, navicularii retenti, mercatores spoliati, esse dicerentur.*" It was not only before they had established universal dominion over the world that they adopted this principle, but it was at a period of their history when they had to fight their battles for empire with other States upon almost equal terms, that they invariably asserted that first right and duty of a State to protect its citizens, and to obtain redress for their wrongs, when they sustained any at the hands of other States. That course, I take it, was not unknown to this country either in one of the most glorious periods of its history. What is it that, in spite of all the dark shades that rest upon his character, has made the memory of Cromwell illustrious? What, but that he would suffer no Englishman to be injured by any State or potentate, no matter how great? But, after all, can the proposition be denied that the Government of a country is bound to obtain redress for, and to afford protection to its citizens when injured? The right hon. gentleman the member for the University of Oxford did not dispute that position; but he qualified it by saying that British subjects living in foreign States, and sustaining any wrong there, either from the Government of the country or any of the subjects of that State, are bound to have recourse to the tribunals of the country for redress, and if redress can be obtained from such tribunals, they are not to call upon the country of which they are the subjects to interfere. I cheerfully assent to that proposition, and I will undertake to make it perfectly manifest that in neither of the cases which have led to the interference of this country was there the slightest or most remote probability—looking to the law of Greece, and the condition of its tribunals—that any English subject, however injured, could succeed in obtaining redress from the tribunals of that country.

Now I will take in the first place the case of Mr Finlay. I do not intend to cite Blue-Books upon this subject—the whole matter is capable of being placed before the House in a very short and succinct form. Mr Finlay, it appears, was the proprietor of some land in Athens. That gentleman, with some other inhabitants at Athens, was anxious, when King Otho was in possession of the actual sovereignty of Greece, to induce the king to fix the seat of Government at Athens; and accordingly, Mr Finlay, with those other inhabitants, presented a memorial to the Government of Greece proposing to give or sell the land which belonged to them to the Government upon certain terms, in order that it might be made applicable for the establishment of the necessary public buildings in Athens, with the view of inducing the Government to fix it there. But they coupled their offer of the land with these conditions, that the land to be taken should be scheduled and set out within six months from the time of taking possession of it. When the Government came to Athens, the land of many of the individuals which had been thus offered to the Government was taken. Mr Finlay's land, however, was not so taken. The land taken by the Greek Government of the other individuals was paid for according to a price which the parties had agreed upon; and it is easy to understand that the inhabitants of a city like Athens, possessing property, and being desirous of bringing the Government to Athens, should be perfectly willing to dispose of a portion of their land at a lower rate, if by so doing they could attain their object, as the existence of the Government at Athens would have the effect of enhancing the value of the remainder of their property. Mr Finlay's land was not, however, taken upon this ground; it was taken some time after by the arbitrary command of the King, without law or ordinance, or without anything whatever which could give a sanction to such a proceeding—nothing except the arbitrary and absolute will of the Sovereign.

That is a matter of fact upon which I defy any man to dispute. That being done, what was the consequence? Mr Finlay's land was taken and converted into the palace garden of the King. Mr Finlay applied for compensation in 1836; and according to the statement of Sir Edmund Lyons — who, I apprehend, notwithstanding the insinuations of the right hon. gentleman the member for the University of Oxford, is in every way worthy of credit—the proceedings of Mr Finlay towards the Greek Government were characterised by the most gentlemanly moderation and forbearance; yet for six long years (until 1842) Mr Finlay continued, from time to time, to put forward kindly and temperately his demand for compensation. Do you tell me that the delay arose from any dispute as to the amount of compensation which should be given to that gentleman? He could not obtain even the slightest answer to his communications. But in 1842, when this injustice became too grievous to be patiently borne any longer, Mr Finlay addressed the noble Lord who was at the head of foreign affairs of this country—not the present Lord, but the Earl of Aberdeen—who instructed Sir Edmund Lyons to apply to the Greek Government, and to enforce by all means in his power the legitimate demands of Mr Finlay. What was the result? After a great deal of difficulty and delay, the King of Greece proposed to issue a Commission to inquire into the claims of Mr Finlay. But of whom was it proposed that the Commission should consist? Of M. Glarakis and M. Manitaki, the Minister of the Interior. One of these persons was a most remarkable character; and Sir Edward Codrington, speaking of him in a public despatch, said that he was a man who had made himself notorious by fostering and encouraging pirates. The other was a mere creature of the King, and would have acted if appointed on the part of the King.

Mr Finlay therefore objected to this Commission. Further communications took place, and no redress could be obtained. This was in 1845. Now a Commission thus constituted Mr Finlay was justified in repudiating. He said very truly, "It is not an inspired tribunal; I can place no confidence in it; I will have nothing to do with it, but will appeal to the Government at home." He did so, and the present noble Lord, then at the head of Foreign Affairs, having inquired into the matter, a despatch was sent to Sir Edmund Lyons, instructing him to enforce the claims of Mr Finlay. The King proposed another Commission, which was appointed, and in the end, after all these years of evasion, shuffling, quirks, and chicanery of every description, it was agreed to refer the matter to arbitration. At first the Greek Government had the assurance to propose that it should have the nomination of the umpire; but being shamed out of this extravagant proposal, a proper umpire was appointed. What was the next trick they resorted to? Why, they delayed the production of the necessary documents beyond the period of three months, within which period, by the law of Greece, an arbitration must be concluded or it falls to the ground. The right hon. gentleman (Mr Gladstone) has stated that the delay had originated with Mr Finlay; but this is not so; the Blue-Book proves directly the contrary. It was the Government who asked for the delay. Now was this fair of the right hon. gentleman? Talk of *nisi prius*, indeed! At least lawyers hold this at *nisi prius*—that though they may use sophistry to induce a jury or a court to adopt their conclusions, it is a sacred duty not to mis-state facts.

Well, then, Mr Finlay could get no redress; but the right hon. gentleman the member for the University of Oxford says, he might have gone to the tribunals of the country. The tribunals of the country, indeed! They say, "a little learning is a dangerous thing"; but this is equally the case when applied to law. The right hon. gentleman possesses every quality which would have made a most brilliant advocate. He has eloquence unlimited, subtlety unrivalled, casuistry unexampled; all he wants is a little knowledge of law. If he had not been a great statesman, he would have been a great lawyer if he only would have condescended to put on the wig and gown, and acquired a little knowledge of the very first principles of law. I would advise him, if he would accept of my humble advice, to confine himself to that science of which he is so great a master—politics, and not to meddle with law. The right hon. gentleman is ignorant of the fundamental principle of law — that a subject cannot sue a Sovereign. That is the rule in every country, with the exception of this. And why is it not the law in England? Simply because, by the established usage and magnanimous practice of this country, the Sovereign, upon the petition of a subject complaining of a wrong sustained from the Crown, refers it to the first law officer of the Crown, and indorses upon the petition the important and solemn words, "Let right be done." And upon that, the Sovereign condescends to submit herself to an equality with her subjects before the throne of law, and allow justice to be administered between her and the meanest of her subjects by the ordinary tribunals of the land. And, thank God! that we have tribunals, and that we have judges, who would administer the law between the Sovereign and her subjects with so much impartiality, with as even a hand, and with as unbiassed a mind, as between any two ordinary persons. But is that the case in Greece? No! I ask, then, what becomes of the position that Mr Finlay could have appealed to the tribunals of the country against the King of Greece? The King of Greece is utterly irresponsible, not only politically, but civilly, to any of his subjects, and you can only seek redress, if you have sustained any injury, against the officers of State. In this case, however, the officers of State were not responsible, because this matter had occurred before the Constitution by which alone even they became responsible, and were called into power. With respect, therefore, to the claim of Mr Finlay, I think that case is pretty well disposed of.

I now come to M. Pacifico, and I rejoice that we shall be able to discuss that case on its merits, and not on the ground of M. Pacifico being a Jew or a usurer, or, as it was ungenerously suggested, and when he could not defend himself, a delinquent, who had committed an act of forgery. All these questions are utterly beside the one at issue. And here, sir, let me say that I never felt stronger indignation than when I read the observations, as to who and what M. Pacifico was and is, which have been repeated over and over again in that portion of the Press devoted to the interests of Russian despotism, and which have been spoken over and over again by certain Lords, who come forward either for their own behoof or that of Continental tyrants. According to these authorities, M. Pacifico is a species of Jew broker, a Jew usurer, a Jew trafficker, a hybrid Jew. And then, sir, forsooth, we are told in the same breath as that in which such phrases are employed, that they are not used to prejudice the individual to whom they are applied! For what purpose then, I ask, are they used? Why, sir, even at *nisi prius* we should not stoop to such shabby artifices as these. Even lawyers would not resort to such mean and dirty acts as these; they would not think themselves justified in saying that, on a man sustaining a civil wrong and demanding justice, the question was to be tried by his character; yet that has been done again and again to prejudice this case. However, the right hon. gentleman, in taking the place of those who had carried on this accusation against the Government elsewhere, thought it necessary to protect himself from being supposed to take any part in such acts as these. But the right hon. gentleman has pursued the course followed elsewhere of making the most of the abused extravagance of M. Pacifico's demand. But I will show the House that the amount of compensation claimed has nothing to do with the question, and for this simple reason, it never was a matter of dispute with the Greek Government. The objection which the Greek Government took was to the principle of the demand, not to its amount. The dispute never advanced as far as to have anything to do with the amount.

As for the wrongs inflicted on M. Pacifico, I need not dwell upon them. They are known to all the world. The man was outraged in his person, in his family, and in his property. The question then is—Was he entitled to redress? He may be a Jew, a broker, a usurer, a hybrid Jew—he may have committed an act of forgery. It is possible—although God forbid that I should believe such a charge against any man without the opportunity of answering it!—he may have been a forger; it did not lie in the mouth of the Portuguese Government to say so, after having appointed him consul—first at Morocco, and then at Athens; but for all that he was injured, and therefore entitled to redress. Now, what are the known facts as to his position? He had been living at Athens for many years in comfort and respectability—a substantial citizen, carrying on his business with the Greek people. Well, he was grievously injured. The right hon. gentleman said he ought to have gone before the Greek tribunals. What tribunals? He did go before one. He tried to proceed in a Criminal Court—with what success we know. A crime had been committed in the broad daylight, at noon, in the midst of Athens. The perpetrators were seen and well known. They were denounced to the police; and the police, in reply, contended that there was no evidence to fix their identity, and so let them loose again. So much for the honour and honesty of Greek tribunals. But the right hon. gentleman says, why did he not go before a civil tribunal? Why did he not sue the rioters for damages? Good God! Is it possible that the right hon. gentleman can be in earnest? Does he really consider us so weak, so fallible, as to be likely to swallow an obvious, a palpable, or gross absurdity such as that? What! seek for compensation from a mob— from a rabble of brigands, vagabonds and ruffians, in rags and tatters, who wrecked his house and stole his furniture? Is he to proceed for damages against such a horde as this? Let me ask the House—let me ask the right hon. gentleman this question: Suppose that, in some time of trouble and popular excitement, a mob were to sack his house, as the mob sacked M. Pacifico's, would he bring an action against each and every member of that mob? We have had instances of such riots taking place, I think. Nottingham Castle was destroyed. It belonged to the Duke of Newcastle. Did he prosecute the mob for damages? The Marquis of Londonderry's house in St James' Square was attacked and damaged. Did he prosecute the mob for damages? The palace of the Bishop at Bristol was burnt down, and property to a great extent destroyed. Did he prosecute the mob for damages? No; you don't proceed against paupers. There is nothing to be got out of them.

Observe the difference between Greece and this country. England, with wiser legislation, proceeding on the principle that for injuries done in times of tumult, it is idle to leave the people to a remedy by civil action against the parties commiting them, provides this wise regulation: that in the case of such injuries the local community, the hundred, should be responsible for the property which has been demolished. If, however, the property fall under a certain category for which the hundred is not liable, the Government is nevertheless bound to make the loss good, so that no owner of property need suffer from the lawless violence of mobs, which it is the business of the executive to keep in order.[1] If, then, this state of things had existed in Athens — if M. Pacifico could have claimed redress from the Greek tribunals, he was no doubt bound to go there. But I say he could not. It is idle to assert that he could. The right hon. gentleman tells us that there are courts of law in Greece, that there is a regular bar there, always ready to undertake the case of anybody applying to them. Is there? Stop a minute. M. Pacifico having been attacked a second time, and having made his complaint, the noble Lord at the head of the Foreign Office instructed Sir Edmund Lyons to institute a prosecution against the parties who had committed the outrage. What was the result? The offending parties had actually been apprehended, when M. Pacifico was told that he

---

[1] A modern instance of the working of this principle was the compensation granted by the Government to the sufferers by the Socialist Riots in the West-end of London in February, 1886.

could not get a lawyer to bring his case on, and that such was the strict compulsion under which the Courts were kept, that they did not dare to place themselves in opposition to the Prime Minister of the country.

But, says the right hon. gentleman, the judges at Athens administer justice impartially and fairly. There is a court called the Areopagus, and its judges are perfectly free to act according to the dictates of their conscience. Let me tell the right hon. gentleman that he never laboured under a more complete mistake. The Constitution undoubtedly provides that the judges shall not be dismissed at the King's pleasure; but they are so dismissed every day. And not only that, but the Greek Government have established this system— and it shows their Greek subtlety, as they have a number of courts of equal jurisdiction and authority—they transplant the judges from one to the other, as the purpose of each case may seem to require. When a particular case which the Government is interested in bringing to a particular decision occurs in a court, why then they transplant the judge on whom they can depend into that court. Let me cite an instance. An action was brought by M. Piscatori, the French Ambassador at Athens, against the editor of a newspaper published there—the *Athena*. This was in 1846. M. Piscatori was, of course, all-powerful with the Government. Well, the sentence was against the editor. Two of the judges pronounced for his acquittal; three for his condemnation. One of the former, called, I believe, Disachi, was summarily dismissed, in the following curt terms: "The King has been pleased to remove you from the bench." Well, the editor appealed to the Court of the Areopagus, and on the eve of his case coming on, two of his judges who were to be were suddenly dismissed, without any reason whatever being assigned. I have these facts from authority upon which I can implicitly rely, and for their exact truth I pledge myself to the House. Again, there was a president of the Court of the Areopagus called Cleonares. He was dismissed upon the instant, without any reason assigned, but for causes of which no one who has listened to what I have stated can for a moment doubt.

And after this you tell me that the Greek tribunals are pure. "Oh, but," says the right hon. gentleman, "I produce Sir Edmund Lyons to prove my case. He says that the Press is free, and the tribunals are fair and independent." True; Sir Edmund Lyons says so; but when? Sir, the reference to Sir Edmund Lyons shows that there are other texts besides those of Scripture which the——which certain persons can quote for their own purposes. The despatch in question was written in 1836, and under what circumstances? King Otho having been advised by his father, as young gentlemen who have lived too fast and extravagantly sometimes are, to go and travel, and look out for a wife—of course, a rich one—obeyed the paternal injunction, and left his kingdom under the charge of Count Armansperg, who took advantage of the absence of his royal master to set matters a little to rights. Well, he began by reforming the tribunals, by making them independent. He set the Press free—he established provincial councils, so as to give the people some sort of means of expressing their opinions on public matters—in short, he set the kingdom so far to rights, hoping, of course that upon the return of his royal master he would reap the reward of his merits in a rich overflow of royal favours. Notice, however, of what Count Armansperg had been doing had, it seems, been conveyed to King Otho, who straightway returned in alarm, and before the boat which conveyed him from the ship touched the soil of Greece, Count Armansperg was ignominiously dismissed. Arbitrary dominion resumed its tyrannical rule—injustice, oppression, and wrong were re-established in their old supremacy; and such is the system which has ruled supreme in Greece ever since.

Well, to proceed. The right hon. gentleman dwelt last night on the case of the man Sumachi, who was tortured; and he set out by saying that he did not believe Sumachi's statement, and that Sir Edmund Lyons was just the man ready to receive and record any unauthenticated case bearing against the Greek Government. Sir, I say that Sir Edmund Lyons is a man who, after eight or nine years' service as Minister of Athens, received, as a token of his Sovereign's approbation, the Grand Cross of the Bath; and I hope that a gentleman who has been thus specially and highly honoured is at least entitled to have his official assertions believed—at all events until the contrary shall have been shown. But is this case of Sumachi a single instance? No. Torture has over and over again been applied in Greece. Torture, I repeat, is commonly applied in Greece. I can prove innumerable instances of it. One is so disgusting that I cannot mention it; yet I ought to mention it—I will mention it. I feel that it ought to be told, that we may at least know what these people, of whom so much has been said, really are. How do they torture women? They attach cats to their naked persons, and then flog the animals, that in their furious struggles they may lacerate the flesh to which they are tied. Another species of torture is this: a man is tied, hands, feet, and head together, and in this position flung upon the ground and bastinadoed. And still, Sir, the right hon. gentleman is right—perfectly right—in saying that all such atrocities are forbidden by the Constitution of Greece. But what is the value of that Constitution? I say, Sir, not so much as that of the paper on which it is written. It has been set aside—violated, outraged in every respect and in every way. It exists but in name; while oppression and corruption reign in unmitigated horror in its room.

And now, Sir, I dismiss the right hon. gentleman and his Greek arguments. I trust I have given him and them satisfactory answers. Transcendent as are the abilities of the right hon. gentleman, I believe that even his talents will not support a case when truth is in the other scale. But truth, if it does not prevail here, will prevail elsewhere. The country is beginning to appreciate what is the truth in this question. The country will fully appreciate, too, the motives which induce you, after four years of silence, now at length to come forward and attack the noble Lord at the head of the Foreign Affairs of this country. But whatever may be the result here, I tell you that the people of England will only rally the more heartily around that Government which stands pledged to extend the safeguard of its power to all its subjects, in whatever land their business may have led them; and which is also able and willing, if on any occasion it may be too late to interfere for the purposes of protection, at all events to stand forward and to demand from them reparation and redress.

SIR BULWER LYTTON[1] ON THE CRIMEAN WAR.

HOUSE OF COMMONS, JUNE 4TH, 1855.

[DURING a six nights' debate on the crisis in the Crimean War, it was seriously recommended to conclude a peace with Russia on terms which, in the opinion of many politicians, did not satisfy the honour of England. Sir E. B. LYTTON spoke on the third night.]

SIR,—The right hon. gentleman the member for Manchester (Mr Milner Gibson), towards the close of his able speech, summed up his strongest objections to the continuance of the war by asking how it would profit the country. In answer to that question, let me remind the right hon. gentleman of the laudable earnestness with which, in a recent debate, he assured the House that he, and those with whom he concurred in the policy to be adopted for the restoration of peace, were no less anxious than we are for the due maintenance of the national honour. I cordially believe him; and when he asks how the continuance of the war can profit the country, I answer, because the continuance of the war is as yet essential to the vindication of the national honour, and because the national honour is the bulwark of the national interests. For there is this distinction between individuals and nations: with the first a jealous tenacity of honour may be a mere sentiment, with the last it is a condition of power. If you lower the honour of a man in the eyes of his equals, he may still say, " My fortune is not attacked,

---

[1] Afterwards Baron Lytton.

my estate is unimpaired, the laws still protect my rights and my person, I can still command my independence and bestow my beneficence upon those who require my aid;" but if you lower the honour of a nation in the eyes of other States, and especially a nation like England, which owes her position, not to her territories, but to her character; not to the amount of her armies, nor even to the pomp of her fleets, but to a general belief in her high spirit and indomitable will—her interests will be damaged in proportion to the disparagement of her name. You do not only deface her scutcheons, you strike down her shield. Her credit will be affected, her commerce will suffer at its source. Take the awe from her flag, and you take the wealth from her merchants; in future negotiations her claims will be disputed, and she can never again interfere with effect against violence and wrong in behalf of liberty and right. These are some of the consequences which might affect the interests of this country, if other nations could say, even unjustly, that England had grown unmindful of her honour. But would they not say it with indisputable justice if, after encouraging Turkey to a war with her most powerful enemy, we could accept any terms of peace which Turkey herself indignantly refuses to endorse? Honour, indeed, is a word on which many interpreters may differ, but at least all interpreters must agree upon this, that the essential of honour is fidelity to engagements. What are the engagements by which we have pledged ourselves to Turkey? Freedom from the aggressions of Russia. Is that all? No; reasonable guarantees that the aggressions shall not be renewed. But would any subject of the Ottoman Empire think such engagements fulfilled by a peace that would not take from Russia a single one of her fortresses, a single one of her ships, by which she now holds Constantinople itself under the very mouth of her cannon?

Sir, both the members for Manchester have the merit of consistency in the cause they espouse. They were against this war from the first. But I cannot conceive how any Government which led us into this war, and is responsible for all it has cost us, should now suddenly adopt the language of Peace Societies, and hold it as a crime if we push to success the enterprise which they commenced by a failure. I approach the arguments of the right hon. member for the University of Oxford (Mr Gladstone), with a profound respect for his rare intellect and eloquence, and still more for that genuine earnestness which assures us that, if he ever does diverge into sophistry and paradox, it is not till he has religiously puzzled his conscience into a belief of their simplicity and truth. The main argument on which the right hon. gentleman rests the vindication of the views he entertains is this : He says, " I supported the war at the commencement, because then it was just ; I would now close the war, because its object may be attained by negotiation." That is his proposition ; I would state it fairly. But what at the commencement was the object of the war, stripped of all diplomatic technicalities ? The right hon. gentleman would not, I am sure, accept the definition of his ex-colleague, the right hon. member for Southwark (Sir Wm. Molesworth), that one object of the war was to punish Russia for her insolence—a doctrine I would never have expected in so accomplished a philosopher as my right hon. friend, the pupil of Bentham and the editor of *Hobbes*. Either in war or legislation, punishment is only a means which has for its object the prevention of further crime. The right hon. gentleman the member for the University of Oxford will no doubt say to me, the object was the independence and integrity of the Ottoman Empire. But how did he describe that object in his speech at Manchester in September 1853 ? He said then to that important audience (I quote his very words) :

" Remember the independence and integrity of Turkey are not like the independence of England and France. It is a Government full of anomaly, of difficulty, and distress."

This is the mode in which, simultaneously with those articles in the *Times*, quoted by the right hon. member for Manchester (Mr Gibson), on the very eve of a war that the right hon. member for the University of Oxford then believed to be just and when he would naturally place the object in the most favourable light his convictions would permit, before the people whose ardour it became his duty to rouse, whose pockets it was his office to tax—this is the laudatory mode in which the right hon. gentleman warmed the enthusiasm of his listeners to acknowledge the justice of his object; and is the statesman who at the onset could take so chilling a view of all the great human interests involved in this struggle, likely to offer us unprejudiced and effective counsels for securing to Turkey that independence and integrity in which he sees anomaly and distress, and in which we see the safeguard to Europe?

The right hon. gentleman complains that the terms in which our object is to be sought are now unwisely extended. Who taught us to extend them? Who made not only the terms but the object itself indefinite? Was it not the head of the Government of which the right hon. gentleman was so illustrious a member? Did not Lord Aberdeen, when repeatedly urged to state to what terms of peace he would apply the epithets "safe" and "honourable," as repeatedly answer, "That must depend on the fortune of war; and the terms will be very different if we receive them at Constantinople, or impose them at St Petersburg"? Sir, if I may say so without presumption, I always discourage that language. I always held the doctrine that if we once went to war, it should be for nothing more and nothing less than justice. [Mr M. Gibson.—"Hear, hear!"] Ay, but do not let me dishonestly catch that cheer, for I must add, and also for adequate securities that justice will be maintained. No redresses should induce us to ask for less—no conquests justify us in demanding more. But when the right hon. gentleman, being out of office, now also asserts that doctrine, why did he not refuse his sanction to the noble Earl, who took the whole question out of the strict limits of abstract justice the moment he made the indefinite arbitration of military success the only principle to guide us in the objects and terms of peace? And if the right hon. gentleman rigidly desired to limit our war to one of protection, how could he have consented to sit in a Cabinet which at once changed its whole character into a war of invasion? All the complications which now surround us—all the difficulties in the way of negotiation which now perplex even the right hon. gentleman's piercing intellect—date from the day you landed in the Crimea and laid siege to Sebastopol. I do not say your strategy was wrong; but wrong or right, when you invaded the Crimea you inevitably altered the conditions on which to establish peace. The right hon. gentleman was a party to that campaign, and he cannot now shrink from its logical consequences. Those consequences are the difficulties comprehended in the Third Article—the lie that your policy would give to your actions if you accepted the conditions proposed by Russia; for why did you besiege Sebastopol, but because it was that fortress which secured to Russia her preponderance in the Black Sea, and its capture or dismantlement was the material guarantee you then and there pledged yourselves to obtain for the independence of Turkey and the security of Europe? And if the fortunes of war do not allow you yet to demand that Sebastopol be disfortified, they do authorise you to demand an equivalent in Russia's complete resignation of a fleet in the Black Sea; for at this moment not one Russian ship can venture to show itself in those waters.

If the right hon. gentleman is perplexed to determine what mode of limiting the Russian preponderance can be invented, one rule for his guidance at least he is bound to consider imperative—namely, that the mode of limitation must be one which shall not content England alone, but the ally to whom the faith of England was pledged by the Cabinet which the right hon. gentleman adorned. It is strange to what double uses the right hon. gentleman can put an ally. When we wished to inquire into the causes of calamities purely our own —calamities which the right hon. gentleman thinks were so exaggerated—an exaggeration that inquiry has not served to dispel—then we are told, "What are you doing? Take care! To inquire into the fate of an English army may offend and alienate your ally, France." But now, when the right hon. gentleman would have desired us to patch up a peace, he forgets altogether that we have an ally upon the face of the globe. He recommends us singly to creep out of the quarrel with Russia, and would leave us equally exposed to the charge of desertion by Turkey, and of perfidy by France. But it has been insinuated—I know not on what authority—that France would have listened to these terms if we had advised it. If this be true, I thank our Government for declining such a responsibility. For if, in that noble courtesy which has characterised the Emperor of the French in his intercourse with us, he had yielded to your instances, and consented to resume and complete negotiations based upon terms he had before refused, who amongst us can lay his hand on his heart and say that a peace which would have roused the indignation even of our commercial and comparatively pacific people, might not so have mortified the pride of that nation of soldiers to which the name of Napoleon was the title-deed to empire, as to have shaken the stability of a throne which now seems essential to the safety and social order of the civilised globe? "Oh," says the right hon. gentleman the member for the University of Oxford, with a solecism in logic which I could never have expected from so acute a reasoner, "see how Russia has come down to terms which she before so contemptuously scouted. In February 1853 she declared such and such terms were incompatible with her honour; she would dictate terms to Turkey only at St Petersburg, under the frown of the Czar, or at the headquarters of the Russian camp; and now see how mild and equitable Russia has become." Yes; but how was that change effected? By diplomacy and negotiations? By notes and protocols? No—these had been tried in vain; the result of these was the levying of armaments—the seizure of provinces—the massacre of Sinope. That change was effected by the sword—effected in those fields of Alma and Inkerman to which the right hon. gentleman so touchingly appealed—effected by those military successes inspired by the passion for fame and glory on which, as principles of action, his humanity is so bitterly sarcastic. The right hon. gentleman dwelt in a Christian spirit, which moved us all, on the gallant blood that had been shed by us, our allies, and even by our foes in this unhappy quarrel. But did it never occur to him that, all the while he was speaking, this question was irresistibly forcing itself on the minds of his English audience: "And shall all this blood have been shed in vain? Was it merely to fertilise the soil of the Crimea with human bones? And shall we, who have buried two-thirds of our army, still leave a fortress at Sebastopol and a Russian fleet in the Black Sea, eternally to menace the independence of that ally whom our heroes have perished to protect?" And would not that blood have been shed in vain? Talk of recent negotiations effecting the object for which you commenced the war! Let us strip those negotiations of diplomatic quibbles, and look at them like men of common sense. Do not let gentlemen be alarmed lest I should weary them with going at length over such hackneyed ground—two minutes will suffice.

The direct question involved is to terminate the preponderance of Russia in the Black Sea; and with this is involved another question—to put an end to the probabilities of renewed war arising out of the position which Russia would henceforth occupy in those waters. Now the first proposition of Russia is to open to all ships the passage of the Bosphorus and the Dardanelles. "That is the right thing," says the right hon. member for Manchester. Yes; so it would be if Russia had not the whole of that coast bristling with fortresses; but while these fortresses remain it is simply to say—Let Russia increase as she pleases the maritime forces she can direct against Turkey, sheltered by all the strongholds she has established on the coasts, and let France and England keep up, if they please, the perpetual surveillance of naval squadrons in a sea, as the note of a French minister well expresses it, "where they could find neither a port of refuge nor an arsenal of supply." This does not, on the one hand, diminish the preponderance of Russia; it only says you may, at great expense, and with great disadvantages, keep standing navies to guard against its abuse; and on the other hand, far from putting an end to the probabilities of war, it leaves the fleets of Russia perpetually threatening Turkey, and the fleets of England and France perpetually threatening Russia. And while such a position could hardly fail sooner or later to create jealousy between England and France, I can scarcely imagine any disease that would more rot away the independence of Turkey than this sort of chronic protection established in her own waters.

The second proposition, which retains the *mare clausum*, not only leaves the preponderance of Russia exactly what it was before the war began, but in granting to the Sultan the power to summon his allies at any moment he may require them, exposes you to the fresh outbreak of hostilities whenever the Sultan might even needlessly take alarm; but with these differences between your present and future position—first, that Russia would then be strengthened, and you might be unprepared; and next, that while, as I said before, now not one Russian flag can show itself on those waters, you might then, before you could enter the Straits, find that flag waving in triumph over the walls of the Seraglio. And, to prove that this is no imaginary danger, just hear what is said upon the subject by the practical authority of Marshal Marmont, which was loosely referred to the other night by the noble Lord the member for London (Lord John Russell), and remember the Marshal is speaking at a period when the force of Russia in those parts was far inferior to what it would be now if you acceded to her terms: "At Sebastopol, Russia has twelve sail of the line, perfectly armed and equipped." Let me here observe that the Marshal recommends that this number should be increased to thirty, and says that if Sebastopol were made the harbour of a powerful navy, nothing could prevent Russia from imposing laws on the Mediterranean—

"In the immediate neighbourhood a division of the army is cantoned; it could embark in two days, and in three more reach Constantinople—the distance between Sebastopol and the Bosphorus being 180 miles, and a speedy passage almost a matter of certainty, owing to the prevalence of northerly winds, and the constant current from the Euxine towards the Sea of Marmora. Thus, on the apprehension of interference from the allied fleet, that of Russia would pass and take up such a position as circumstances might dictate, while an army of 60,000 men would cross the Danube, pass the Balkan, and place itself at Adrianople ; these movements being effected with such promptitude and facility that no circumstances whatever could prevent their being carried into execution."

And now I put it to the candour of those distinguished advocates for the Russian proposals, whose sincerity I am sure is worthy of their character and talents, whether the obvious result of both these propositions for peace is not to keep your Powers in the unrelaxing attitude of war—one of those Powers always goaded on by cupidity and ambition, the other three always agitated by jealousy and suspicion ? And is it on such a barrel of gunpowder as this that you would ask the world to fall asleep? But, say the hon. gentlemen, "The demand of the Western Powers on the Third Article is equally inadequate to effect the object." Well, I think there they have very much proved their case—very much proved how fortunate it was that negotiations were broken off. However, when a third point is to be raised again let us clear it of all difficulties, and raise it not in a Congress of Vienna but within the walls of Sebastopol.

Sir, before I pass from this part of the subject, let me respectfully address one suggestion to those earnest and distinguished reasoners who would make peace their paramount object. You desire peace as soon as possible ; do you think you take the right way to obtain it ? Do you think that when Russia can say : " Here are members of the very Government who commenced the war declaring that our moderation has removed all ground for further hostilities ; they are backed by the most conspicuous leaders of the popular party ; the representatives of those great manufacturing interests which so often influence, and sometimes control, the councils of a commercial State ;" do you think that Russia will not add also : " These are signs that encourage us, the Russian Empire, to prosecute the war; they are signs that our enemy foresees the speedy exhaustion of its means, the relaxing ardour of its people, and must, after some bravado, accept the terms which are recommended in the National Assembly by experienced statesmen and popular tribunes"? You are leading Russia to deceive herself, to deceive her subjects. You are encouraging her to hold out, and every speech you make in such a strain a Russian general might read to his troops, a Russian minister might translate to trembling merchants and beggared nobles, if he desired to animate them all to new exertions against your country. I do not wish to malign and misrepresent you. I respect the courage with which you avow unpopular opinions. I know you are patriots as sincere as we are. You have proved your attachment to the abstract principle of freedom; but do you reflect whether you make a right exercise of your powers if, when we are sending our sons and kinsmen to assist a cause which would at least secure weakness from oppression, and the free development of one nation from the brute force of another, you take the part of the enemy against your country? [Mr M. Gibson.—"No, no!"] "No, no?" What means that denial? You take part with the enemy when you say he is in the right, and against your country when you say we are in the wrong. You transfer from our cause to his that consciousness of superior justice, which gives ardour to the lukewarm, endurance to the hesitating, and by vindicating his quarrel you invigorate his arms.

If I now turn to the Amendments before the House, I know not one that I can thoroughly approve; not, of course, that by the hon. member for the University of Oxford (Sir Wm. Heathcote), not that of the hon. member for Kidderminster (Mr Robert Lowe); for I feel no regret that Russia should not have terminated hostilities by accepting proposals inadequate in my judgment to secure our object; while I think it scarcely consistent with the prerogative of the Crown, and might furnish a dangerous precedent hereafter, if we were to contest the right of Her Majesty to judge for herself whether the means of peace on the basis of the Third Negotiation are exhausted or not. The Amendment of the right hon. member for Portsmouth (Sir F. Baring) would have been more complimentary to the quarter whence he stole it if he had not added the crime of murder to that of theft. He takes an infant from the paternal cradle, cuts it in half, and the head which he presents to us has no longer a leg to stand upon. The original motion of my right hon. friend the member for Buckinghamshire (Mr Disraeli), in censuring the Government for ambiguous language and uncertain conduct, gave a substantial reason for conveying to Her Majesty that we, at least, would support her in the conduct of war. Omit that censure—imply by your silence that there is no reason to distrust Her Majesty's responsible advisers—and the rest of the Resolution becomes an unmeaning platitude. It is with great satisfaction that I think of the effect produced by the original motion of my right hon. friend; for to my mind that effect atones for its want of success in meeting with the sanction of the House. It has not, it is true, changed the Government, but it assuredly has changed its tone. I do not know whether that change will be lasting, but I hope that we are not to take, as a test of the earnestness of a Government thus suddenly galvanised into vigour, the speech of the noble Lord the member for London (Lord John Russell), which, before the division, implied so much, but which, after the division, was explained away in so remarkable a manner. I rejoice that, in wringing direct declarations from the Government, it leaves us free to discuss that which is before us, not as Englishmen against Englishmen, but as citizens of one common State equally interested in surveying the grounds of a common danger.

Much reference has been made, in the course of this debate, as to the position of Austria. The mediation of Austria is withdrawn for the present, but Austria is still there, always ready to mediate as long as she hesitates to act. It is well to consider what may be our position with regard to a Power with which we have constantly been brought into contact.

I cannot too earnestly entreat you to distinguish with Austria and the alliance with Austria. I think it is of the utmost importance, if you would confine this war within compact and definite limits, that you should maintain friendly terms with a Power which, as long as it is neutral, if it cannot serve does not harm you, and which you could not seriously injure without casting out of the balance of Europe one of the weights most necessary to the equilibrium of the scales. It is easy to threaten Austria with the dismemberment of her ill-cemented Empire—easy to threaten her with reduction to a fourth-rate Power. But she has this answer to the practical sagacity of England and the chivalrous moderation of France: "Is the Empire of Austria not less essential as a counterpoise to France than the integrity of Turkey is essential as a barrier against Russia? If the balance of power be not a mere dream, I trust my cause to every statesman by whom the balance of power is respected." But though, for this and for other reasons, I would desire you to maintain friendly relations with Austria, pardon me if I doubt the wisdom of having so earnestly solicited her alliance. Supposing you had now gained it, what would you have done? Just what a Government here might do if it pressed into its Cabinet some able and influential man, with views not congenial to its own, and who used his power on your councils to modify the opinions and check the plans upon which you had before been united. Add Austria now, while she is still timid and reluctant, to the two western Powers—give her a third co-equal voice in all the conduct of the war, and it could only introduce into their councils a certain element of vacillation and discord. But if you bide your time, preserving Austria in her present attitude of friendly neutrality, if you do not threaten and affront her into action against you, the natural consequences of continued war, the common inclinations of her statesmen and her people—which I have reason to know are not favourable to Russia—will bring her to you at length with coincidence in your objects, because according to the dictates of her own sense of self-interest. As far as I can judge, our tone with Austria has been much too supplicating, and our mode of arguing with her somewhat ludicrous. It reminds me of the story of an American who saw making up to him in the woods an enormous bear. Upon that he betook himself to his devotions, and exclaimed, "O Lord, there is going to be a horrible fight between me and the bear. All I seek is fair-play and no favour. If there is justice in Heaven, you ought to help me; but if you won't help me, don't help the bear."

But now comes the grave and solemn problem which the withdrawal of all negotiations forces still more upon the mind of every one who thinks deeply, and which the right hon. gentleman the member for Manchester has so properly raised. War being fairly upon us, of what nature shall be that war? Shall it assume that vast and comprehensive character which excites in the hon. member for Aylesbury (Mr Layard) hopes for the human race too daring even for him to detail to this sober House? In plain words, shall it be a war in which, to use the language of Mr Canning in 1826, you will enlist "all those who, whether justly or unjustly, are dissatisfied with their own countries;" in which you will imitate the spirit of revolutionary France, when she swept over Europe, and sought to reconcile humanity to slaughter by pointing to a rainbow of freedom on the other side of the deluge? Does History here give to the hon. member an example or a warning? How were these promises fulfilled? Look round Europe! You had the carnage—where is the freedom? The deluge spread, the deluge rolled away—half a century is fled, and where is the rainbow visible? Is it on the ruins of Cracow? on the field of Novara? or over the walls of defeated Rome? No; in a war that invokes liberal opinion against established rules, what I most dread and deprecate is, not that you will fulfil your promises and reap the republics for which you sowed rebellions; what I dread far more is, that all such promises would in the end be broken—that the hopes of liberty would be betrayed—that the moment the monarchies of England and

France could obtain a peace that realised the objects for which monarchs go to war, they would feel themselves compelled by the exhaustion of their resources, by the instincts of self-conservatism, to abandon the auxiliaries they had lured into revolution—restore to despotism "the right divine to govern wrong," and furnish it with new excuse for vigilance and rigour by the disorders which always distinguish armed revolution from peaceable reforms.

I say nothing here against the fair possibility of reconstructing in some future Congress the independence of Poland, or such territorial arrangements as are comprised in the question, "What is to be done in the Crimea, provided we take it?" But these are not all that is meant by the language we hear, less vaguely out of this House than in it, except when a minister implies what he shrinks from explaining. And woe and shame to the English statesman who, whatever may be his sympathy for oppressed subjects, shall rouse them to rebellion against their native thrones, not foreseeing that in the changes of popular representative Government, all that his Cabinet may promise to-day a new Cabinet to-morrow may legally revoke; that he has no power to redeem in freedom the pledges that he writes in blood! And woe still more to brave populations that are taught to rest Democracy on the arms of foreign soldiers, the fickle cheers of foreign popular assemblies, or to dream that liberty can ever be received as a gift, extorted as a right, maintained as a hereditary heirloom, except the charter be obtained at their own Runnymede, and signed under the shadow of their own oaks! But there is all the difference between rousing nations against their rulers and securing the independence and integrity of a weak nation against a powerful neighbour. The first is a policy that submits the destinies of a country to civil discord, the other relieves those destinies from foreign interference; the one tends to vain and indefinite warfare—the other starts, at the outset, with intelligible conditions of peace.

Therefore, in this war, let us strictly keep to the object for which it was begun—the integrity and independence of the Ottoman Empire, secured by all the guarantees which statesmen can desire, or victory enable us to demand. The more definite the object, the more firm you will be in asserting it. How the object is to be effected, how these securities are to be obtained, is not the affair of the House of Commons. The strategy must be planned by the allied Cabinets, and its execution entrusted to Councils of War. We in this House can only judge by results; and, however unfair that may seem to Governments, it is the sole course left to us, unless we are always dictating to our allies, and hampering our generals. But we thus make the end of the war purely protective; we cannot make the means we adopt purely defensive. In order to force Russia into our object we must assail and cripple her wherever she can be crippled and assailed. I say, with the right hon. gentleman the member for the University of Oxford, do not offer to her an idle insult, do not slap her in the face, but paralyse her hands. "Oh," said a noble friend of mine the other night (Lord Stanley), "it is a wretched policy to humble the foe that you cannot crush; and are you mad enough to suppose that Russia can be crushed?" Let my noble friend, in the illustrious career which I venture to prophesy lies before him, beware how he ever endeavours to contract the grand science of statesmen into scholastic aphorisms. No, we cannot crush Russia as Russia, but we can crush her attempts to be more than Russia. We can, and we must, crush any means that enable her to storm or to steal across that tangible barrier which now divides Europe from a Power that supports the maxims of Machiavelli with the armaments of Britain. You might as well have said to William of Orange, "You cannot crush Louis XIV.; how impolitic you are to humble him!" You might as well have said to the burghers of Switzerland, "You cannot crush Austria; don't vainly insult her by limiting her privilege to crush yourselves." William of Orange did not crush France as a kingdom—Switzerland did not crush Austria as an empire; but William did crush the power of

France to injure Holland; Switzerland did crush the power of Austria to enslave her people; and in that broad sense of the word, by the blessing of Heaven, we will crush the power of Russia to invade her neighbours and convulse the world.

The right hon. gentleman the member for Manchester has sought to frighten us by dwelling on the probable duration of this war; but if you will only be in earnest, and if you will limit yourselves strictly to its legitimate object, I have no fear that the war will be long. I do not presume on our recent successes, important though they are, for Kertch is the *entrepôt* of all the commerce of the Sea of Azoff; nor on the exaggerated estimate of the forces which Russia has in Sebastopol, or can bring to the Crimea; nor on her difficulty through any long series of campaigns to transport and provision large armies from great distances; nor on many circumstances which, of late especially, tend to show that for exertions at once violent and sustained, her sinews are not strong enough to support her bulk. But I look only to the one fact, that in these days war is money; and that no Power on earth can carry on a long war with a short purse. Russia's pecuniary resources are fast failing her. In no country is recruiting so costly, or attended with such distress to the proprietors of the soil. Every new levy, in depriving the nobles of their serfs, leaves poverty and discontent behind; while in arresting her commercial intercourse, you exhaust the only springs that can recruit the capital which she robs from the land. In the great "History of Treaties," now publishing by the Count de Garden, and which must supersede all other authorities on that subject, he speaks thus of Russia in 1810:—

"The closing of her ports, which was the result of her war with England, deprived Russia of all outlet for her exportations, which, consisting chiefly of raw materials, such as timber, potash, iron, etc., could only be transported by sea. The balance of commerce thus fixed itself entirely to the detriment of Russia, and producing there a disastrous fall in the course of exchange, and a depreciation of the currency, menaced with ruin all the financial resources of the State."

You have, therefore, always at work for you, not only your

fleets and armies, but the vital interests of Russia herself. She cannot resist you long, provided you are thoroughly in earnest. She may boast and dissimulate to the last, but rely on it that peace will come to you suddenly—will, in her proper name, knock loudly at the door which you do not close against peace herself, but against her felonious counterfeit, who would creep through the opening disguised in her garments, and with the sword concealed under her veil.

The noble Lord, who has just spoken with so much honesty of conviction (Lord Archibald Hamilton), ventured to anticipate the verdict of History. Let me do the same. Let me suppose that when the future philanthropist shall ask what service on the human race did we, in our generation, signally confer, some one—trained, perhaps, in the schools of Oxford, or in the Institute of Manchester—shall answer: "A Power that commanded myriads—as many as those that under Xerxes exhausted rivers in their march—embodied all the forces of barbarism on the outskirts of civilisation. Left there to develop its own natural resources, no State molested, though all apprehended, its growth. But, long pent by merciful nature in its own legitimate domains, this Power schemed for the outlet to its instinctive ambition. To that outlet it crept by dissimulating guile, by successive treaties that, promising peace, graduated spoliation to the opportunities of fraud. At length, under pretexts too gross to deceive the common-sense of mankind, it prepared to seize that outlet—to storm the feeble gates between itself and the world beyond." Then the historian shall say that we in our generation—the united families of England and France—made ourselves the vanguard of alarmed and shrinking Europe, and did not sheathe the sword until we had redeemed the pledge to humanity made on the faith of two Christian sovereigns, and ratified at those distant graves which Liberty and Justice shall revere for ever.

THE EARL OF ELLENBOROUGH ON THE POLISH INSURRECTION.

House of Lords, June 8th, 1863.

[The immediate cause of this insurrection was an attempt on the part of the Russian Government to press into the army all the young men of the towns who betrayed the least sympathy with the patriotic movement. Escaping into the woods near the Austro-Polish frontier, the insurgents were able to harass the Russians, and also make good their retreat into a friendly country when pressed too hard. Their chief hope was to hold out until some of the European Powers should take up their cause.]

My Lords,—I rise to ask the noble Earl the Secretary of State for Foreign Affairs (Earl Russell) whether there has been such progress in the negotiations as to afford a reasonable hope of a satisfactory settlement of the affairs of Poland. I do not think the question can be considered premature. The insurrection in Poland, which the Emperor ordered the authorities of the country to put down in ten days, has existed for four months and a half; and according to the last accounts, it was rapidly extending itself to various distant points in the ancient provinces that belonged to Poland before 1772. While diplomatists are writing and consulting, plunder, massacre, and incendiarism are extending through the whole country. My Lords, this is not an ordinary case of diplomacy. Generally, diplomacy originates with the Governments which conduct it; but in this instance, I think it may be considered to have originated with the nations which those Governments represent; for in all parts of the world, except perhaps in Prussia, deep sympathy has been expressed for Poland. When, some years ago, the diplomatic intervention which preceded the Crimean war was undertaken, that diplomacy proceeded from statesmen who had in view not a distant but a coming danger, and endeavoured to avert that danger by diplomatic arrangement; but the evil with which diplomacy now deals is a present existing evil, which has existed for more than thirty years, and has been increasing in intensity until it has arrived at a degree of enormity which has compelled the people of Poland to rise in arms, and makes it impossible for the people of Europe to view their condition with indifference.

This is a question of humanity. From one end of the kingdom of Poland to the other, war is carried on with an atrocity unknown in ordinary warfare. It is a question of justice, because the Poles have never had the Constitution which was promised to them. It is more than that, it is a question of policy affecting not only Russia, but affecting every State in Europe. It is impossible that insurrection can continue in Poland without exciting an insurrectionary feeling among the turbulent spirits of every State in Europe. For over 160 years Russia has been endeavouring to establish her power in Europe—to secure to herself an entrance into Europe. That entrance into Europe is, at the present moment, denied to her. While Poland remains as she is, or even as she has been for several years, it will be impossible for Russia to move an army into Europe. She would require more than 100,000 men to protect her communications; and the longer this state of things remains in Poland, the greater will become the difficulties of Russia. Depend upon it, that whenever any part of the Russian Empire presents a weakness, it will be discovered by those who are anxious to take advantage of any opportunity that may be afforded for acting against her. Circassia will be responsible to Poland, and everywhere there will be a material alteration in that position of strength which I confess, for my part, I am desirous that Russia should maintain.

When the Powers assembled at the Congress of Vienna, they

participated in the general feeling of distrust and apprehension of Russia. Things were then somewhat different from what they are now. In France, the ancient monarchy had been restored; France had suffered great losses; her frontiers had been thrown back to their ancient limits; she was deemed to be in a state of abeyance, and no injury or encroachment was apprehended from that quarter. In Belgium, and on the Rhine, and in Italy, what were then deemed securities had been taken against France. The great danger seemed to be on the side of Russia. Russia had performed great services for Europe, but she stood in her strength, and certainly evinced a disposition to use that strength in a manner that threatened the independence and security of other States. With these feelings, this country desired, in connection with Austria and Prussia, to establish in Poland a state of things which, unfortunately, they did not succeed in bringing about. They desired to establish in Poland an independent kingdom. Russia insisted on uniting the kingdom of Poland to herself. I confess that even at the present time, if I could see the map of Europe arranged as I should most desire, I should rejoice to see the re-establishment of the kingdom of Poland in all its integrity, and within the ancient limits, but under a better Government and with a hereditary monarchy; but I know how visionary is my hope of seeing that great act of moral retribution accomplished. I cannot be insensible to the changes that have taken place in France. We have seen a change of dynasty in France; we have seen her great increase of strength, and we have seen that strength used with great effect in Europe. We have seen other material changes in the distribution of power and of territory as established in 1815.

Having regard to those events, I do not think it would be expedient to take any measures which would permanently deprive Russia of her power of interfering, and I hope usefully interfering, for the maintenance of a Conservative policy in Europe. We cannot now preserve the balance of power in Europe without the intervention of Russia. It is upon that account that, as a friend of Russia as well as a friend of Poland, I do earnestly desire to see an end put to the state of things which now exists. When the Congress of Vienna imposed on Russia the duty of giving a representative national Constitution to Poland, she imposed on her a condition which, in the political condition of Russia, it was impossible for her to perform. I say impossible, because I hold it to be impossible to give a really good government, of a Constitutional form, to a country of which the Sovereign is a foreign despot of enormous power, educated in the practice of despotism, and ready on all occasions to exercise his despotic authority, and throw the sword of Brennus into the scale to turn it in his favour. There was, and still is, that difficulty, which it is impossible to overcome, and which must at all times make it impossible to establish a really good government in Poland under a despotic foreign Sovereign, capable of using on all occasions his arbitrary power. My Lords, a Constitutional government can only exist with benefit to the people where there is mutual confidence between the Sovereign and the people, and where there are mutual interests, where there is a mutual desire to support the Constitution, and where, above all, the Sovereign is attached to his people, and depends on them for his position.

All these circumstances are wanting in the case of Russia. Even were she so disposed, the difficulties which she has to encounter it would be impossible for her to overcome. But, my Lords, there never has been any attempt to overcome those difficulties. We are told in the papers which have been laid on the table of the House, that up to 1831 no attempt had been made to give that Constitution to Poland which she had a right to, in accordance with the Treaty of Vienna. We know what has taken place since. We know that there has been no security either for property or for person. Nothing could be more cruel and exhaustive than the conscription. Every man must have felt that his family, his life, and his property depended on the will of a despot; and it was utterly impossible for the country to prosper or to be contented. That was the case before the last instance of violent despotism—which the noble Earl the Foreign Secretary properly called a "proscription"—was perpetrated in Russia. That proscription came on the people of Poland as one of the plagues of Egypt, destroying in one night the first-born in every family. It created a deep chasm between the people and the Sovereign, which it was impossible ever to pass. It destroyed all confidence, all possibility of ever trusting the word of the Sovereign, who had violated his obligations. If the Emperor puts forth his hand and offers it to the people of Poland, how can they take it? There is blood upon that hand. It is the blood of the people of Poland, of the families of those to whom he offers it—blood shed in the perpetration of an iniquity which has no parallel in Europe.

My Lords, I can come to no other conclusion than this: That to attempt to give good government to the people of Poland while the Emperor of Russia directly exercises authority in that country is a thing impossible, and that there are no guarantees—of which the noble Earl spoke some time ago—which could secure it. It is a thing impossible, and therefore it is a thing which no prudent person would endeavour to obtain. But it is most desirable that Russia should endeavour to accomplish two objects—that she should give good government to Poland, and, at the same time, preserve her power of entering Europe by the Vistula. I know but one course of proceeding by which that double object can be accomplished. The wise course for Russia to pursue would be to propose to dissever the connection which was established at Vienna between the Russian Empire and Poland, then declared inseparable, and to place Poland, with such arrangements as to the political relations between her and Russia as might be deemed expedient, as an independent country with respect to internal government, under the Sovereignty of a Prince of her own family. I do trust that Her Majesty's Government and the other Powers of Europe which were parties to the Treaty of

Vienna would willingly accept this compromise, and consider it as a sufficient performance of the obligations which were imposed upon Russia at the Congress of Vienna. Further, I do hope that the Poles themselves would have the good sense to accept it, and that no visionary ideas of future grandeur, however gratifying they might be to their pride as a nation—great as their pride justly is—would induce them to decline to accept that which, for the present at least, would give security for the government of Poland and the permanent peace of that country.

My Lords, I do not know what value is to be attached to the statements I have seen in the foreign rather than the English papers; but I see it there stated that it has been suggested by the Government of this country, and has been at last acquiesced in by foreign Powers, that an armistice should be proposed to the Emperor of Russia and to the insurgents in Poland. I believe that measure to be utterly impracticable. There are wanting on the side of the Poles three things essential, as it has always been supposed, to the making of an armistice—an ostensibly acknowledged Government with which to contract it; an army for which to contract; nor is there any possibility of making that demarcation of limits which is essential in all cases of armistice. The only force possessed by the Poles is one which is here and everywhere, which is here to-day and gone to-morrow. The Polish insurgents collect only to strike. They disappear when they have struck their blow. They have no regular, no acknowledged limits within which they act. In an armistice the two sides keep their arms. But what is required here is that one side should lay down its arms. There is no other mode by which the Poles can perform their part of the arrangement. But what is it to lay down their arms? You may maintain, and you may extend an insurrection, but you cannot renew it when you have once thrown down your arms. And what is to be the position of the insurgents in the interval during the time in which the diplomatists—who are proverbially not the most rapid in their movements—attempt to bring about a permanent arrangement? From the penalties of treason the Poles might be relieved, but they would be still subject to the criminal law. Russian officers now rule throughout every parish in Poland. They have at their back what are called peasant guards. Every man who has property, who is supposed to have patriotic feelings, is denounced, and there is a general sequestration of the property of such persons. Even in Lithuania, which is not a part of the Kingdom of Poland, no peasant is now permitted to pay rent to his landlord. He pays it to the State, and the State hereafter, if satisfied of the good conduct of the proprietor, will give him the balance which is due to him.

This is a state of things which we know not as having existed at any time in any part of the world, and all this machinery would remain to afflict Poland during the long period of negotiation which must ensue if an armistice were agreed upon. Does the noble Earl, or does Her Majesty's Government, suppose that in diplomacy by itself there is any strength at all? Its strength is in the force by which it is supported—in the force behind. The strength of the Poles in diplomacy is the strength of the insurrection. It is no other. And, depend upon it, great as the sufferings of the Poles have been, they might have suffered for years longer; but if they had suffered in tranquillity and in silence, never would the sympathy of Europe have been extended to them. They have now the sympathy of Europe because they have had the courage and the spirit to rise against their oppressors. It is because they show themselves worthy of Liberty that all Europe feels they ought to possess it. All I can say to the Poles is: "Persevere! Keep your arms! Strike down your enemies wherever you can reach them! You have embarked in a career of honour, of patriotism, and of glory. You may fall in the field; but it is better to fall there than to die in the ranks of your enemies. Persevere! And depend upon it, having adopted this course—adopted, perhaps, by despair, but sanctioned by reason and by justice—you will have the respect of all men, and I trust that Providence will bless your efforts."

JOHN BRIGHT ON SUSPENSION OF THE HABEAS CORPUS ACT.

HOUSE OF COMMONS, FEBRUARY 17TH, 1866.

[THE disturbed state of Ireland rendered it necessary, in the opinion of the Government, to suspend the Habeas Corpus Act, and so give the Lord-Lieutenant unlimited power to arrest and detain suspected persons. For this purpose an extraordinary sitting was called in both Houses of Parliament on Saturday, February 17th, 1866, and the Bill was run through at once, receiving the Royal Assent at twenty minutes to one o'clock on Sunday morning.]

I OWE an apology to the Irish Members for stepping in to make an observation to the House on this question. My strong interest in the affairs of their country, ever since I came into Parliament, will be my sufficient excuse. The Secretary of State (Sir George Grey), on the part of the Government of which he is a member, has called us together on an unusual day and at an unusual hour, to consider a proposition of the greatest magnitude, and which we are informed is one of extreme urgency. If it be so, I hope it will not be understood that we are here merely to carry out the behests of the Administration; but that we are to be permitted, if we choose, to observe upon this measure, and if possible to say something which may mitigate the apparent harshness which the Government feels itself compelled to pursue. It is now more than twenty-two years since I was permitted to take my seat in this House. During that time I have, on many occasions, with great favour, been allowed to address it; but I declare that during the whole of that period I have never risen to speak here under so strong a feeling, as a member of the House, of shame, and of humiliation, as that by which I feel myself oppressed at this moment. The Secretary of State proposes—as the right hon. gentleman himself has said—to deprive no inconsiderable portion of the subjects of the Queen—our countrymen, within the United Kingdom—of the commonest, of the most precious, and of the most sacred right of the English Constitution: the right to their personal freedom. From the statement of the Secretary of State it is clear that this is not asked to be done, or required to be done, with reference only to a small section of the Irish people. He has named great counties, wide districts, whole provinces over which this alleged and undoubted disaffection has spread, and has proposed that five or six millions of the inhabitants of the United Kingdom shall suffer the loss of that right of personal freedom that is guaranteed to all Her Majesty's subjects by the Constitution of these realms.

Now, I do not believe that the Secretary of State has overstated his case for the purpose of inducing the House to consent to his proposition. I believe that if the majority of the people of Ireland, counted fairly out, had their will, and if they had the power, they would unmoor the island from its fastenings, and move it at least two thousand miles to the west. And I believe, further, that if by conspiracy, or insurrection, or by that open agitation to which alone I ever would give any favour or consent, they could shake off the authority, I will not say of the English Crown, but of the Imperial Parliament, they would gladly do so. An hon. member from Ireland a few nights ago referred to the character of the Irish people. He said, and I believe it is true, that there is no Christian nation with which we are acquainted amongst the people of which crime of the ordinary character, as we reckon it in this country, is so rare as it is amongst his countrymen. He might have said, also, that there is no people—whatever they may be at home—more ndustrious than his countrymen in every other country but their own. He might have said more—that they are a people of a cheerful and joyous temperament. He might have said more than this—that they are singularly grateful for kindnesses shown to them, and that of all the people of our race they are filled with the strongest sentiments of veneration. And yet, with such materials, and with such a people, after centuries of government—after sixty-five years of government by this House—you have them embittered against your rule, and anxious only to throw off the authority of the Crown and Queen of these realms. Now, this is not a single occasion we are discussing. This is merely an access of the complaint Ireland has been suffering under during the lifetime of the oldest man in this House : of chronic insurrection. No man can deny this. I dare say a large number of the members of this House had, at the time to which the right hon. member for Buckinghamshire referred, heard the same speech on the same subject from the same Minister to whom we have listened to-day. [Sir G. GREY.—"No!"] I certainly thought I heard the right hon. gentleman the Secretary of State for the Home Department make a speech before on the same question, but he was a Minister of the Government on whose behalf a similar speech was made on the occasion referred to, and no doubt concurred in every word that was uttered by his colleague.

Sixty-five years ago this country undertook to govern Ireland. I will say nothing of the manner in which that duty was brought upon us except this—that it was by proceedings disgraceful and corrupt to the last degree. I will say nothing of the pretences under which it was brought about but this—that the English Parliament and people, and the Irish people, too, were told, if you once get rid of the Irish Parliament it will dethrone for ever Irish factions, and with a united Parliament we shall become a united, and stronger, and happier people. Now, during these sixty-five years—and on this point I ask for the attention of the right hon. gentleman who has just spoken (Mr Disraeli)—there are only three considerable measures which

Parliament has passed in the interests of Ireland. One of them was the measure of 1829, for the emancipation of the Catholics and to permit them to have seats in this House. But that measure, so just, so essential, and which, of course, is not ever to be recalled, was a measure which the chief Minister of the day, a great soldier, and a great judge of military matters (the Duke of Wellington), admitted was passed in the face of the menace and only because of the danger of civil war. The other two measures to which I have referred are the measure for the relief of the poor, and the measure for the sale of the encumbered estates; and those measures were introduced to the House and passed through the House in the emergency of a famine more severe than any that has desolated any Christian country of the world within the last four hundred years.

Except on these two emergencies, I appeal to every Irish member, and to every English member who has paid any attention to the matter, whether the statement is not true that this Parliament has done nothing for the people of Ireland. And, more than that, their complaints have been met—complaints of their sufferings have been met— often by denial, often by insult, often by contempt. And within the last few years we have heard from this very Treasury Bench observations with regard to Ireland which no friend of Ireland, or of England, and no Minister of the Crown, ought to have uttered with regard to that country. Twice in my Parliamentary life this thing has been done—at least, by the close of this day will have been done—and measures of repression—measures for the suspension of the civil rights of the Irish people—have been brought into Parliament and passed with extreme and unusual rapidity. I have not risen to blame the Secretary of State, or to blame his colleagues, for the act of to day. There may be circumstances to justify a proposition of this kind, and I am not here to deny that these circumstances now exist; but what I complain of is this: there is no statesmanship merely in acts of force and acts of repression. And more than that, I have not observed since I have been in Parliament anything on this Irish question that approaches to the dignity of statesmanship. There has been, I admit, an improved administration in Ireland. There have been Lord-Lieutenants anxious to be just, and there is one there now who is probably as anxious to do justice as any man. We have observed generally in the recent trials a better tone and temper than were ever witnessed under similar circumstances in Ireland before. But if I go back to the Ministers who have sat on the Treasury Bench since I first came into this House—Sir Robert Peel first, then Lord John Russell, then Lord Aberdeen, then Lord Derby, then Lord Palmerston, then Lord Derby again, then Lord Palmerston again, and now Earl Russell—I say that, with regard to all these men, there has not been any approach to anything that History will describe as statesmanship on the part of the English Government towards Ireland. There were Coercion Bills in abundance—Arms Bills Session after Session—lamentations like that of the right hon. gentleman the member for Buckinghamshire, that the suspension of the Habeas Corpus Act was not made perpetual by a clause which he laments was repealed. There have been Acts for the suspension of the Habeas Corpus Act, like that which we are now discussing; but there has been no statesmanship. Men, the most clumsy, and brutal, can do these things; but we want men of higher temper—men of higher genius—men of higher patriotism to deal with the affairs of Ireland.

I should like to know if those statesmen who hold great offices have themselves comprehended the nature of this question. If they have not, they have been manifestly ignorant; and if they have comprehended it, they have not dealt with it; they have concealed that which they knew from the people, and evaded the duty they owe to their Sovereign. I do not want to speak disrespectfully of men in office. It is not my custom in this House. I know something of the worrying labours to which they are subjected, and I know how, from day to day, they bear the burden of the labour imposed upon them; but still I lament that those who wear the garb, enjoy the emoluments—and I had almost said, usurp the dignity of statesmanship—sink themselves merely into respectable and honourable administrators, when there is a whole nation under the Sovereignty of the Queen calling for all their anxious thoughts—calling for the highest exercise of the highest qualities of the statesman. I put the question to the Chancellor of the Exchequer (Mr Gladstone). He is the only man of this Government whom I have heard of late years that has spoken as if he comprehended this question, and he made a speech in the last Session of Parliament that was not without its influence both in England and in Ireland. I should like to ask him whether this Irish question is above the stature of himself and his colleagues? If it be, I ask them to come down from the high places which they occupy, and try to learn the art of legislation and government before they practise it. I believe myself, if we could divest ourselves of the feelings engendered by party strife, we might come to some better results. Take the Chancellor of the Exchequer. Is there in any legislative assembly in the world a man, as the world judges, of more transcendent capacity? I will say even, Is there a man with a more honest wish to do good to the country in which he occupies such a conspicuous place? Take the right hon. gentleman opposite, the Leader of the Opposition (Mr Disraeli). Is there in any legislative assembly in the world, at this moment, a man leading an Opposition of more genius for his position, who has given in every way but one in which proof can be given that he is competent to the highest duties of the highest offices of the State? Well, but these men—great men whom we on this side and you on that side to a large extent admire and follow—fight for office, and the result is, they sit alternately one on this side and one on that. But suppose it were possible for these men, with their intellects, with their far-reaching vision, to examine this question thoroughly, and to say for once, whether this leads to office, and to the miserable notoriety that men call Fame, which springs from office, or not: "If it be possible, we will act with loyalty to the Sovereign and justice to the people; and if it be possible, we will make Ireland a strength and not a weakness to the British Empire." It is on account of this fighting with party, and for party, and for the gains which party gives, that there is so little result from the great intellects of such men as these. Like the captive Samson of old—

> "To grind in brazen fetters, under task,
> With their Heaven-gifted strength"—

and the country and the world gain little by those faculties which God has given them for the blessing of the country and the world.

The Secretary of State and the right hon. gentleman opposite, even in stronger language, have referred to the unhappy fact that much of what now exists in Ireland has been brought there from the United States of America. That is not a fact for us to console ourselves with; it only adds to the gravity and the difficulty of this question. You may depend upon it that if the Irish in America, having left this country, settle there with so strong a hostility to us, they have had their reasons; and if, being there with that feeling of affection for their own country which in all other cases in which we are not concerned we admire and reverence, they interfere in Ireland and stir up there the sedition that now exists, depend upon it there is in the condition of Ireland a state of things which greatly favours their attempts. There can be no continued fire without fuel, and all the Irish in America, and all the citizens of America, united together, with all their organisation and all their vast resources, would not in England or in Scotland raise the very slightest flame of sedition or of insurrectionary movement. I want to know why they can do it in Ireland. Are you to say, as some people say in America and in Jamaica, when speaking of the black man, that "nothing can be made of the Irishman"? Everything can be made of him in every country but his own. When he has passed through the American school—I speak of him as a child, or in the second generation of the Irish emigrant in that country—he is as industrious, as frugal, as independent, as loyal, as good a citizen of the American Republic as any man born within the dominions of that Power. Why is it not so in Ireland? I have asked the question before, and I will ask it again; it is a pertinent question, and it demands an answer. Why is it that no Scotchman who leaves Scotland—and the Scotch have been taunted and ridiculed for being so fond of leaving their country for a better climate and a better soil—how comes it, I ask, that no Scotchman who emigrates to the United States, and no Englishman who plants himself there, cherishes the smallest hostility to the people, to the institutions, or to the Government of his native country? Why does every Irishman who leaves his country and goes to the United States immediately settle himself down there, resolved to better his condition in life, but with a feeling of ineradicable hatred to the laws and institutions of the land of his birth? Is not that a question for statesmanship? If the Secretary of State, since his last measure was brought in, now eighteen years ago, had had time in the multiplicity of his duties to consider this question, possibly, instead of now moving for the suspension of the Habeas Corpus Act, he might have been rejoicing at the universal loyalty which prevailed, not throughout Great Britain only, but throughout the whole population of Ireland. I spent two autumns in Ireland in the years 1849 and 1852, and I recollect making a speech in this House not long afterwards which some persons thought was not very wide of the mark. I recommended the Ministers of that time to take an opportunity to hold an Irish Session of the Imperial Parliament—to have no great questions discussed connected with the ordinary matters which are brought before us, but to keep Parliament to the consideration of this Irish question solely, and to deal with those great matters which are constant sources of complaint; and I said that a Session that was so devoted to such a blessed and holy work would be a Session, if it were successful, that would stand forth in all our future history as one of the noblest which had ever passed in the annals of the Imperial Parliament:

Now, Sir, a few days ago everybody in this House, with two or three exceptions, was taking an oath at that table. It is called the Oath of Allegiance. It is meant at once to express loyalty, and to keep men loyal. I do not think it generally does bind men to loyalty, if they have not loyalty without it. I hold loyalty to consist, in a country like this, as much in doing justice to the people as in guarding the Crown—for I believe there is no guardianship of the Crown, in a country like this, where the Crown is not supposed to rest absolutely upon force, so safe as that of which we know more in our day probably than has been known in former periods of our history, when the occupant of the throne is respected, admired, and loved by the general people. Now, how comes it that these great statesmen whom I have named, with all their colleagues, some of them as eminent almost as their leaders, have never tried what they could do—have never shown their loyalty to the Crown by endeavouring to make the Queen as safe in the hearts of the people of Ireland as she is in the hearts of the people of England and of Scotland? Bear in mind that the Queen of England can do almost nothing in these matters. By our Constitution the Crown can take no direct part in·them. The Crown cannot direct the policy of the Government—nay, the Crown cannot, without the consent of this House, even select its Ministers; therefore the Crown is helpless in this matter. And we have in this country a Queen who, in all the civilised nations of the world, is looked upon as a model of a Sovereign, and yet her name and fame are discredited and dishonoured by circumstances such as those which have twice during her reign called us together to agree to a proposition like that which is brought before us to-day. Now, there is an instructive anecdote to be found in the annals of the Chinese Empire. In a remote province there was an insurrection. The Emperor put down the insurrection, but he abased and humbled himself before his people, and said that if he had been guilty of neglect, he acknowledged his guilt, and he humbled himself before those on whom he had brought the evil of an insurrection in one of his provinces. The Queen of these realms is not so responsible. She cannot thus humble herself; but I say that your statesmen for the last sixty—for the last forty—years are thus guilty, and they ought to humble themselves before the people of this country for their neglect.

But I have heard from members in this House—I have seen much writing in newspapers—and I have heard of speeches elsewhere, in which some of us, who advocate what we believe to be a great and high morality in public affairs, are charged with dislike to the institutions, and even disloyalty to the dynasty which rules in England. There can be nothing more offensive, nothing more unjust, nothing more utterly false. We who ask Parliament, in dealing with Ireland, to deal with it upon the unchangeable principle of justice, are the friends of the people, and the really loyal advisers and supporters of the Throne. All history teaches us that it is not in human nature that men should be content under any system of legislation and of institutions such as exists in Ireland. You may pass this Bill, you may put the Home Secretary's five hundred men in gaol—you may do all this, and suppress the conspiracy, and put down the insurrection; but the moment it is suppressed here will still remain the germs of this malady, and from these germs will spring up, as heretofore, another crop of insurrection and another harvest of misfortune. And it may be that those who sit here eighteen years after this moment will find another Ministry and another Secretary of State to propose to you another administration of the same ever-failing and ever-poisonous medicine. I say there is a mode of making Ireland loyal. I say that the Parliament of England, having abolished the Parliament of Ireland, is doubly bound to examine what that mode is, and, if it can discover it, to adopt it. I say that the Minister who occupies office in this country merely that he may carry on the daily routine of administration, who dares not grapple with this question, who dares not go into Opposition, and who will sit anywhere except where he can tell his mind freely to the House and the country, may have a high position in this country, but he is not a statesman, nor is he worthy of the name.

Sir, I shall not oppose the proposition of the right hon. gentleman. The circumstances, I presume, are such, that the course which is about to be pursued is perhaps the only merciful course for Ireland. But I suppose it is not the intention of the Government, in the case of persons who are arrested, and against whom any just complaint can be made, to do anything more than that which the ordinary law permits, and that when men are brought to trial they will be brought to trial with all the fairness and all the advantages which all the ordinary law gives. I should say what was most unjust to the gentlemen sitting on that (the Treasury) Bench, if I said aught else than that I believe they are as honestly disposed to do right in this matter as I am, and as I have ever been. I implore them, if they can, to shake off the trammels of doubt and fear with regard to this question, and to say something that may be soothing—something that may give hope to Ireland. I voted the other night with the hon. member for Tralee (The O'Donoghue). We were a very small minority. Yes, I have often been in small minorities. The hon. gentleman would have been content with a word of kindness and sympathy, not for conspiracy, but for the people of Ireland. That word was not inserted in the Queen's Speech, and to-night the Home Secretary has made a speech urging the House to the course which, I presume, is about to be pursued; but he did not in that speech utter a single question which lies behind, and is greater and deeper than that which he discussed. I hope, Sir, that if Ministers feel themselves bound to take this course of suspending the common right of personal freedom to a whole nation, at least they will not allow this debate to close without giving to us and to that nation some hope that before long measures will be considered and will be introduced which will tend to create the same loyalty in Ireland that exists in Great Britain. If every man outside the walls of this House who has the interest of the whole Empire at heart were to speak here, what would he say to this House? Let not one day elapse, let not another Session pass, until you have done something to wipe off this blot—for blot it is—upon the reign of the Queen, and scandal it is to the civilisation, and to the justice of the people of this country.

THE RIGHT HON. ROBERT LOWE[1] ON PARLIAMENTARY REFORM.

HOUSE OF COMMONS, APRIL 26TH, 1866.

[THE Reform Bill of 1866, introduced by Mr Gladstone on March 12th, had for its object the reduction of the County Franchise from £50 to £14, and of the Borough Franchise from £10 to £7. The popular interest in this measure was unbounded; not since the passing of Lord Russell's Reform Bill in 1832 had any Parliamentary measure excited so much curiosity or alarm.]

SIR,—My hon. friend the member for Westminster (Mr John Stuart Mill) has come out in a new character. I do not speak of the excellent speech which he has made, because, having known him for many years, I was quite sure that, when he took the trouble to give us his best thoughts, instead of dealing in impromptus, those great abilities which are acknowledged to be his would be apparent. But my hon. friend has taken a new stand. He has taken many positions with regard to this subject, as those who are acquainted with his works well know; but he has now come forward in the capacity of the advocate of my second principle, the doctrine of class representation. He demands the franchise for the working classes; because, he says, they are not sufficiently represented now, although they have a fourth of the votes in boroughs. He offers no argument in support of his assertion; I therefore pass it by, as I wish to deal with arguments, and not assertions. My hon. friend does

---

[1] Afterwards Viscount Sherbrooke.

say, however, that the working classes have not so much influence as they might be supposed to have, because they are so distributed that they are usually outvoted, and thus they are in a position little better than if they had no votes at all. He regrets, on their behalf, that some law is not in force for giving to minorities representation. I believe that is a fair statement of my hon. friend's argument. (*Mr Mill was understood to assent.*)

Now, I think my hon. friend ought, in passing, to have adverted to the argument which I have so frequently insisted upon in this House—namely, that if the working classes have only 128,000 votes in the present constituencies, it is very much their own fault, because many more of them have the means, if they choose to live in £10 houses. The law, therefore, is not to blame in this respect. He might have adverted to a case which I may mention as the type of many others. The Southwick glass manufactory, at Sunderland, is a large establishment where many workmen are employed, earning from £4 to £5 a week. It is complained that none of these persons have the franchise. But whose fault is that? These workmen are earning, some £200 and some £250 a year, and yet they live in houses under £10 a year in value. Is it the fault of the law? Of course, I must not say whose fault it is. Every gentleman is free to say anything that is complimentary of the working classes in general, and his own constituency in particular; but any gentleman who says anything in the slightest degree not pleasing to them is thought to have grossly misconducted himself. But now, having adopted the theory of classes, we cannot, as my hon. friend was inclined to do, take it up in order to make an argument in favour of the working classes, and lay it down when it makes against them. His logical mind will tell him that he must follow the principle out to its legitimate conclusions, and so he is bound to show us that the extension of the franchise which he asks for the working classes, though a wide extension, can be given without injury to the other classes. He must not take the theory up for the working classes alone, but for all classes. Now, he has not condescended to show us how the extension which he approves would influence the position of any other class; for I view this question not as one between working classes and those who employ them, but between those who have property and those who have not.

Now, Sir, I would refer my hon. friend and the House to the Preface of the third edition of his work on "Political Economy." It was published in 1852, so that my hon. friend has had time to change his mind since, and he is entitled to do it. This is what he said. I am very glad that I didn't—

"The only objection to which any great importance will be attached in the present edition, is the unprepared state of mankind in general, and the labouring classes in particular; their extreme unfitness at present for any order of things which would make any considerable demand on either their intellect or their virtue."

That was in 1852; but we have the opinion of my hon. friend in 1861. In his work on "Representative Government" he says—

"I regard it as wholly inadmissible that any person should participate in the suffrage without being able to read, write, and, I will add, perform the common operations of arithmetic. Universal teaching must precede universal enfranchisement. No one, but those in whom an *à priori* theory has silenced common sense, will maintain that power over others, over the whole community, should be given to people who have not acquired the commonest and most essential requisites for taking care of themselves."

My hon. friend himself cheers these remarks. I hope he will take some opportunity of telling us what was the process of investigation he entered upon for the purpose of satisfying himself that the electors in £7 houses will be found prepared for the exercise of the franchise. I hope he will tell us what evidence he has to produce of their intellect and their virtue I hope he will satisfy us, if he has satisfied himself, of their being able to read and write, and to perform all the common operations of arithmetic, including—I suppose, though he did not state it in that passage—the Rule of Three. I hope he has satisfied himself that universal teaching has preceded universal enfranchisement. Of course the word "universal" might be struck out, and the sense would remain the same—namely, that instruction must precede enfranchisement. I hope he will show us how he has satisfied himself that those persons whom he proposes to enfranchise—to whom he would entrust the interests of others—are persons who have acquired the commonest and most essential requisites for taking care of themselves. If not, how can he reconcile his present position with any principle, but that *à priori* theory of which he speaks? I do not say my hon. friend cannot do it. He can do most things, and perhaps he can do this; but I only say, as things stand, he has not done it, and that his own writings are against the principle which he now supports by his speech.

My hon. friend half took up the challenge which I threw out when I asked in what this Parliament—which has only just come into existence, and which was condemned before it was born—has been found wanting. He pointed out our old friend the Cattle Plague. I am not going to argue that question over again; but my hon. friend said, that if the working classes had been represented here, they might have objected to persons being twice compensated for their cattle. Now, Sir, I cannot persuade my hon. friend, but I think, if I had the working men here, I could show them that the persons to whom the hon. member for Westminster alludes will not be compensated twice. Suppose a farmer has a hundred head of cattle, which are killed to prevent the spread of the disease. He is compensated at less than their value, and then it becomes necessary for agricultural purposes that he should go into the market and buy another hundred head of cattle. The loss which he sustains is not only the difference between the value of his former cattle and the compensation which he got for them, but also the amount by which the price of cattle has been enhanced by the disease, and enhanced in some degree by the slaughter. I cannot persuade my hon. friend, because he is a philosopher, but I think I could persuade the working men whom he seeks to bring among us, that so far from being paid twice over, the farmer in that case has never been paid once. You can put a case which will be the other way. If a man has a large herd of cattle, and is compensated for a few of them, he may be paid over again by the enhanced prices of the remainder. You can put the case both ways, but what I complain of is the narrowness and illiberality of saying that this is a matter which cannot admit of two aspects—that those who differ from my hon. friend must be wrong, and that if it were not for the faulty constitution of this House, we should see and judge things in the same manner as he does. [Mr MILL.—I wish to correct the last assertion of my hon. friend. I never imputed to hon. gentlemen in this House, or to the landed interest, that they were wilfully wrong.] I may remark that I suppose no one in this House would have any objection to working men coming here if the constituencies wished to send them. They can do so now if they like, and therefore we need not take up time in arguing the point, because I am sure that, whenever the constituencies may think proper to send working men here, we shall receive those representatives properly, and listen to them with respect. But my hon. friend told us of the subjects which the working classes might wish to debate here. He referred to "the right of labour." That sounds very like the right *to* labour, of which we heard in 1848. Are we to have the doctrines of Fourier and St Simon discussed here? We are told that in so doing we shall educate the working man. I protest against this. We are here to legislate for this country, and if we look after the Executive Government pretty sharply—if we take care of our finance, and if we watch the Foreign Office, we shall be doing better than we should by converting this House into an academy or gymnasium for the instruction even of the *élite* of the working classes.

My hon. friend said that if the working classes were here they would establish a school in every parish in a few years. Well, that is a subject on which I ought to know something; and I may say that the main object I had in view, in the changes which I proposed on the part of the Government in the education system, was to benefit the working classes.

Under the old system the poor children were not properly taught. The upper children, the children of richer parents, were examined, and the money was paid; but the lower and poorer children were neglected. The upper children had generally had some education at home; but the poorer children had received no education at home, and they were not done justice to in the schools. The object of the Revised Code was to ensure that education should be given to the poor just as much as to the rich; so that the object was one mainly—indeed entirely—for the working classes. But in that object I never received the slightest assistance in any way from the working classes. The opposition to it was very much from the members of the large towns in which the working classes form a considerable portion of the constituencies; but the working classes themselves never interfered in the matter. They did not care about it. The schoolmasters interfered, and got members of Parliament to oppose the Code; but the working classes never entered into the matter at all. How, therefore, my hon. friend can think that working men will deal with this question, in which they have never shown any interest, and which is very intricate and difficult, I cannot understand. Again, my hon. friend ought to be prepared to show how he means to resist the course of what he calls false economy. If the working classes, in addition to being a majority in the boroughs, get a redistribution of the seats in their favour, it will follow that their influence will be enormously increased. They will then urge the House of Commons to pass another Franchise Bill, and another Redistribution Bill to follow it. Not satisfied with these, yet another Franchise Bill and another redistribution of seats will, perhaps, follow. It will be a ruinous game of see-saw. No one can tell where it will stop, and it will not be likely to stop until we get equal electoral districts, and a qualification so low that it will keep out nobody.

There is another matter with which my hon. friend has not dealt: I mean the point of combination among the working classes. To many persons there appears great danger that the machinery which at present exists for strikes and trades' unions may be used for political purposes. And that this use of such machinery has not escaped the attention of thinking men, I will show you, from a speech made by the hon. member for Birmingham in January 1860. In that speech he said—

"Working men have associations; they can get up formidable strikes against Capital—sometimes for things that are just, sometimes for things that are impossible. They have associations, trade societies, organisations; and I want to ask them why it is that all these various organisations throughout the country could not be made use of for the purpose of obtaining their political rights?"

Why is it that these various organisations have not been so made use of? The hon. gentleman asked that question in 1860, and I admit that hitherto he has received no answer. Why? I will tell you why. The working classes, to use his own expression, are the lever. But they must have a fulcrum before they can act. They have not got it. Give them the majority of the voters in a number of boroughs, and it is supplied to them. It is not by passing resolutions and making speeches they coerce their masters. They watch their opportunity; they wait for the time when large orders are in, and they refuse to work: that is the fulcrum they work on. Give them the majority of voters—that will be their political fulcrum; and if the hon. gentleman repeats his advice, no doubt they will use it with avidity. I want to call the attention of the House, in a few words, to the condition of the trades' unions, because we are all anxious to discover, if we can, the future of that Democracy, which, I believe, this Bill will be the first means of establishing. I take one class, the operative stonemasons—a very influential association, numbering 80,000 members, and having a large capital. Last year, after a strike of nineteen weeks, this body of masons beat the masters. Let me call the attention of the House to a letter which they sent to the employers—

"We present you with the wishes of our trade union, requesting a reply on or before Saturday next:—Mr Thomas and all non-society plasterers to be discharged ; all non-society carpenters and improvers to be discharged ; piecework to be abolished, etc. On behalf of the United Building Trades, JOHN BRAY, Chairman."

Mark what that is. See the power unions have of drawing men within their own circle. You say, if they become political bodies, men who want to have nothing to do with politics will have nothing to do with them. Can they help themselves? They will be overborne, overawed; they are like men contending with a mäelstrom, into which, and struggle as they may, eventually they will be sucked. This is a paragraph which I have taken from an Edinburgh paper—

"The tailors' strike may now be considered at an end, the men having agreed to accept the London 'log,' with payment at the rate of 5½d. an hour, as offered by the masters. These terms the men seem to consider as highly satisfactory, entailing, as they will, an increase of from 15 to 25 per cent. on their wages. We have been informed that the men have made it a condition with the masters that the 'black sheep,' or those who have continued working during the lock-out, shall not obtain employment until they become members of the Society, besides paying a fine of ten shillings each."

You will say these men do not want to join these societies— I daresay they do not; but what choice have they? The truth is—and of this I want to convince the House—that these trades' unions are far more unions against the best, the most skilful, the most industrious, and most capable of the labourers themselves, than they are against their masters. Listen to another rule which is taken from the printed book of the Co-operative Society of Masons—

"Working overtime, tending to our general injury by keeping members out of employment, shall be abolished, except in case of accident or necessity."

This is your future political organisation. Again—

"It is also required that lodges harassed by piecework or sub-contracting do apply at a reasonable time for a grant to abolish it."

That is to say, men are first to be driven into these unions by pressure such as I have explained to the House, and then, once they are got within the limits, whatever their necessities, whatever the pressure of their families, they are not to be allowed to eke out their income by working overtime. To do so might enable a man, a poor man, to raise himself out of that sphere of life, and furnish him with some still better occupation. But although his good conduct might have invited the confidence, and attracted the notice of his master, he is not allowed to take a sub-contract, to make a little money in that way. The object of all these proceedings is obvious. It is to enclose as many men as can be got into these societies, and then to apply to them the strictest democratic principle; and that is to make war against all superiority, to keep down skill, industry, and capacity, and make them the slaves of clumsiness, idleness, and ignorance. One extract more, and I have done—

> "In localities where that most obnoxious and destructive system generally known as 'chasing' is persisted in, lodges should use every effort to put it down. Not to take less time than that taken by an average mason in the execution of the first portion of each description of work, is the practice that should be adopted among us as much as possible; and where it is plainly visible that any member or other individual is striving to overwork or 'chase' his fellow-workers, thereby acting in a manner calculated to lead to the discharge of members, or a reduction of their wages, the party so acting shall be summoned before the lodge, and if the charge be satisfactorily proved, a fine shall be inflicted on the party implicated."

That is to say, when a poor workman, naturally quicker and more skilful than those about him, and with a wish to distinguish himself, shows his capacity, so as to oblige his fellow-workmen to exert themselves more than goes to what they please to call the time taken by an average mason in the execution of his work, he is to be fined and put down. Add to this—what does not appear in any of the rules and regulations, but what we know well — the system of terrorism that exists behind these trades' unions, and makes the lives of the "knob-sticks" and "black sheep" miserable till they are driven into them. And then look at this tremendous machinery; if you only arm it with the one thing it wants—the Parliamentary vote!

It remains for us to consider the result of the step that you are invited to take. I assume that this is really a very large and sweeping change in the democratic direction, giving, as I believe, the majority of votes in boroughs to the working classes. On that point we are compelled to differ, because the Government will not give us the materials necessary for making an accurate calculation. This change is to be followed by a further and very large change in the redistribution of seats. It does not depend upon any Government, upon any Minister, perhaps upon any House of Commons, to say where those changes will stop. One hon. member speaks of this as a change that will last fifty years. He has put the matter as entirely out of his power as a man who, rolling a stone down the side of a mountain, fixes beforehand in his own mind the time it will take to reach the bottom. We have had this matter put before us from one very peculiar and invidious point of view. It seems to have been thought that the manner to discuss the probable results of a great democratic change in this country was, on the one side, to praise the working man, especially those among our own constituents, and on the other, to remain silent, because nothing except praise, it is presumed, would be borne. I think that is not the way to approach this question. There is considerable risk that in this way the basis of our institutions may be complimented away. We are rich in experience on this subject. We have the experience of our own state and condition, which, compared with that of other countries, may be called a stationary state; we have the experience of our Colonies all over the world, which may be described as in a transition state; and we have the experience of those two great democracies, France and America, where Democracy may be said to have run its course, and arrived at something like its ultimate results. It is inexcusable in us, if we do not apply our minds to the consideration of this subject, and draw from this rich field of observation conclusions more trustworthy and more reliable than those to be gained from our own isolated experience, particularly as this is so often contradictory.

The hon. gentleman the Under-Secretary for the Colonies (Mr Cardwell) began his speech the other night by telling us, that if the working men had a fault in the world, it was their too great reverence for authority, and then he went on to tell us, that if we did not accede to their present moderate requests, it would be a question, not of how much we should give, but of how much they would take. That was the sum of the hon. gentleman's remarks; he told us that the burden of proof would be effectively shifted, and he said what we all understood the Chancellor of the Exchequer (Mr Gladstone) to say before he wrote his preface, and made his two speeches to explain away his meaning. The working men entered the hon. gentleman the Under-Secretary's speech like lambs, and they left it as lions; and so his estimate of them may be said to answer itself. The question of peace or war has been a good deal touched upon in this debate. The Chancellor of the Exchequer, at Liverpool, was very much struck with the magnificent spectacle put forth by Democracy in the recent war. I would rather he had commended it for something it had done in peace. I never doubted that Democracy was a terrible warlike power. It is not the educated and reflective who are influenced by ideas, but the half-educated and the unreflective; and if you show to the ignorant and poor and half-educated wrong, injustice, and wickedness, anywhere, their generous instincts rise within them, and nothing is easier than to get up a cry for the redress of those grievances. We feel the injustice, too; but we look not merely at the injustice itself—we look before and after; we look at the collateral circumstances, at what must happen to the trade, revenue, and our own position in the world, and we look also at what must happen to those very poor persons themselves, before we commit ourselves to a decided course. Persons, also, who have something to lose are less anxious to lose it than those who have little at stake often, even though these last may by the loss be reduced to absolute poverty. At the time of the Crimean war, we actually got up an enthusiasm on behalf of that most abominable and decrepit despotism—the Turkish Empire. Nothing would have been more popular in England than a war on behalf of Hungary in 1849, or one lately on behalf of Poland. Wherever cruelty or injustice exists, the feelings of the humbler class of Englishmen—to their honour be it said—revolt against it, and, not possessing the quality of circumspection, their impulse is to go straight at the wrong and redress it, without regard to ulterior consequences.

Therefore, to suggest that in making the institutions of the country more democratic we have any security from war, that we do not greatly increase the risk of war, seems to me supremely ridiculous. What is taking place in the Australian Colonies? Victoria and New South Wales are both governed by universal suffrage, and it is as much as we can do to prevent their going to war with each other. Look at America. A section of the American Democracy revolted and broke up the Union, the rest fought to preserve it; the war was fought out to the bitter end, and now that the war is concluded, they are almost ready to go to war again to prevent the doing of that which they took up arms to accomplish. Look at Free Trade. If we have a precious jewel in the world, it is our Free Trade Policy. It has been everything to us. With what eyes do Democracies look at it? Let us turn to History, and not enter into particular cases of particular working men. Take the facts. Canada has raised her duties enormously, and justified them upon Protectionist principles. The Prime Minister of New South Wales at this moment is a strong Protectionist. The Ministry in Victoria were Free Traders, but by the will of the people they have been converted, and have become Protectionists. So vigorously has the question been fought, that destruction is threatened to the second branch of the Legislature, though equal in power to the other, in defiance of the laws of the country, and all to carry out a policy of Protection. Then we come to America. America out-protects Protection—there never was anything like the zeal for Protection in America. With a revenue that needs recruiting, by every means in their power they persist in sacrificing the most valuable resources; with a frontier that bids defiance to any effectual attempts to guard it, they persist in maintaining duties that provoke to wholesale smuggling rather than reduce them by a single penny. And, as if anxious at once to illustrate the Free Trade and Peace proclivities of Democracy, they terminate the Treaty with Canada, which was a step in the direction of Free Trade, and then seek to enforce by violence the very rights which the Treaty they have put an end to secured. I will add one word as to Communism. The hon. member for Lambeth has certainly furnished us with a very good argument in favour of the proposition of having working men to represent themselves. He has drawn such a picture of them as they would scarcely have given themselves. What does he say? He says, in the first place, that they are entirely unable to understand that wages depend on the laws of supply and demand; that, he says, is entirely out of their conception. Then he tells us that they have no conception of any difference between the remuneration of the strong and the weak; the strong are to work for the weak, and all are to be paid alike. Then, as far as Government is concerned, the working men—so far from having a horror of a paternal and interfering Government—want us to prevent their going to public-houses, and this in the name of universal Liberty, Equality, and Fraternity. Not only so, but they insist that the money of their fellow-taxpayers ought to be spent in building houses for them to live in, forsooth, to appropriate a sufficient proportion of their own incomes to pay the amount of rent required to accomplish this object on commercial principles.

I now come to the question of the representatives of the working classes. It is an old observation that every Democracy is in some respects similar to a despotism. As courtiers and flatterers are worse than despots themselves, so those who flatter and fawn upon the people are generally very inferior to the people—the objects of their flattery and adulation. We see in America, where the people have undisputed power, that they do not send honest, hard-working men to represent them in the Congress, but traffickers in office, bankrupts, men who have lost their character, and been driven from every respectable way of life, and who take up politics as a last resource. There is one subject of immense importance to a constitutional House—viz., the expenses of elections. The member for Westminster (Mr J. S. Mill) thinks this Bill will abridge the influence of wealth. Will it do so? Let us see. These expenses are of two kinds—legitimate and illegitimate. The Bill now before the House will enormously increase the electoral districts, and in many it will double, and in some treble, the legitimate expense of elections. I am speaking among people who are thoroughly acquainted with this subject, and they know too well that the expenses of elections depend as much on the illegitimate as on the legitimate agencies employed. Can it be argued, then, that by admitting occupiers of houses between £10 and £7 you will diminish the illegitimate expenses of elections? Yes, it can, for it has been thus argued by the right hon. gentleman the President of the Board of Trade (Mr Milner Gibson). The right hon. gentleman—and I am happy to have his authority—says (mind, I do not) that the people in a great many of the boroughs are very corrupt. [Mr M. GIBSON.—I said, "Some voters."] Well, some voters in some boroughs. I wish to be cautious. Some of these voters have political opinions, but their minds are so sluggish that they cannot be influenced without a certain *lene tormentum*, or reminder in the shape of a five-pound note; while others, who have no political opinions, are slow and procrastinating, being never able to make up their minds until about three o'clock on the day of the poll, when by some inscrutable influence they are urged on to a little activity. Others are judicial, and cannot decide till they have been paid on both sides. It is said, Here is a disease; cure it, dilute its poison by admitting a large number to the franchise. Well, this would be a very good argument if health were catching as well as disease. If I had half-a-dozen diseased cattle, and I turned one hundred sound cattle among them, I might infect the new ones, but I do not think that I should do much good to the sick ones.

And now let me say that I have never been answered as to

the effect which the lowering of the franchise would have upon this House, and I suppose that I never shall be. One great mistake is made—it is almost a childish oversight—and that is to speak of this House as if it were merely a legislative body. The members of this House have a position, a consideration, and a weight in this country such as no legislative body ever had in any country in the world. This is not because of any extraordinary skill in legislation; we have other functions. The House is the administrator of the public funds, but besides that, it is a main part of the Executive Government of the country. It can unmake the Executive, and it can go a long way to make it. It is, therefore, well to consider that you are dealing with a Legislature entirely different from either the Assembly of France or the Congress of America. We all know that while our legislation has been more vigorous and better since the Reform Bill, the Executive Government has shown weakness and languor. If you exaggerate, if you intensify the causes already at work, you will find it necessary to do what has been done elsewhere—to separate the functions of the Executive Government from the House of Commons altogether, to break up that most salutary union which exists between them, and to have a Government which shall not depend for its existence upon a majority in this House.

Now, that is a consideration the seriousness of which it is perfectly impossible to exaggerate. In the Colonies they have got Democratic Assemblies And what is the result? Why, responsible Government becomes a curse, instead of a blessing. In Australia there is no greater evil to the stability of Society, to industry, to property, and to the well-being of the country, than the constant change which is taking place in the Government, and the uncertainty that it creates, and the pitting of rival factions against each other. The same thing, I think, is wonderfully exemplified in Victoria, where you have a Government which is now under the influence of universal suffrage, and which is at war at once with the judicial authorities and the Upper Chamber, because neither will yield to its illegal exactions. The Supreme Court decides against the levy of taxes by resolution of the Assembly, and the Government dissolves Parliament and appeals to universal suffrage against the decision of the Supreme Court. What does this tend to? It tends to Anarchy, and from that Anarchy these Colonies must be relieved. They can, however, only be relieved by depriving them of that boon which in an unfortunate hour they received— that of responsible Government coupled with universal suffrage —and by placing their Government in some permanent hands, so that the Executive shall not be in a perpetual state of change. Look a little further, and see what happened in France, where there was a limited constituency in the time of Louis Philippe, and Parliamentary Government until the Revolution of 1848. Then came the Assembly elected by universal suffrage, and still with a responsible Government. But that responsible Government became weaker every day until the *coup d'état*, and I doubt if there are many gentlemen here who could tell me the name of the nominal Premier under whom the liberties of France were overthrown. The great men who founded the Constitution of America foresaw this, and they took means to obviate the difficulty. They knew perfectly well of what the enormous advantage of our system of Government consisted. They knew that Democracy required checks, and they sought to check it by various means. They, in fact, checked Democracy with Democracy, and elected a President. They added, too, what we have not got—the principle of federalism, which resisted the downward tendency of Democracy by a lateral pressure. To use a familiar illustration, they held a piece of coal up by a pair of tongs. That has been the course adopted in America. And now let us see what has come of it. They have fought out a Civil War, and gained a great victory. But we must remember that men's opinions were divided. One side wanted to prevent the South from regaining the power it possessed before the Civil War, and the other to reconstruct the Union on the principle of State rights. In this country the question would be decided by a vote displacing or retaining the Government; and those who were displaced would carry into the wilderness their offences, as the scapegoat carried off the offences of the people of Israel. But mark what happens in America. You cannot get rid of the President, who sits for four years; nor the Congress, which sits for two years. Therefore you have an internecine duel, and those who ought to combine and coalesce for the good of the country are in factious opposition. The whole frame of the Constitution is thus stretched until it cracks—to try, not who shall hold the supreme power, but which of the two rival institutions shall gain the victory over the other. You have seen Senators expelled in order to secure a majority of two-thirds, and things have arrived at such a pitch that no man need be surprised at seeing a second Civil War, from the inability of the Constitution to solve the difficulty in which the first Civil War had placed the country.

Let us apply this to our own country. We have in our own Government an invaluable institution, and let us not rashly or foolishly put it in peril. I do not know whether hon. gentlemen have read the report of the debate which took place the other day in the French Chamber between M. Thiers and M. Rouher on the subject of the introduction into France of a responsible Government. Though my sympathies, as an Englishman, are with M. Thiers, I confess that in my opinion the argument of M. Rouher was unanswerable, for the question was whether responsible Government could co-exist with universal suffrage? If you were to have responsible Government back, said M. Rouher, you must also have back the *pays legal*, the old constituencies containing 200,000 voters; for, without that, he argued, M. Thiers was asking for a thing without being prepared to realise the only conditions under which it could exist. Now, Sir, Democracy has yet another tendency, which it is worth while to study at the present moment. It is singularly prone to the concentration of power. Under it individual men are small, and the Government is great. That must be the character of a Government which represents the majority, and which absolutely tramples down and equalizes everything except itself. And Democracy has another strong peculiarity. It looks with the utmost hostility on all institutions not of immediate popular origin which intervene between the people and the Sovereign power which the people have set up. To use the words of the right hon. gentleman the Chancellor of the Duchy of Lancaster, it likes to have everything as representative as possible, but that which is not representative it likes to have swept away. Now, look what is done in France. Democracy has left nothing in that country between the people and the Emperor except a bureaucracy, which the Emperor himself has created. In America it has done almost the same thing. You have there nothing to break the shock between the two great powers of the State. The wise men who framed the Constitution tried to provide a remedy by dividing functions as much as possible. They assigned one function to the President, another to the Senate, a third to the Congress, and a fourth to the different States. But all their efforts have been in vain, and you see how two hostile camps have arisen, and the terrible duel which is now taking place between them.

Now, apply that to England, which, above all countries in the world, is the country of intermediate institutions. There are between the people and the throne a vast number of institutions which our ancestors have created. Their principle in creating them seems to have been this—that they looked a great deal to Liberty, and very little to Equality. If there were something to be done, they sought for some existing institution which was able to do it. If some change were required, they altered things as little as they could, and were content to go on in that manner. This is a country of privileges above all other countries; but the privileges have been given, not as in other countries—as in France before the Revolution, for instance—for the benefit of the privileged classes, but because our ancestors, in all moderation, believed this to be the best way to ensure order, and good government, and stability. It may be difficult to prove upon theory how all this should be, because ancient Governments, as Burke finely remarks, are seldom based on abstract principles, but rather are the materials from which abstract principles are drawn. I think we should act more wisely and more worthily to the country if we were to ascertain what lessons of wisdom may be drawn from the signal success of our own Government, instead of trying to borrow from the people of America notions which lead to such results as I have been endeavouring to depict. But, Sir, have we succeeded? I will quote, not my own words, but an unexceptional witness. Says the speaker whom I quote—

"It has been our privilege to see a process going forward in which the throne has acquired broader and deeper foundations in the affections of the country; in which the law has commended itself more and more to the respect and attachment of the people; in which the various sections of the community have come into close communion the one with the other; in which the great masses of our labouring fellow-countrymen have come to be better supplied than they were in the time of their immediate forefathers; and in which, upon the whole, a man desirous of the welfare of his kind, looking out on the broad surface of Society, may thank his God, and say, 'Behold, how good and pleasant a thing it is for brethren to dwell together in unity!'"

Well, those eloquent words were the words of the Chancellor of the Exchequer, and they were spoken on the 14th of September last, just two months before he began the concoction of the Bill which has been so very successful in illustrating the manner in which brethren dwell together in unity.

Now, let us suppose Democracy to be established in a greater or less degree in this country. With what eyes would it look upon the institutions which I have alluded to? What would be the relation of this House with the House of Peers? I will call a witness. Eight years ago the hon. member for Birmingham (Mr John Bright) inverted his present process. He is now anxious to secure means; he was then proclaiming ends. He then said—

"See what I will do for you, if you will only give me Reform."

But now he says—

"Give me Reform, and be assured that I will do nothing."

But the Bill does not say that. The words he uttered eight years ago remain. They have never been retracted, and I have no reason to suppose that the hon. gentleman wishes to retract, or is ashamed of any one of them. The hon. member said on one occasion—I am speaking from memory; but, though I am not sure about the words, I am about the meaning which the hon. member intended to convey—that, as far as the House of Peers was concerned, he did not believe that even the Peers themselves could suppose that they were a permanent institution in this country. What do you suppose would become of a House of Peers in America? What has become of the House of Peers in France? The name alone remains; but where is the power of that brilliant aristocracy which surrounded the throne of the Louises, and gave a glitter even to their vices? Then, what shall we say of the Church? I am speaking of it merely from a secular point of view, as a large and wealthy institution, not exactly of popular origin, nor looked upon with particular affection by persons who stand well with the masses. I call a witness again. What does the hon. gentleman the member for Birmingham say? He speaks of

"That portion of the public estate which is for a time permitted to remain in the hands of the Church of England."

What would be the position of the judges? Looking at the differences in this respect between the two countries, it will be seen that we have fenced round our judges with every safeguard, and given them more and more power, until we have made them practically an irresponsible class in the country. We have been content to witness the melancholy sight of a person actually blind, and we have still a man of ninety years, sitting upon the judicial bench. We submit to this, not because we think it right in itself, but because we think it better to err to a small extent than to give rise to the slightest suspicion that a judge has been influenced in the least way by this House. Now, what state of things exists in America?

In the great State of New York the judges are appointed for six years only, and further West the term decreases, until in Mississippi two years is the *maximum*. And why? In order that they may be able to administer the law, not in accordance with the law, but in accordance with the popular sentiment. That we should continue to have judges I do not doubt, but do you think they would occupy such a position as they occupy now, and be so utterly independent of popular power?

And now, let us come to ourselves. Our position, as I have remarked already, is much more honourable than that of the members of any other Legislative Assembly in the world. Do you think Democracy would look with a favourable eye upon that? Would it not judge by analogy that such a state of things ought, in some degree, to be altered, and that we should be made to approach nearer to the level of our constituents? Now, we have a privileged class of electors who hold houses above £10. That class is a humble one, but it has discharged its duty up to the present time in a manner which almost defies criticism. But now, without any reason, but merely on account of an abstract principle of right, we have an attempt made to sweep that class away and swamp it in the class below it. Without enlarging upon this topic, I must say it is manifest to me, that if the House of Commons is democratised, it will not rest under such modified circumstances until it has swept away those institutions which at present stand between the people and the throne, and has supplied the place of them, as far as it can, by institutions deriving their origin direct from the people; being, as the Chancellor of the Duchy of Lancaster said, as representative as possible, and not having the *quasi* independence which the present privileged institutions and corporations possess. You will then have face to face, with no longer anything to break the shock between them, the monarch of the time and a great Democratic Assembly. Now, History has taught us little, if we are to suppose that these two powers would go on harmoniously, and that things would continue to work as they do now. The event no one can predict. We saw what a duel there was in France in 1851, when the President and the Assembly were each grasping at the sword, and endeavouring to exterminate the other. The Emperor conquered, and Cæsarianism followed. Had the Emperor failed, France would have had the very worst form of Government—namely, a Convention, a deliberative Assembly, attempting through its Committees to exercise Executive power, and endeavouring to do that which ought to be done through responsible Ministers; and such a Government would only last for a time, to be destroyed by some Cromwell or Napoleon, or to dissolve by its own vices and weakness. Look, again, on the state of things in America, where the President wields the Executive power, and where an opposition to him is raised in Congress. And then see how Congress works. It works through Committees, and every officer in the Government has a corresponding Committee in Congress to thwart and to overrule him.

But I need not follow that question further. Probably, many gentlemen may even think that I have endeavoured to look too far into futurity. At all events, I do not base my case on mere vague conjecture; I base it upon History and experience. The right hon. gentleman the Chancellor of the Duchy of Lancaster (Mr Goschen) has told us that England is a country totally different from America or Australia, and that no argument could be drawn from either of the two latter applicable to the position in which we stand. Well, Sir, there is, of course, no doubt that England is a country entirely different from America or Australia, but the difference is in their favour as regards the working of a Democracy. They possess boundless tracts of land. In America land acts as a sedative to political passion; in England it operates as an irritant. Here land is held up by democratic politicians to their followers as a thing to be desired and secured—as the spoils, in fact, of political warfare; in America it is, comparatively speaking, of no value; it is easily obtained, and much inflammable matter is, in consequence, removed, which would, under other circumstances, prove dangerous to the system. Everybody knows that if America were altogether governed by the great towns, the result would be most disastrous, and that it is the cultivators of the land who moderate their influence, and prevent them from rushing on to their destruction. Upon this point I should like to quote the words of Lord Macaulay, one of the most able of the advocates of the Reform Bill of 1832, from which he never went back a hair's-breadth. He, in replying to an American gentleman who sent him a "Life of Jefferson," says, speaking of this country—

"In bad years there is plenty of grumbling here, and sometimes a little rioting; but it matters little, for here the sufferers are not the rulers. The supreme power is in the hands of a class, numerous indeed, but select—of an educated class—of a class which is, and knows itself to be, deeply interested in the security of property and the maintenance of order."

Then he writes as follows—

"It is quite plain that your Government will never be able to restrain a distressed and discontented majority, for with you the majority is the Government, and has the rich, who are always a minority, absolutely at its mercy. The day will come when, in the State of New York, a multitude of people, not one of whom has had more than half a breakfast, or expects to have more than half a dinner, will choose a Legislature."

He adds—

"Is it possible to doubt what sort of Legislature will be chosen? On one side is a statesman preaching patience, respect for vested rights, strict observance of public faith; on the other is a demagogue ranting about the tyranny of capitalists and usurers, and asks why anybody should be permitted to drink champagne and ride in carriages, while thousands of honest folks are in want of necessaries. Which of the two candidates is likely to be preferred by the working man who hears his children crying for more bread? I seriously apprehend that you will, in some such season of adversity as I have described, do things which will prevent prosperity from returning. Either some Cæsar or Napoleon will seize the reins of Government with a strong hand, or your Republic will be fearfully plundered and laid waste by barbarians in the twentieth century, as the Roman Empire was in the fifth; with this difference, that the Huns and Vandals who ravaged the Roman Empire came from without, and that your Huns and Vandals will have been engendered within your own country and by your own institutions."

Now, observe the argument of Lord Macaulay. It is this—

"You have a Democracy in America; but you have there, also, plenty of elbow-room, and abundant means of subsistence for its whole population; but when this state of things comes to an end, then the institutions of the country will be tried, and a crash may follow."

In England we have not a Democracy, but we have a state of Society in which, in the event of pressure, distress and misery must to a great extent prevail. Now, if we add here with our hands Democracy to population, as the course of time may in America add population to Democracy, we shall have done all in our power to bring about exactly the state of things which Lord Macaulay describes, and we may expect that something like the same consequences will be the result. Sir, it appears to me we have more and more reason every day we live to regret the loss of Lord Palmerston. The remaining members of his Government would seem, by way of a mortuary contribution, to have buried in his grave all their prudence, statesmanship, and moderation. He was scarcely withdrawn from the scene before they set to work to contravene and contradict his policy. That policy, acted upon by a statesman who perfectly understood the wants of the English people, had been crowned with unexampled success; and they, I suppose, must have thought that the best way to secure a continuance of that success was to aim at doing that which he above all other things disapproved. The noble Lord at the head of the Government, and the right hon. gentleman the Chancellor of the Exchequer, have performed a great feat; they have taken the great mass of their supporters, who are, I believe, men of moderate views and moderate opinions, and laid them at the feet of the hon. member for Birmingham. They have thus brought them into contact with men and with principles from which, but six short months ago, they would have recoiled.

That is what has happened to a portion of those who sit upon these benches. As to the rest of us, we are left like sheep in the wilderness, and after the success of this extraordinary combination, to use no harsher word, we who remain precisely what we have been, are charged with inconsistency, while the bonds of political allegiance are being strained until they are ready to crack for the purpose of keeping the Liberal Party together. We are told that we are bound by every tie which ought to bind mankind to act in accordance with the policy of Earl Russell; but I, for one, Sir, dispute the justice of that proposition. I have never served under that noble Lord. I have served under two Prime Ministers for a period, I am sorry to say, of little less than ten years. The one was Lord Aberdeen, the other Lord Palmerston. Earl Russell joined the Government of each of those Ministers; both Governments he abandoned, both he assisted to destroy. I owe the noble Lord no allegiance. I am not afraid of the people of this country. They have displayed a good sense, which is remarkable, indeed, when contrasted with the harangues which have been addressed to them. But if I am not afraid of the people, neither do I agree with the right hon. gentleman the member for Huntingdon, in fearing those by whom they are led. Demagogues are the commonplace of History. They are to be found wherever popular commotion has prevailed, and they all bear to one another a strong family likeness. Their names float lightly on the stream of time; they are in some way handed down to us; but then they are as little regarded as the foam which rides on the crest of the stormy wave, and bespatters the rock which it cannot shake. Such men, Sir, I do not fear; but I have, I confess, some misgivings when I see a number of gentlemen of rank, of character, of property, and intelligence carried away, without being convinced, or even over-persuaded, in the support of a policy which many of them in their inmost hearts detest and abhor. Monarchies exist by loyalty, aristocracies by honour, popular assemblies by political virtue and patriotism; and it is in the loss of these things, and not in comets and eclipses, that we are to look for the portents that herald the fall of States. I have said that I am utterly unable to reason with the Chancellor of the Exchequer for want of a common principle to start from; but there is happily one common ground left to us, and that is the Second Book of the *Æneid* of Virgil. My right hon. friend, like the moth which has singed its wings in the candle, has returned again to the poor old Trojan horse, and I shall, with the permission of the House, give them one more excerpt from the history of that noble beast, first premising that I shall then turn him out to grass, at all events for the remainder of the Session. The passage which I am about to quote is one which is, I think, worthy the attention of the House, because it contains a description of the invading army of which we have heard so much, but also a slight sketch of its General—

> "Arduus armatos mediis in mænibus adstans
> Fundit equus, victorque Sinon incendia miscet
> Insultans; portis alii bipatentibus adsunt,
> Millia quot magnis, nunquam venêre Mycenis."

In other words—

> "The fatal horse pours forth the human tide,
> Insulting Sinon flings his firebrands wide,
> The gates are burst; the ancient rampart falls,
> And swarming millions climb its crumbling walls."

I have now, Sir, traced as well as I can what I believe to be the natural results of a measure which, it seems to my poor imagination, is calculated, if it should pass into law, to destroy one after another those institutions which have secured for England an amount of happiness and prosperity which no country has ever reached, or is ever likely to attain. Surely the heroic work of so many centuries, the matchless achievements of so many wise heads and strong hands, deserve a nobler consummation than to be sacrificed at the shrine of revolutionary passion, or the maudlin enthusiasm of humanity! But, if we do fall, we shall fall deservedly. Uncoerced by any external force, not borne down by any internal calamity, but in the full plethora of our wealth and the surfeit of our too exuberant prosperity, with our own rash and inconsiderate hands, we are about to pluck down on our own heads the venerable temple of our liberty and our glory. History may tell of other acts as signally disastrous, but of none more wanton, none more disgraceful.

THE RIGHT HON. GATHORNE HARDY[1]
ON THE IRISH CHURCH.

House of Commons, March 31st, 1868.

[The great speech of Mr John Francis Macguire on the state of Ireland on March 16th led to a motion for Irish Disestablishment. It was valiantly championed by Mr Gladstone, and, in spite of all opposition, was carried in the course of the following Session.]

We are called on at a special and peculiar moment to go into Committee upon a question of the greatest possible importance, and one that cannot be settled or terminated—I will not say in this Parliament, nor probably in the next, nor for many years to come, in my opinion. This is met by an Amendment on the part of my noble friend (Lord Stanley, afterwards second Earl of Derby), to which great exception has been taken. I will for a moment take notice of a remark that has been made on that Amendment. My noble friend claimed for himself freedom of acting in future Sessions on this great question, without expressing his full opinion now; but at the same time he said that he wished to make it manifest by the earlier part of his Resolution that the present course of the Government was not adopted from mere motives of obstruction, from no conviction that there was nothing to redress, or nothing to reform in the Irish Church, for an admission to the contrary was made by the issuing of the Commission now sitting, which may be taken as an acknow-

---

[1] Afterwards Viscount Cranbrook.

ledgment that there are reforms to be effected and Amendments to be made; and though some wish to go far beyond what I should desire, yet many who think as I do acknowledge, as I have already done before this time, that there are evils within the Church; that, as has been said by many of her Bishops, many of her clergy, many of her attached friends, with a view to strengthening and giving more effect to the administration of that Church, great reforms, great alterations, and, if I may without great offence to gentlemen opposite use the word, great "modifications" are needed. It would have been idle and absurd, after having assented to a Commission upon the Irish Church, if the Government had not been prepared to act upon the facts which may be proved before that Commission, and to ameliorate where it was found necessary. I do not mean to say that the present Parliament is not competent to deal with the subject, because it is obvious that so long as this House is in existence it must have all the powers and functions of a legislative Assembly. It is not a question of competence, but of time, occasion, and opportunity. The facts are these: At a comparatively late period of the Session, with very little progress made in Supply; with Boundary Bills involving the interests of eighty-one burghs and one or two counties; and with Reform Bills—one for Scotland and one for Ireland—in which Amendments of great importance will be moved, and which must take a long time—it is with these things before us, and with the necessity of calling for an early dissolution of the House and an appeal to the country; I say, with these things before us, are we not right in saying that the House is encumbered with business; measures of great importance are pressing upon us, and therefore this is not the time to come forward with an abstract Resolution. The first Resolution of the right hon. gentleman (Mr Gladstone) is distinctly and solely an abstract Resolution, which cannot pledge the new Parliament that will have to assemble in a few months, and which he himself admits cannot be carried into effect by legislation in the course of the present Session.

I say, then, that this question is one which has been suddenly started upon the country; it has taken the people by surprise. If it had not been started so suddenly, if it had not come but recently on the minds of those who produced it, why —when the opportunity was afforded by the motion of the hon. member for Cork (Mr Maguire) to go into Committee on the state of Ireland, of submitting this question of the Irish Church to the consideration of the House—why did not the right hon. gentleman produce his Resolutions then, and ask the House to consider them in connection with the state of Ireland? If this had been done we should have had time to consider them, and they would certainly have been discussed at an earlier period of the Session than they have. Is it unreasonable that we should ask for time to consider so important a matter? Is it unreasonable to ask for time in order that the country should consider the question upon which it must eventually decide? Even within the short week we have had the rustle of petitions increasingly heard from both sides of the House day by day. As time goes on I venture to say that more and more petitions will be brought here, and as the question becomes more thoroughly understood in the country they will yet increase. Already, too, I notice that many of the Nonconformist body have petitioned against the Resolutions of the right hon. gentleman, so that the feeling against them is not confined to Churchmen. And, after all, the right hon. gentleman himself stated last night he did not anticipate that this great measure which he had in hand could be carried into effect under much less than thirty years' time; and yet now, forsooth, it is a question of hours; it is not to be adjourned for a few months in order that it may be placed in all its integrity before the country. I will show before I sit down that the proposition is one which evades the chief difficulties of the question, and only deals with those portions of it upon which unity of action can be obtained; whereas, if the right hon. gentleman had developed his whole plan, it would be certain to split his supporters into many sections.

The Resolutions aimed a blow at the property of the Irish Church, which I, as a Churchman, maintain has, during the last three hundred years at the very least, and indeed, as I believe, for a much longer time, passed down in regular succession into the hands by which it is now held. If this be so, where are the Acts of Parliament transferring the right to that property at any time before or during those three hundred years? In what way has that transfer been made? I will not, however, enter into that question, because if I did so, it might possibly call up opposition on the other side. But I contend that when we are dealing with a mass of property of so much importance and of so long prescription, it is not a matter for haste; and you have no right to force it upon the country until it has the whole case before it, and until we have an opportunity of consulting the constituencies upon it.

I would ask whether this question of the Irish Church is to be disposed of hastily and without discussion? Is this Church, which has stood for so long a time, and has battled for centuries in defence of the truth, to be at once given up without consideration, and are all the arguments of the many great men who defended her in former days to be ignored, or declared to be of no avail? Am I to be afraid to say that the Union of Great Britain and Ireland was a compact—a treaty of a solemn and a binding character. Am I to be forbidden to say that the 5th Article of that Union was so important that it was made the fundamental basis and the very essence of that Union? Let those who doubt this look at the Act of Union itself, and see how differently other conditions are treated which were not regarded as fundamental or essential. This Article respecting the Church was made, if I may say so, the very bait for the Irish Protestants to yield to that Union. It was put forward on all occasions as an inducement to them to establish their Church upon what was represented as a firmer footing, by uniting it, as was supposed, indissolubly to the Church of England. And have we any right now, because this connection may, in the opinion of some, be a burden or

... weakness to us, to throw it aside and say: "We will
... the Union of the Churches, and leave the Irish Church
... care of itself"? Let us see what has been said in
... debates by eminent politicians; what, for instance,
... by the Lord Chief-Justice of England as to the effect
... Union upon the united Churches of England and
I... On the 13th of May 1805, Lord Ellenborough
... ended this Article of the Treaty in his place in
Parliament —

"... 5th Article of the Union it is declared that the continuance and
... of the said United Church, as the Established Church of Eng-
... Ireland, shall be deemed and taken to be an essential and funda-
... part of the Union. By fundamental is meant, with reference to the
matter, such an integral part of the Compact of Union formed
... the two kingdoms as is absolutely necessary to the support and
... of the whole fabric and superstructure of the Union, raised
... upon; and such as, being removed, would produce the ruin and
... the political union founded upon this Article as its immediate
..."

... right hon. gentleman the member for South Lancashire
Mr Gladstone) escaped from this point by saying: "Oh, but
Mr Pitt meant to do this in connection with other things," that
... expressed, not in the Act of Union, but in State
... which are now accessible to us. But there was no
... either in the Act of Union or in any statement on
... part of Mr Pitt that anything would be done more than
... by that Statute. Nothing can be produced that ever
... by Mr Pitt to show that anything forming part of
... compact was, in the slightest degree, neglected or left
... by him.

My right hon. friend opposite says that there were other
... ments. I am sorry to say that there were, and that the
Irish Parliament of that day may be said to have been corrupt
... sense of the term. But the Parliament of
... land, which accepted that compact and joined in that
... was it also as corrupt a Parliament? [Mr BRIGHT.—
"Hear, hear!"] The hon. member for Birmingham says it was,
... I presume that, in his opinion, the Acts of that

Parliament are not to be attended to, or, at least, are not to be attended to in the same way, as he would doubtless conceive they ought to be if they were the Acts of some more perfect legislative Assembly. [Mr BRIGHT.—" I did not say so."] I am perfectly aware of that. But just now, when I was asking whether the Parliament of England, which also joined in the Act of Union, was as corrupt as the Irish Parliament, the hon. gentleman interrupted and said "It was." And that either has some meaning, or it has not. If it has a meaning, does it mean that the Acts of that Parliament are in any sense invalidated? If so, we shall be entering upon a very difficult question. And if we are to question the intentions of Parliament and its freedom from corruption, and so to judge of the Acts which it performed, I am afraid that some of our creditors will not be in a very favourable position for obtaining payment of their debts.

The right hon. gentleman the member for South Lancashire had stated that, whatever else might be the ultimate effect of his Resolutions, they could not be injurious to the Protestant faith; and he went into statistics as to the population and the proportions of different creeds. With regard to these, I will only say that anyone who heard the statistics given as to the different creeds and different professions in Ireland must have felt that the sources from which they were derived were not such that they would be treated as a particular and demonstrative statement with regard to the population. The only statistics, I may say, that were thoroughly gone into were those in 1834 and 1861. The right hon. gentleman said that when the Penal Laws were most strictly enforced, the Protestants had increased; but that when the Penal Laws ceased to be enforced and liberty was freely accorded, the Protestants began to diminish in proportion to the Roman Catholics; the right hon. gentleman taking these things as cause and effect. Now, if there were a period during which there was a more general relaxation of the Penal Laws, it was that between 1834 and 1861, and yet it will be found that the proportions of the petitions had then increased in favour of the Protestants. I know that the right hon. gentleman says that such increase is to be accounted for by the emigration of the labouring classes, which he assumes to be all of the Roman Catholic faith. But the right hon. gentleman has made no allowance whatever for the emigration of Protestants from Ireland. I believe there is not an Irish member who will fail to tell you that among the emigrants there were a very large number of Protestants, who carried themselves and their religion to another country. But the right hon. gentleman says that the Disestablishment of the Protestant Church in Ireland will not be injurious to the Protestant faith. I should be ashamed of the religion which I profess, if I thought it would be unable to meet any other form of religion with or without the aid of endowments; but am I on that account to say that I think it is encumbered by having endowments? If so, that seems to me an argument which goes far beyond the case of the Irish Church. I do not know why in one country it is to be considered advantageous to be without endowments, and in another to possess them. And if religion in this country can exist, although cumbered, as the right hon. gentleman would have us think, with large endowments, why do you object to our Protestant friends in Ireland retaining that which they believe to be of service to them, and that to which they believe they have a right?

In respect to the Voluntary principle, there is a great part of Ireland in which the Voluntary principle is hardly applicable—parts where the Protestants are but thinly scattered, and where it would be almost impossible, without parochial organization, that they could obtain for themselves the means of grace; and therefore it is necessary that in these parts of the country there should be some means of providing them with the means of grace to which they are now entitled by law. The right hon. gentleman, in holding out these Resolutions as an olive branch to Ireland, forgets how much he is alienating—how much he is distressing those who are members of the

Church, and those who, though not actually members of the Church, feel towards it a friendly interest. We are here, as it were, lookers-on at a picture which is passing before us in the distance; but it touches the hearts and the homes of many. It is to such not only a sentimental grievance, but a practical wrong. While they feel deeply upon the matter, is it for us, in our apathetic indifference, to give up the dearest interests of those with whom we are united by the ties of religion, of honour, of treaty, and of compact—to allow such considerations to be thrown over without regard to their feelings, with the view of reconciling others who may, after all, remain hostile to us, whilst we alienate our old friends who have ever been faithful to us? Now, Sir, the right hon. gentleman said he did not think that anyone would venture to use the argument that the subversion of the Irish Church would tend also to the subversion of property. It is, however, an argument that has been used by some of our greatest authorities, and, not the least, by that great man, Sir Robert Peel, whose memory probably the right hon. gentleman opposite respects. It was an argument that Sir Robert Peel did not disdain to use, and urge with great force, on more than one occasion. He did so at some length; but I will merely read a short extract from a speech of his on the Appropriation Clause, to show the terms in which he spoke of the Church property. He said—

"If long possession and the prescription of three centuries were not powerful enough to protect the property of the Church from spoliation, there is little safety for any description of private property; and much less for that property which is in the hands of lay corporations."

And it was no idle fear, for there are symptoms that property in the hands of lay corporations is in danger, and language has been used in this House on the Irish Land Question which seemed to verge very near an attack on the Irish property of the City Companies. Language has been used with reference to their possession of land in Ireland which must certainly give them the hint that the time may soon come when they will have to set their houses in order.

And with reference to another great corporation possessing land in Ireland—the Law Life Assurance Society—language has been used which shows there is a design in some persons to carry the attack beyond the property of the Irish Church, and not stop short of the landed interest; for I do not hesitate to state that the schemes proposed for dealing with the land in Ireland are in themselves on a revolutionary scale. The schemes do attack the rights of property, and those who argue that you may justly take corporate property from the Church, depend upon it, will not be very squeamish hereafter in dealing with other property. Well, Sir, in speaking of this question, I will not hesitate to adopt what may be considered a legal statement upon the question of corporate property made by the Lord Chancellor. He says—

"It was always admitted that so long as the corporate property which possessed the title to ecclesiastical property remained, so long as the property is not greater in amount than can be usefully applied by that corporate body, there is no right of principle on which Parliament can interfere to alienate property of that kind."

I concur in that principle. It is a principle acted on with respect to all charity property by the Court of Chancery. I believe it is a just rule, and one which we cannot violate without assailing the interests of property. The right hon. gentleman says we are going to deal tenderly with our victims, for we are going to preserve vested interests, and we even propose going beyond that; but at that moment the cheer which had greeted the maintaining of vested rights died away—and at the more than vested rights, the interests of curates and those who had entered on some miserable benefice with the hope of advancing to better things—I found that cheering checked; and it is manifest that it will not be so easy for the right hon. gentleman to carry into act his tender regard for those who have no vested interest in the property of the Irish Church. The rights to which he alluded were the vested rights of the clergy. But how are you going to deal with the rights of the laity? You may deal with the clergy, so far as they are personally concerned, by paying them off, pensioning them, or by arranging with them in any other manner you please; but when you come to the vested interests of the laity, which are held in trust for them by the Bishops and clergy, and not for themselves, how are you to compensate them for the vested interests you are about to rob them of?

The right hon. gentleman says it is absurd to talk of what was promised in former years in order to gain concessions when engagements were made that if a particular thing were done, it would produce peace and harmony, and that at length we should see our efforts in respect of Ireland crowned with success. Certainly those who prophesied, at the periods to which I allude, that those efforts would not follow have had their fears amply justified by the result. I think it a great misfortune for Ireland that the hopes which then actuated those who were pleading the cause of the Catholics, and the promises which they made, have not been fulfilled. Those who are now advocating the Disestablishment of the Protestant Church in Ireland do not hold the opinions of Plunket, Blake, and Peel, or of the Roman Catholic Prelates, or of the Canonists of Maynooth, who said that the title of the Established Church in Ireland would be recognised by Rome itself, which only requires a prescription of a hundred years, while the Protestant Church in Ireland has lasted for three hundred years. I am bound to say that on this occasion we are not in danger of being led away by promises, for no promises are held out that what we are asked to do will in any way tend to the pacification of Ireland, or that are to be more than a step to new departures. It is true that in speeches in this House something of that kind may be said; but those for whose benefit the property of the Church is to be taken away are holding out no promises. They are not saying that they have not in reserve a demand for concessions which they regard as of much greater importance. Those "calm men of Limerick" to whom the right hon. gentleman the member for Calne (Mr Robert Lowe) alluded a few nights ago, say that they do not believe anything will do

... of the people of Ireland except a repeal
... Irish interests to an Irish Parliament
... friend the member for Honiton (Mr R.
... speech last night, quoted a remarkable pas-
... was not heard by as many as ought to
... it shows that the persons who are agitat-
... in Ireland put aside the Church altogether
... At a meeting of the Meath Tenant-Right
... the Bishop and the Roman Catholic Vicar-
... members, this statement was put forward, the
... presiding on the occasion—

..., the sole question for Ireland is the Land Question.
... such as that against the Established Church, got up for
... will infuse an element of bigotry into the already dis-
... lord and tenant, would effect the ruin of thousands
... precipitate that social catastrophe which we are anxious to

... told that, by holding out this olive-branch to
... we are doing all that is required ; whilst Lord
... own the Land Question over as unworthy of his
... and bids us bestow on the Roman Catholic
... what they themselves regard as a concession
... [*Cries of* "No, no!"]
I now come to an important question, one which
... by the Resolutions of the right hon. gentleman,
... speech he offered us no solution, and without
... which, I say, we cannot fairly and honestly vote
... It is essentially necessary that we should
... of the scheme that is to be proposed. Are
... going to secularize the revenues of the
... in Ireland? If you are going to secularize
... do you propose to apply them? The main
... "What are you going to do with the funds
...? And until we have an answer to it, you
... together a number of persons to vote on
... question without any idea of the principles that

are to guide them hereafter. The hon. member for Westminster (Mr J. S. Mill) has his scheme, and would apply the funds to unsectarian education. But, I would ask, is that the way to conciliate the Roman Catholics of Ireland? If there is one thing which they have been setting their faces against more than another, it is unsectarian education. The right hon. gentleman told us yesterday that it was not to be endured that the tithes of Connaught should be taken and applied for the benefit of Churchmen in Ulster; but I want to know whether it is to be endured that the tithes of Connaught are to be applied to the building of lighthouses near Dublin or anywhere else, and whether, when improvements are made, the funds are to be applied for Irish purposes generally, or expended in the locality whence they are derived? If the funds are to be taken in order to supply the wants of the people of Ireland generally, such a plan will be quite as inconsistent with the right hon. gentleman's powers of endurance as the application of the tithes of Connaught for the benefit of the Churchmen of Ulster. This is not a separate property, and does not belong to the people of Connaught in particular. It belongs neither to the landlord nor to the tenant, but to the laity of Ireland; and if it is for the improvement of their religious instruction, I say it may fairly be taken and applied in any part of Ireland where it may be wanted. I pass by Earl Russell's scheme of redistribution, which no one is ready to adopt, and which the noble Lord himself condemned with such great effect very recently before he adopted it. We might, therefore, rely on his condemnation as sufficient for our purpose.

The hon. member for Birmingham (Mr Bright), as I understand it, would leave something to the Church, though he would take away a good deal and secularize it; but he has not told us what particular mode of procedure he would recommend. We do not know, therefore, in what way the money is to be dealt with. That there is to be an unsettlement of everything is clear, and it is also clear that there is to be a settlement of nothing. You say that this is a

grievance, and I, for one, do not assert that the
… of a grievance being sentimental is not enough
… to resent it; but I maintain that, when
a sentimental grievance on the one side, and are
make a more than sentimental grievance on the
… fair and just that the persons on whom you
to make the experiment should know what is to be
… of the funds of which you are about to despoil
… I am told, of all things, that it is not legitimate
in this debate that the question of the Irish Church
… stability of the English and Scotch Churches. I
understand that there are those who are like the
her extremity, who threw away her children to save
… the devouring wolf; but, at the same time, I do
… that incident to have been regarded as a very
… of maternal feeling. The course taken by that
… does not commend itself to those who feel
… bound to Ireland by sympathy and the ties of
… religion. I am not so disposed to throw her
… and I am still less disposed to do so when a
taken which affects and materially affects—the
… upon which the Church Establishment rests in
… country; for, whatever may be said, the main
which have been used by the right hon. gentleman
… members who sit below the gangway, and with
… by the latter, in support of these
… are in favour of religious equality. Now,
equality I do not understand, either in principle
… to apply to only one part of the Empire. I say,
it is not unreasonable in us to object, if you are
touch part of our Church, that on that principle
in fact, touching the whole, and upsetting the
upon which alone the Establishments of the
Church and State—can be defended. If it is
for religious equality that there should be no
… or privileges accorded to the ministers of the

Established Church, then I understand the argument. It is the Voluntary system, pure and simple, and one fairly to be debated and argued; but you cannot justly put forward religious equality when you are only going to apply the principle to a small part of the Empire.

What will be gained by this great sacrifice of principles on our parts if we are to accede to it? You have promised us nothing, and you have brought nothing before us to justify such a sacrifice; but if you can show that at this dear rate you can bring perfect harmony and concord in every part of our dominions, Heaven knows how many prejudices—how many sacrifices of a deeper nature—everybody would be ready to make to obtain so desirable an object. If justice required that we should give up those things on which our hearts are set—that the interests of the whole country required it, and there was before us a certainty of obtaining that which we all desire, then there are reasons for renouncing opinion, and I, for one, if I could not assent, would at least withdraw out of my way, and let others carry this measure for the benefit of all. But when I do not see that the desired end would be attained, I then continue advocating on this side of the House principles which I advocated from the opposite side; and if changes in those principles are to be made, it shall not be by my hand that the stab shall be given, and not on these Benches that the change shall be made. I will leave to others to effect purposes which I may no longer be able to resist. Well, Sir, what is the general emergency that has arisen, calling on us to make those enormous sacrifices, which likewise, if we had made, we should have been taunted for making them on an occasion which did not require it to be done? Is it the miserable Fenianism that has prevailed in this country, or the base Fenianism in Ireland spoken of the other night, calling on us to make this sacrifice of our time, of our duty, of all that is dear to us, in order to get rid of what would not be affected by it for a moment?

Is it the suspension of the Habeas Corpus Act? We have had the suspension of the Habeas Corpus Act for many years. Has it interfered practically with the liberties of Ireland in the way it has been used? Has it interfered with the ordinary progress of business? Has it interfered with religious freedom? Has it interfered with ordinary freedom of intercourse? Has it not rather been used in emergencies, in order to give greater security to the real freedom of Ireland, by checking that which is lawless, and upholding real loyalty and liberty? If you are to take this ground, you will only be adding another to the right hon. gentleman's list of dates which were last night cited to prove the imbecility and weakness of the English Parliament—its injustice, its unfairness, its readiness to do wrong so long as the wrong could be done with impunity; and he told us that up to the present time we had abstained from doing justice to Ireland, but now these things must be swept away, and he threw it in the teeth of Parliament that it had never done an act of justice to Ireland without having been compelled to do so. That, I think, is one of the censures of Parliament, which ought not to be recorded as a merit, or held up as an example to be followed on the present occasion.

Well, I think I have shown that the present is not a fitting time at which such a change, if it were necessary, should be made; and I state boldly that nothing which has been put forward by the right hon. gentleman is sufficient to convince the House that the people of this country repose any reliance in the views of the right hon. gentleman the member for South Lancashire on this question. Surely, then, the people ought to be consulted before such a change is made. I further say that the first Resolution, if you should pass it, is not binding on the Parliament to which it will pass on from the hands of this House. I say that if you throw aside a compact statute made as a treaty, and say, "That is not to bind us any more," how can you say that this Resolution, passed by a dying Parliament, is to bind its successor? You are putting this branch of the Legislature in an undue position. There is a complaint that the House of Lords has nothing to do. The reason is because you will not test its power to work. But it is an Assembly equal to this; and when you are calling upon us to proceed upon this dangerous and revolutionary path— for so it was called by the right hon. baronet the member for Morpeth (Sir George Grey)—you ought, at all events, to call into council that branch of the Legislature without which you cannot legislate. Again, I say, suppose you carry this Resolution, you do not show us the object in view, or that you obtain the peace of Ireland. On the contrary, you would increase many of her evils. You complain of absenteeism; well, by the adoption of your scheme, I believe that you would increase it, and cause it to extend among the landlords as well as the clergy. [*Laughter.*] In answer to that laugh, I may observe that the right hon. gentleman the member for South Lancashire admitted that in all the great emergencies the clergy in Ireland had been found at the bedside of the sick and in the cottages of the poor. I believe that the charities of Ireland owe more to the clergy than to any other class of the community.

We have been asked what course we intend to take upon this question. In the first place, if, in spite of the objection that we have taken, I believe justly, to the Resolutions of the right hon. gentleman, you succeed in overthrowing the Amendment, our course is clear. We shall oppose the Resolutions themselves. If you ask what we would do—not in this Parliament, because it would have no opportunity of doing anything, but in the next Parliament—in the event of the Resolutions being carried, my reply is that I will give the right hon. gentleman no other pledge than this—that we will act in accordance with the former part of the Amendment, and if, on the report of the Commission, we are satisfied that it would be for the benefit of the Irish Church that certain modifications in it should be made, we will make them with a fearless hand. But if you ask us to go further, I will say, at least for myself, as I have upon former occasions, that I will not be a party to a measure of disestablishing the Irish Church. I am not prepared to sever Ireland from England in religious matters, and present the spectacle of a Government in Ireland of a purely secular character, and a Government in England partially religious. *[Laughter.]* My form of expression is not, I am aware, as perfect as I would wish; but what I meant to say was, that I will not consent to an anomaly that Church and State should be dissevered in Ireland, and remain connected in England. The right hon. gentleman said that the disestablishment of the Irish Church would, as respected the Irish people, "Pluck from the memory a rooted sorrow; Raze out the written troubles of the brain"; but he quite omitted to quote the preceding line, "Can'st thou minister to a mind diseased?" It is the mind of Ireland that is diseased—a disease caused by a long traditionary hatred of the Saxon, and kept alive by constant agitation and misrepresentation. It is thus you have, as I believe, diseased the kindly and generous mind of Ireland, which, but for that pernicious agitation, I believe would have been in harmony with us at the present moment. The drug, however, which the right hon. gentleman proposes to administer would not be a "sweet oblivious antidote," to appease the distempered mind of the disloyal, who would rather ask for some "purgative to scour these English hence." The measure proposed by the right hon. gentleman would not tend in any degree to the desired end—to conciliate those who first of all told them that the Land Question was to be settled on a basis and in a way to which the present Parliament would never assent, and that in the end there is to be a repeal of that Union the inviolable and fundamental basis of which was the United Church of England and Ireland.

I have looked through the speeches that have been made in the House for a statement of the specific wrongs—wrongs which call for specific remedies. I have looked in vain to find out to whom you are to give these funds which you are going to take away from those now in possession of them. I have looked in vain for any statement in former debates or in this which will lead me to a conclusion upon this vital question. I say your Resolutions are founded on principles repugnant to, and far away from, the theory and the practice of the Constitution of this country, and will be provocative of strife, of enmity, and of dissension, instead of paving the way for peace and harmony between England and Ireland. If they conciliate one party, they will irritate another; and although I will never believe that the Protestants of Ireland will become disloyal, yet there can be no doubt that it will excite among them discontent and disaffection; there will be the injustice which is done them, which must in the end react upon England. I feel bound, where no wrong has been done in the use of property by those to whom it belongs, to protest against the spoliation of it. I feel doubly bound, both as a just man and as an Englishman, to be true to the compact which is in force between the two countries. As a Churchman I cannot be indifferent to the condition of my brethren in the faith in Ireland. I cannot be indifferent to the clergy who so zealously and so effectually have performed their duties in that country. To that fact I call to witness those gentlemen who are most opposed to the old endowments. I cannot be a party to sever that union between Church and State, under which it is the glory and the privilege of the State to uphold the light of the Reformation in Ireland.

EARL RUSSELL ON THE BALLOT.

HOUSE OF LORDS, JULY 8TH, 1872.

[It is well known that LORD JOHN RUSSELL was always a vigorous opponent of the Ballot. The following speech during the debates on the Parliamentary and Municipal Elections Bill exhibits his peculiar views on this subject.]

I THINK I may venture to address your Lordships on the present occasion, as my attention has been directed to the subject of the Ballot for more than forty years. When, in 1831, the Ministry of the late Earl Grey was formed on the principle of introducing the question of Parliamentary Reform as a Ministerial question, I was one of a Committee of the Ministers to whom was committed the charge of drawing up the scheme of the first Reform Bill. The proposals of that Committee contained a recommendation of the Ballot. When Earl Grey spoke to me of the scheme, he said that while the Cabinet cordially approved of the measure as a whole, there was one part of it to which they could by no means assent—namely, the Ballot. He asked me whether I attached much importance to the point, and whether I was willing to give it up. My answer was that, in fact, I had used every argument to induce the Committee not to insert the Ballot in their proposals. The question of the Ballot was consequently omitted from the Reform Bill which I introduced into the House of Commons, and it never appeared in any of the subsequent Bills. Since that time I have watched all the discussions that have been raised upon the Ballot question, and have taken part in some, and have seen no ground for changing the opinions I entertained forty years ago. The late Sir Robert Peel was as much opposed to the Ballot as Earl Grey. Many noble Lords will remember the speech of wonderful argumentative force and eloquence which he delivered against Mr Grote's motion in 1838. The result of the debate on that occasion was that the motion of Mr Grote was rejected by a majority of 117. The present Prime Minister (Mr Gladstone) has eight or nine times voted against the Ballot in the House of Commons.

It was therefore with no little surprise that I heard the year before last that Mr Gladstone had suddenly announced that he had become a convert to it. The reason given for this sudden conversion was twofold—first, that secret voting had been adopted all over the world; and, secondly, that now every adult person in England had the right of voting. These two reasons are no doubt plausible; but the allegations on which they rest are totally inadequate. With regard to the first, it is far from being true that the Ballot has been introduced all over the world. It has not been adopted even in all our own Colonies. The good sense of the people of the Dominion has refused to accept its introduction in Canada, and if I do not mistake, the use of secret voting has not been practically adopted in our great Colony of Victoria. Secret Ballot does not really exist in half of the States of the American Union. In the New England State of Massachusetts a law was passed by which a voter might go to a public office and ask for an envelope in which he might enclose his vote, and thus if he chose keep the way in which he voted a secret. That was, if anything, an "optional Ballot"—the secrecy was in the absolute power of the voter himself. At the end of three or four years some curious people wished to know how many of those envelopes had been taken, and whether any great number of the electors had chosen to vote secretly. It was found that very few, if any, of the electors had taken those envelopes, or chosen to vote secretly. The law was therefore repealed, and everyone voted openly. No doubt, open voting gives opportunity for intimidation; but, in my opinion, the system embodied in the present measure will increase personation, will increase bribery, will increase fraud and falsehood of every kind—indeed, in whatever light secret voting is viewed, it seems a bad system; it is nothing but an increased power of corruption in every direction. It will encourage falsehood, for it is quite possible under the Ballot that a voter may be intimidated by his landlord into promising his vote; but having the power to vote, will secretly vote against his promise. He would then go to his landlord and say, "I voted as you asked me; I quite agree in your opinions, and have voted with you." It was some such argument as this that Mr Grote put forward in proof of the value of the Ballot in checking the influence of the landlord and employer, and he maintained that the tenant would be perfectly justified in acting in this way.

It seems, however, to me that though the intimidation may fail as to the actual vote, the Ballot will introduce a new form of fraud and distrust which will not be much preferable to the old fashioned intimidation. The Englishman's privilege of public voting should be as sacredly respected; he should have the same right of voting openly as he has by the existing law; and at least there is no reason why the electors of Old England should be deprived of a privilege of open voting which is enjoyed by the voters of New England. It seems to me a great argument in support of open voting that a man who is desirous of promoting some great public question; of something that would improve the condition of his fellow-creatures is more likely than any other man to give his vote publicly, and will be proud of proclaiming his support of a candidate who holds large and liberal views. When Sir Samuel Romilly was engaged in his endeavours to mitigate the severity of our criminal code, and was a candidate for Westminster, an elector, sympathising with his efforts, was proud to say, "I vote for Samuel Romilly!" Why should not a voter feel proud to proclaim his sympathy with a man whose life is devoted to mitigating the sufferings of his fellow-men? Or again, when Wilberforce stood before the great constituency of Yorkshire, the champion of the abolition of slavery throughout the world—a great and noble aspiration—surely the electors should not be prohibited from proclaiming openly, in the face of all men, "I vote for Mr Wilberforce and the Emancipation of the human race!" This Bill will make the revelation of his vote an offence and a crime on the part of the official persons who are in the polling-booth at the time. It is provided by this Bill that the voter, having secretly marked his vote on the ballot-paper, and folded it up so as to conceal his vote, shall place it in a closed box. There is, indeed, no penalty imposed on the voter for telling his vote, but every officer, clerk, and agent in attendance at a polling-station who shall communicate at any time, to any person, any information obtained in a polling-station, as to the candidate for whom any voter in such station is about to vote, or has voted, will be liable, on summary conviction before two Justices of the Peace, to imprisonment for any term not exceeding six months, with or without hard labour.

I feel ashamed that such a proposition should have come up from the other House. Surely it is a degradation to which the country will never submit. As to the allegation that every adult man in England has the right of voting, it is allowed by Mr Gladstone himself not to be an accurate statement, and he rebukes Mr Disraeli for supposing that every man who marries has the right of voting. I must, in addition, point out that our whole progress for the last century and a half has been in favour of publicity. There was a time when the proceedings of Parliament were published under the disguise of "Debates in the Senate of Lilliput," and notes of the speeches were prefixed by fictitious names. I remember, in my own time, seeing the Serjeant-at-Arms bring before the House a man whom he found making notes in the Gallery. Since that time we have gone on introducing more and more publicity in the transaction of public affairs. The debates in Parliament are reported day by day, under the real names of the speakers, and are openly discussed the next morning in the journals throughout the kingdom. The proceedings of the Courts of Law are public, and the man who is called upon to give evidence in a Court of Law is not allowed the shelter of secrecy even where—as is too often the case in Ireland—his giving evidence may be attended with risk to his life. No exemptions are made; all questions affecting life and property are decided in public. Yet it is now proposed that if a man comes to the polling-booth, and says, " I wish to vote for Lord Enfield," so essential is secrecy in the performance of public duty, that the open declaration of a man's wish and opinion by an officer in the polling-booth is declared to be a disgrace and a crime. We declare that publicity must be the rule of our Law Courts, whatever the consequences. In one of our Courts, presided over by a member of this House, cases arise of which the publicity is injurious to morality and offensive to decency; nevertheless, no exception is made. Proposals have been made that in the Divorce Court proceedings may be taken in secrecy, if the Judge shall think fit; but no—the noble and learned Lord who presides over that Court approves of publicity; and by means of this publicity all persons may read the details of these trials in the public journals. At whatever cost, the Law must be administered in public; but when you come to the election of the law-givers—secrecy is so essential in the performance of this form of public duty—the vote must be so entirely in the bosom of the voter that it is impossible that publicity can be allowed—the vote must be given in secret. The man who is in office in the booth, and hears a person say, " I vote for Lord Enfield," or, " I vote for Lord George Hamilton," is liable to six months' imprisonment.

This is simply monstrous. The people of England have for hundreds of years been free to go to the poll and say, " I vote for such and such a man, because I look upon him as the most fit." But this is no longer to be allowed,—secrecy, in the form of voting, is henceforth to be the rule.

I will not go into the question of the ulterior results of secret voting, but I do not believe it will long stand alone. Probably it will lead in no very long time to Universal Suffrage. I cannot forbear from noting the language of the Administration of Earl Grey in reference to the great plans for Parliamentary Reform which they had laid before Parliament. In 1831 there appeared the following passage in the Speech from the Throne—

> "I have availed myself of the earliest opportunity of resorting to your advice and assistance after the dissolution of the late Parliament. Having had recourse to that measure for the purpose of ascertaining the sense of my people on the expediency of a Reform in the Representation, I have now to recommend that important question to your earliest and most attentive consideration, confident that, in any measures which you may prepare for its adjustment, you will carefully adhere to the acknowledged principles of the Constitution, by which the prerogative of the Crown, the authority of both Houses of Parliament, and the rights and liberties of the people are equally secured."

That was firm and clear language. No such language is heard in these days. On the contrary, when a question arises affecting the hereditary rights of your Lordships, the Prime Minister says, "I will think once, twice, or thrice before touching such a question." That, however, was not the course adopted by the people of England upon a recent occasion. When the people of England found that the life of the Heir to the Throne was in peril, they did not think thrice, or twice, or even once; but by one unanimous voice, as if impelled by instinct, in supplication for the Heir to the Throne, they put up prayers to Heaven for his recovery. It is not by measures of this kind, but by feelings such as those which animated the whole people during that crisis—and which, I trust, will ever be the sentiments of the people of England—that the Constitution can be preserved, and the rights and liberties of the people secured.

ISAAC BUTT ON HOME RULE.

HOUSE OF COMMONS, MARCH 20TH, 1874.

[IN the debate on the Address to be presented in answer to the Queen's Speech on the assembling of the New Parliament, MR BUTT seized the opportunity to introduce a Motion which, though at the time rejected, was destined to play an important part in the history of the country. This was the earliest intimation of the Home Rule Movement, since the time of Daniel O'Connell, in Parliament.]

IN moving an Amendment to the Address, I am fully aware of the objection that may be raised to a course being followed which will bring controversial questions to the vote on such an occasion as the present. I venture at the same time to think that, if the House favours me with a hearing, I shall be able to satisfy hon. members that I am justified in acting as I do; I hope, in short, to show that there is an absolute necessity for giving Ireland a new system of internal Government. The proposal I desire to submit to the House is that the following passage be added to the Address—

"We also think it right humbly to represent to Your Majesty that dissatisfaction prevails very extensively in Ireland with the existing system of Government in that country, and that complaints are made that under that system the Irish people do not enjoy the full benefits of the Constitution and of the free principles of the law; and we humbly assure Your Majesty that we shall regard it as the duty of Parliament, on the earliest opportunity, to consider the origin of this dissatisfaction with a view to the removal of all just causes of discontent."

I think there is one result of this dissatisfaction in Ireland, as exhibited by the recent elections, to which no person can be indifferent, and which no wise statesman can disregard. For the first time since the Act of Union, a majority—I will call it a decisive majority—of Irish members has been returned pledged to seek such a modification of the arrangements of the Union as would give to Irishmen in Ireland the right of managing their own affairs. I refer to this fact as evidence of dissatisfaction with the existing state of things. The Irish members who have been returned as Home Rulers are a decisive majority of the Irish representatives, and these have not been pledged to any mere vague declaration in favour of Home Rule. Those who have thought it right to endeavour to excite the attention of the country to the question of Home Rule have deliberately prepared and put before the country the plan contained in the Resolution, which, I venture to say, is framed in terms as clear and distinct as possible. We ask that Ireland shall have the management of exclusively Irish affairs. Our plan would relieve the House of business which it has not the time, and, I may say, without disrespect, the capacity, to manage. Our plan would not in the slightest degree affect the prerogative of the Crown or the stability of the Empire. We see no reason why an Irish Parliament could not manage exclusively Irish affairs without endangering the stability of the Empire. Has the grant of Parliaments to Canada, Australia, and other Colonies endangered the stability of the Empire? I believe I speak for every member who has been returned for Ireland on the Home Rule principle, when I say that we repudiate, in the strongest terms, the slightest wish to break up the unity of the Empire, or to bring about a collision between England and Ireland. We make no secret that they have all been elected to put forward the claim of Ireland to Home Rule, and, whether rightly or wrongly, we have come to an agreement among ourselves that we will act separately and independently of all existing political combinations in this House.

Whether this course is wise or not, it certainly is a new feature in Irish politics, and one that cannot be overlooked. We take up this position because we cannot acquiesce in anything that appears to us to imply that there is nothing in the state of Ireland that requires a remedy. In taking up this position I feel that we have taken a great responsibility upon ourselves, and I know the difficulty of our position. I know the prejudice which the statement that we have determined to act independently of political combinations must naturally provoke, but I would ask this House to judge us by our conduct. We would pursue a course very different from anything of faction. I think I may base the first part of this Amendment upon the mere fact that a majority of the Irish members are returned expressly to endeavour to obtain for Ireland self-government. I know not what stronger proof can be given of the dissatisfaction existing in Ireland. This dissatisfaction has been constitutionally expressed. It has not been expressed by any disturbances, such as on former occasions have been noticed in the Queen's Speech. The Irish people have made this great political movement at a time when perfect tranquillity prevails throughout the country, and in all the agitation by which the result has been brought about there has been nothing unconstitutional or illegal. It has been expressed through that political franchise which has been given to them for the purpose of declaring their political opinion. Ireland at present is in a state of perfect tranquillity. The Assizes that have just closed have ended in every place with congratulations from the Judges upon the peaceableness of the different counties. In the Last Summer Assizes in the city I have the honour to represent (Limerick), white gloves were given to the Judges, there not being a single prisoner to be tried. In the city of Cork, another great city in the south of Ireland, the very same thing occurred. I think the dissatisfaction in Ireland calls upon the House, I will not say to alter or reverse the policy that has been hitherto pursued with reference to Ireland, but certainly to review calmly and deliberately that policy, and ascertain the causes that have given rise to the opposition to the management of Irish affairs by this

I think I need not go far to justify the second part of this Amendment, which affirms that the Irish people complain that they have not had the full benefits of the Constitution of England. I believe that at this moment Ireland is under a code of law which for severity has not its parallel in any European State. I will not speak for a moment of the law that prevails all over Ireland independently of the will of the Lord-Lieutenant. The Lord-Lieutenant has power, by proclamation, to make it illegal in any district to carry arms without a licence from a police magistrate; and any man having a gun, a pistol, or dagger is liable, unless he have a magistrate's licence, to imprisonment for two years. Of the thirty-two counties in Ireland, twenty-six have been proclaimed; the greater part of five others has been proclaimed; and there is just one county in Ireland, designated Tyrone, which is free from proclamation. Of the eight counties and cities, Carrickfergus only is free from proclamation. Now this, I think, is a very startling state of things in Ireland. But more than this—at any time of the night, in any district where this law prevails, any policeman holding a warrant may demand to be admitted into any house in a proclaimed district, and may break open the door if admittance be refused, to search the house for arms; and one hundred and nineteen of these general warrants are now in operation. Even this is not all. By proclamation the Lord-Lieutenant may make it a crime to be out of doors after dark; while by another proclamation he can empower the police to seize any stranger; and a large portion of Ireland is at present under this law. By another proclamation any magistrate or police officer may demand admittance to any man's house, and ransack his papers for the purpose of comparing the handwriting with the handwriting of a threatening letter. Let it not be insinuated that these powers are never used. On one occasion a number of young men, one of whom was the son of a respectable merchant, determined to play "Hamlet." A police inspector, hearing of this, went to the theatre, arrested the young gentleman, and kept him in prison from Saturday

... till Monday morning, when he was brought before a magistrate on a charge of having arms in his possession. Cases like this are of frequent occurrence in Ireland. Under the pretext of searching for arms the police often seek to procure evidence of robberies and thefts, and these powers may be abused for many other purposes. I care not how these provisions may be defended, for I am sure they are not necessary.

This, I think, amply justifies me in saying that Ireland does not enjoy the advantages of the British Constitution, nor the true principles of the English law. These powers are in constant use. With regard to arresting persons after sunset, I will tell the House what occurred on the fifth of the present month, according to an account which appeared in a very respectable newspaper. Early in the morning on that day a band went to attend an election meeting. In going through the town they played some tune—which, however, was not a party tune—and the young people of the place were naturally attracted by the music. The crowd cheered, and then a policeman thought fit to think an offence had been committed against the law. Subsequently the constable followed two young men, whom he knew perfectly well, a distance of two miles, and at six minutes to six o'clock, just after sunset, he told them they were out under suspicious circumstances. Thereupon he carried them to gaol, where they were detained until they were brought before a magistrate the next day. Is this a state of things that ought to be endured in a country which is nominally under the British Constitution? The police in Ireland are in truth a military force. A high Conservative authority said they are ten times as numerous as they need be for the purpose of keeping the peace; and the late Lord Mayo said that, by converting them into a military force, their efficacy as detectors of crime has been destroyed. These exceptional laws make the police the masters of the daily life of the people. Indeed the police have been termed an "army of occupation," and when the civil power of a country is confided to an army, the law is identified with the idea of conquest.

But how does Ireland stand with regard to other matters? In the first place, the franchise is not the same as in England. When the late Reform Act was passed for England, household suffrage was introduced into the boroughs; whereas in Ireland no one can vote in a borough unless he have a rating qualification above £4. Moreover, the franchise in Ireland is encumbered by so many vexatious rules about rating that it is difficult for anybody to obtain a vote. In England, with a population of 26,000,000, as many as 1,200,000 enjoy the town franchise; while in Ireland, with a population of 5,000,000, there are just 50,000 town voters, of whom 30,000 are to be found in Belfast, Dublin, Cork, and Limerick. In the whole of the rest of Ireland only 20,000 persons are admitted to what ought to be a popular franchise. Perhaps it may be said that the town population of Ireland is not so large as that of England. This is doubtless true, but in England one man out of every eight has the franchise, whereas in Ireland only one man out of every twenty has it. I will ask you whether the Irish people have the full benefit of the Constitution which has been established in England? It is a strange circumstance that the progress of Liberal opinions lead to this divergence between the English and the Irish franchises. Formerly they were the same in both countries, but shortly after the passing of Catholic Emancipation the 40/ freeholders were abolished, and by the Reform Act the franchise in Ireland was made higher than in England. There is also a difference between the municipal franchises in the two countries. In Ireland—the poorer country, be it remembered—a man cannot take part in a municipal election unless he occupies a house worth £10 a year; but in England every householder has a right to vote. Again, how are fiscal affairs managed in Ireland? A Grand Jury is summoned in every county for the purpose of finding bills and discharging the criminal administration of justice, and the members of this body, who are not elected by the people, are made the guardians of the whole county expenditure, which amounts throughout the whole of Ireland to £1,200,000 a year. In fact, the whole system of Government in Ireland is based on distrust of the people, just as the whole system of Government in England is based upon trust of the people.

This circumstance, I think, justifies the complaint of the people of Ireland that they have not the benefit of the Constitution. In accordance with an old principle of the British Constitution, sheriffs in all towns are elected by the people, and this was the case in Ireland until Liberal legislation reformed the corporations, and took from them this power of electing sheriffs. Do not the facts I have mentioned justify me in asking the House to recede from its policy of coercion and distrust? The conclusion has been reluctantly forced upon me, that conceding to Ireland a Parliament to manage its own affairs is the only way to establish a perfect Constitutional Government in that country. I am persuaded that any candid Englishman who will examine the peculiar condition of Ireland, and the differences which exist between Ireland and England, will arrive, as I have done, at the conclusion that the only way to have a really Constitutional Government in Ireland is to allow the representatives of the people, freely chosen by the people, to administer their own affairs. However, the Amendment I am about to move does not express any opinion on this point. All I now ask the House to say is that Ireland has not the benefit of the Constitution, and to consider a remedy. The Amendment ought to commend itself to the common sense and candour of English gentlemen. A new state of things has arisen in Ireland, and an opportunity is now given to the House of Commons to review its policy with regard to that country. I do not at present ask the House to concede Home Rule to Ireland. That question it may be to be discussed, and perhaps to be discussed for many years. But first the advocates of Home Rule must satisfy the English people that they are not seeking separation. Ireland has given up the idea of separation, because she has before her the prospect of obtaining another and a far better remedy. I do not believe Ireland will ever be content with the existing state of things; but if Englishmen approach the subject with unprejudiced minds, there will be no difficulty in framing a measure which will make Ireland contented, while the integrity of the Empire will be perfectly maintained.

We are now entering upon a new phase of Irish politics. It is not my wish to say one word of disrespect towards the right hon. gentleman opposite (Mr Disraeli), who by his genius has raised himself to the exalted position he at present occupies. The right hon. gentleman is now for the first time in his life in power, although he has previously been in office. Ireland is a field large enough for the ambition of any man if he can reconcile that country cordially to the British nation, and dispel every trace of disloyalty to the British Crown. I believe it is possible to do this by wise legislation. There may be a veiled policy as well as a veiled rebellion. It will be a mistake, however, if the right hon. gentleman conceives that other questions will not have to be dealt with. If a policy of conciliation is pursued towards Ireland, the right hon. gentleman will not find himself obstructed by Irish representatives; but if he unfortunately pursues a different course, he will find himself disappointed. But however great our wish to relieve the House of Commons from the management of exclusively Irish affairs, for which we believe the House unfit, while these affairs are managed in the House, and we continue members of it, a duty devolves upon us which will be discharged by offering factious opposition to any measures for the benefit of Ireland, from whichever side of the House such measures may emanate.

I think I have shown that a crisis has arisen in the affairs of Ireland presenting new phases; that those gentlemen who have associated themselves for the purpose of obtaining self-government for Ireland are bound not to acquiesce in an Address which infers that things shall remain as they are; and it is with this view that I now place in the hands of the Speaker the Amendment which I have prepared.

A. M. SULLIVAN ON THE IRISH NATIONAL DEMANDS.

House of Commons, January 17th, 1878.

[On the opening of Parliament the Home Rule Members took exception to the Queen's Speech on the ground that it contained no reference to Ireland's Demands for Home Rule. They therefore proposed an Amendment to be inserted in the Address in these words:—"We humbly assure Your Majesty that we shall regard it as the duty of Parliament, in the present condition of public affairs, on the earliest opportunity, to consider in a wise and conciliatory spirit the National Demands which the Irish people have repeatedly raised." To speak against this Amendment the Government put up Mr David Plunket, the Member for Dublin University, a grandson of that Lord Plunket who in the Irish Parliament had most violently opposed and denounced the Act of Union, and who had declared that, if that measure was passed, he would, like another Hannibal, take his children to the altar of his country, and there swear them to eternal enmity against the power which had so basely wronged their native land.]

Sir,—The House stands indebted to the hon. and gallant gentleman the member for Waterford. His motion has broken "the cold shade of silence" that hung over the Government benches, and extracted from the hon. and learned gentleman (Mr Plunket) a speech which, whatever its other characteristics, we have all admired for its varied play of humour, eloquence, and ability. He had no need to apologise to the House for the time he was occupying. This is the business, and this of all others the subject, with which the time of the House should most rigidly be occupied. Parliament has been assembled three weeks earlier than usual, and within these three weeks there should be good time for discussing and considering the Irish question —for fully considered and discussed we are fixedly determined it shall be. Mr Speaker, that hon. and learned gentleman said of the men amidst whom I stand that they were " masquerading as Home Rulers." The phrase is not offensive, I suppose, or he would not have applied it; so I may use it too, and say that the thing which is really intolerable is to see the grandson of the great Plunket masquerading on the floor of the House as an Imperialist. We are supposed to be concerned just now with the Turkish question. One of the cruelest wrongs which the subject Christians under the Moslem yoke were made to feel was that oftentimes the children of Christian parents were seized and carried into the Turkish camp, trained up in Turkish ideas, embraced the faith and the banner of the conqueror, and appeared many a time, scimitar in hand, to wage war upon their kindred and their race! Even so it has been with us in Ireland through many a sad chapter of our country's history. Sometimes by force, sometimes by guile, sometimes by one influence, sometimes by another, the British power has been able to tear away from us children who bore great names, and might have greatly served their country; and we have seen these converts, as to-night, skilfully set in the fore-front of the assault when their countrymen were to be cut down.

Who is our accuser? The voice is the voice of an Irishman; the wit, the ability, the brilliant play of fancy and of genius, the rhetoric, the skill—all, all are Irish, but all are used against Ireland! Who, I repeat, is our accuser? If we stand here to-night, as we do, upon the floor of this House to maintain in the face of the Empire and of Europe the protest of Ireland against the memorable crime that robbed her of her Constitutional liberties, whose behests are we fulfilling?—who pledged us to undying hate and eternal war against the crime? The hon. and learned gentleman had the temerity to use a phrase for ever notable in the history of his family when he spoke of men "swearing upon the altar." Who was that great Irish-

... ... distinguished Constitutional lawyer, who declared ... ... Parliament were successfully overthrown he ... ... child—oh, why did he not say his grandchild? ... ... upon the altar of his country to wage relentless ... against that tremendous wrong? How little did he ... in that hour that to-night the representatives of Ireland ... over in the ranks of their Imperial adversaries the ... of his great name, and in no small degree of his genius, ... principles and his teachings, false to his lineage and ...!

But, Sir, I turn from the man to his arguments. He drew for us a picture of Ireland. Many years ago O'Connell was ... a sheep-stealer. In his speech to the Jury he drew a ... picture of the prisoner at the bar as a model husband ... (he was not married at all), a dutiful son, an exemplary citizen, virtuous, pious, industrious, inoffensive. At ... point the prisoner in the dock could stand it no longer, and ... him to those around him, "I never knew before that I ... such a character." Well, Sir, we have heard to-night ... leader of British rule in Ireland extolling the virtues and ... of his client; and well may the prisoner at the bar ... exclaim, "I never knew I was so beautiful, so virtuous ... meritorious as all that." Only believe the hon. and learned ... man, and there is not the slightest need of ... anything, the slightest possibility of improving ... in Ireland. Everything there is already perfect in ... of government, law, and administration. There is ... if you believe him, a more fortunate spot on the face of the ... globe. It is the home of happiness, peace, ... of beneficent rule and abounding loyalty. Hon. ... to its cheer. You evidently think so too. You ... about it. You know Ireland better than we do. You ... to speak for it than we, the Irish majority, ... But, pray, by what right does your party hold ... and rule the destinies of England but by the ... majority? In virtue of a Parliamentary ... you are entitled to speak to the world for

England, while in virtue of a Parliamentary minority you would claim to speak for Ireland.

But, Sir, the question before the House is much wider, and greater, and more serious than the merits of the Irish "Bills" which the Government has promised. If it were a matter of a better or a worse Grand Jury Law, or a better or a worse Intermediate Education Bill, I, for one, should hesitate to concur in an interposition like the present. The question we raise is that for which it may be said Parliament has been specially convoked. We have been told in the Royal Speech of a possible danger near at hand, of precautions and preparations that may be necessary for the defence of the power and stability of the Empire. Well, we have come forward to suggest the wisest precaution and the most potential preparation which the Government could make. The matter is glossed over by smooth phrases, but the danger that you all mean is war—a war in which England will have to fight for her very existence as a nation. If that war break out, if it be not averted, as I hope it may be, England will find herself in such desperate strait as she has not known for four hundred years. Your army, small, but brave and fearless as ever, will behave with its traditional valour; wherever it may be sent, on whatever field it may fight, the army of this country will exhibit those splendid qualities that have justly given it a world-wide fame. I would say as much for it, even were it not composed as largely as it is of my own brave countrymen. But there is not a military man sitting in this House who does not know and feel the truth of what I say—that a recent memorable war in Europe has demonstrated that courage and prestige no longer compensate as largely as they used to do sixty years ago against overwhelming odds; and that your army of a hundred thousand, or a hundred and fifty thousand men, would be utterly powerless before the hosts that now stand arrayed and disciplined on the Continent of Europe. Should this calamity befall, should this trouble for your existence arise, think you that it is upon inanimate sword and bayonet, and ship and gun,

r ... r than up on stalwart arms and patriotic enthusiasm, your
... will be? Should that crisis come, right sure am I
... the English masses a patriotic fervour will answer to
... Through out England and throughout Scotland it will
... will it be so in Ireland? In the spirit of the oath which
I ... table — nay, higher obligations still, by the duty I
... conscience and to truth—I dare all misconception and
... liver at this momentous crisis my solemn testimony
... that if this Empire enters upon a struggle of such
... while Ireland is in the attitude which Hungary
... d towards Austria previous to Sadowa, the popular
... n which you will receive in England and Scotland
... not respond to you in Ireland. [*Cries of* "Oh! oh!"]
I was prepared for your exclamations, and I do not complain;
for the statement I have made is serious, and naturally un-
w......; but time will vindicate the truth of my words and the
... rity of my motives.

Twenty or twenty-five years ago there stood upon the floor
of this House a band of Irish members, struggling, as we
... now, to persuade you to listen to Irish demands.
... yourselves what was their fate; read for yourselves
... of that time. They were voted down, they were
... down, they were laughed at, they were denounced or
... l. You had in that day—as you always have—some
... eloquent Irishman in your service to get up and do
... against his countrymen—to contradict their testi-
... to tell you pleasant tidings which you hailed as gospel
... honest warnings of danger were shrieked against
... motives. John Francis Maguire and others
... say in this House, as I say now, that there was
... and disaffection in Ireland. They were set upon
... traitors. They were contradicted and con-
... House, by overwhelming voice, declared their
... and that Ireland was peaceable, contented,
... etc. Alas! a year or two barely passed when
... a true light on all this. At that very moment

my unfortunate countrymen were being sworn in by the thousand in a secret conspiracy for armed insurrection. Barely a few years passed away when the crowded dock, the convict ship, the penal gang, the triangle, and the bloody lash—nay, the scaffold itself—furnished a frightful contradiction to the pleasant testimonies which you preferred to believe; a frightful corroboration to the warnings you denounced and despised. What happened then? Like the story of the recent Fenian amnesty which we have heard to-night, measures prayed for in vain in the hour of your tranquillity, when concession would have grace and efficacy, were conceded amidst public disquietude and almost panic. Writing some six weeks ago to a friend in the north of England—a fair-minded, a kindly-hearted, and a high-principled Englishman—yes, I believe in the existence of such men, not in scores or hundreds, but in hundreds of thousands—I complained of this, and asked how and why it was that English statesmen and politicians should thus put a premium on turbulence and revolt.

Just look what has been the history of any great political measure passed for Ireland in our own generation. The argument of Catholic Emancipation was exhausted in 1801. Its justice was as patent to all men in 1812 as at any time afterwards; yet it was resisted and refused until, as the Duke of Wellington declared, civil war seemed inevitable. Was not that a mischievous lesson to Irishmen? The Tithe Question you resisted until our land was reddened with blood. The Church Question and the Land Question—it is a story of recent years. A Land Bill was passed in 1870, after passions had been aroused, hearts broken, homes desolated by the thousand; after you had filled America with combustible elements that are at this moment a serious menace to England. In that struggle you broke the heart of Lucas, and drove Gavan Duffy into exile—robbed Ireland of the services of a man whose genius and worth you have been glad to recognise at the Antipodes. The Land Bill, prayed for in 1850, was granted in part in 1870, after the terrible tragedy

of Ballycohey had startled the Empire. In 1868 you
utterly overthrew the Irish Church, because, as you avowed,
of the spread of Fenianism. In the face of the men whose
warnings you had angrily resented a few years previously,
you came down to this House to concede in an hour of alarm
what you had refused in the time of tranquillity. Is this
narration true or false? Am I, or am I not, reciting facts
known to you all? What do these facts show? That, by
some fatal fatality, some calamitous coincidence, if nothing
more, you scoff at men, like my colleague and myself, who
beseech you to be just in time. You resist concession in
time of calm, and yield it only in the face of real or fancied
peril. If it be not so, let some one get up to-night, and name
for us any great national concession made to Ireland under
any other circumstances. As it has been, perhaps it is still
to be. You will complain of my words; you will say I do
not warn but threaten, and you will prefer to believe those
who tell you the Irish masses are contented and well-affected,
as enthusiastically ready as Englishmen could be to pour out
their blood in your defence; but I dare all risk of temporary
misrepresentation and blame.

I look into the future, and can await my vindication. Do
not affect to mistake our position in this crisis of the Empire.
We are not so many members of a party or a section of this
House. We are not so many advocates of this or that Bill.
We are the national representation of Ireland, here in overwhelming majority to demand the restoration of Parliamentary
and Constitutional Government. We are projecting no
novelty, like the friends of this or that great reform or
innovation. We are here to call for the restitution of what
you conveyed and possessed, but which you wrung from us by
a fraud held to vitiate and render illegal every public
transaction between man and man, between nation and
nation. Possession gives you no title to it; for no time runs
against a claim asserted and renewed, as ours has been, from
the hour of its spoliation. Legally we stand to-day where we

stood seventy years ago. Restore to Ireland the reign of law! It is all she asks as the price of her friendship—a price cheap indeed, for it takes nothing from you that belongs to you. The price of her friendship! You are now, in view of a terrible emergency, possibly at hand, searching Europe through for allies. Here we are to-night empowered to offer you one worth the best you could elsewhere find—the alliance, the hearty friendship, the enthusiastic support of Ireland. I own I have deep reason to wish this question settled, and to see a cordial feeling established between the two countries before dark clouds grow darker, and while yet the reconciliation can be free and generous and efficacious. The peace, the happiness, the tranquillity of Ireland are most dear to me; and I do not wish to see my country desolated and destroyed by being made, perhaps, a battle-field of the coming struggle. I do not want the ghastly episode of some Continental despot making what he would call a diversion in Ireland—wasting the blood and blasting the hopes of my country in a mere stroke of tactics to serve his own ends. I shudder when I think of such a possibility; and I appeal to you—yes, unchilled by the foregone conclusion of your unwise refusal—I nevertheless raise and record my appeal to you and the English nation to-night to let us clasp hands in friendship on the only terms on which we can be allies or friends. Be simply just. That you will do so yet, despite your customary refusals now, I am as convinced as I am of my own existence. It is the time which, with your customary unwisdom, you may select for such a step that alone disquiets me. Austria tried your present policy towards Hungary, and changed it after Sadowa. I hope and pray you will wait for no such hour to accept the proffered hand and secure the ready aid of the brave and gallant Irish nation.

THE EARL OF BEACONSFIELD ON THE BERLIN CONGRESS.

Carlton Club Banquet, July 27th, 1878.

[On his return from the Berlin Congress, Lord Beaconsfield was at the summit of his popularity. Enthusiastic crowds cheered his progress through the City to the Foreign Office, from one of the windows of which he addressed the multitude, saying, "I have brought you peace, but I trust, peace with honour." These words became memorable. The speech, which follows, by him at the Carlton Club Banquet in the Duke of Wellington's Riding School, Knightsbridge—the largest available hall in the West End—was a development of that brief address to the people. The Duke of Buccleuch occupied the Chair.]

My Lord Duke and Gentlemen,—I am sure that you will acquit me of affectation if I say that it is not without emotion that I have received this expression of your goodwill and sympathy. When I look around this chamber I see the faces of some who entered public life with myself, as my noble friend the noble Duke has reminded me, more than forty years ago; I see more whose entrance into public life I witnessed when I had myself gained some experience of it; and lastly, I see those who have only recently entered upon public life, and whom it has been my duty and my pleasure to encourage and to counsel when they entered that public career so characteristic of this country, and which is one of the main securities of our liberty and welfare.

My Lord and Gentlemen, our Chairman has referred to my career as that of all public men in this country, as one of toil and vicissitude; but I have been sustained, even in the darkest hours of our party, by the conviction that I possessed your confidence, I will say your indulgent confidence; for in the long course of my public life, that I may have committed many mistakes is too obvious a truth to touch upon; but that you have been indulgent there is no doubt, for I can, I hope, I may say proudly, remember that it has been my lot to lead in either House of Parliament this great party for a longer period than has ever fallen to the lot of any public man in the history of this country. That I have owed that result to your generous indulgence more than to any personal qualities of my own no man is more sensible than myself; but it is a fact that I may recur to with some degree of proud satisfaction. Our noble Chairman has referred to the particular occasion which has made me your guest to-day. I attended that high assembly which has recently dispersed with much reluctance. I yielded to the earnest solicitations of my noble friend near me (the Marquis of Salisbury), my colleague in that great enterprise. He thought that my presence might be of use to him in the vast difficulties he had to encounter; but I must say now, as I shall ever say, that to his lot fell the labouring oar in that great work, and that you are, I will not say equally, but more indebted to him than to myself for the satisfactory results which you kindly recognise. I share the conviction of our noble Chairman that it is one which has been received with satisfaction by the country, but I am perfectly aware that that satisfaction is not complete or unanimous, because I know well that before eight-and-forty hours have passed the marshalled hosts of opposition will be prepared to challenge what has been done, and to question the policy we hope we have established.

My Lords and Gentlemen, as I can no longer raise my voice in that House of Parliament where this contest is to take place, as I sit now in a House where our opponents never unsheath their swords, a House where, although the two chief plenipotentiaries of the Queen sit, they are met only by innuendo and by question, I hope you will permit me, though with extreme brevity, to touch on one or two of the points which in a few hours may much engage the interest and attention of the Parliament. My Lords and Gentlemen, it is difficult to describe the exact meaning of the charge which is brought against the plenipotentiaries of the Queen, as it will be introduced to the House of Commons on Monday. Drawn as it is, it appears at first sight to be only a series of congratulatory regrets. But, my Lords and Gentlemen, if you penetrate the meaning of this movement, it would appear that there are two points in which it is hoped that a successful onset may be made on Her Majesty's Government, and on those two points, and those alone, I hope with becoming brevity, at this moment, perhaps, you will allow me to make one or two remarks. It is charged against Her Majesty's Government that they have particularly deceived and deserted Greece.

Now, my Lords and Gentlemen, this is a subject which is, I think, capable of simpler treatment than hitherto it has encountered in public discussion. We have given at all times, in public and in private, to the Government of Greece and to all who might influence its decisions but one advice—that on no account should they be induced to interfere in those coming disturbances which two years ago threatened Europe, and which concluded in a devastating war. And we gave that advice on these grounds, which appear to me incontestable. If, as Greece supposed, and as we thought erroneously supposed, the partition of the Ottoman Empire was at hand, Greece, morally, geographically, ethnographically, was sure of receiving a considerable allotment of that partition when it took place. It would be impossible to make a re-settlement of the East of Europe without largely satisfying the claims of Greece; and great as those claims might be, if that were the case, it was surely unwise in Greece to waste its treasure and its blood. If, on the other hand, as Her Majesty's Government believed, the end of this struggle would not be a partition of the Ottoman Empire, but that the wisdom and experience of all the Powers and Governments would come to the conclusion that the existence and strengthening of the Ottoman Government was necessary to the peace of Europe, and without it long and sanguinary and intermitting struggles must inevitably take place, it was equally clear to us that when the settlement occurred, all those rebellious tributary principalities that have lavished their best blood and embarrassed their finances for generations would necessarily be but scurvily treated, and that Greece, even under this alternative, would find that she was wise in following the advice of England and not mixing in a fray so fatal. Well, my Lords and Gentlemen, has not the event proved the justice and accuracy of that view? At this moment, though Greece has not interfered, fortunately for herself—though she has not lavished the blood of her citizens and wasted her treasure, under the Treaty of Berlin she has the opportunity of obtaining a greater increase of territory than will be obtained by any of the rebellious principalities that have lavished their blood and wasted their resources in this fierce contest. I should like to see that view answered by those who accuse us of misleading Greece. We gave to her the best advice; fortunately for Greece she followed it, and I will hope that, following it with discretion and moderation, she will not lose the opportunity we have secured for her in the advantages she may yet reap.

I would make one more remark on this subject, which will soon occupy the attention of many who are here present. It has been said we have misled and deserted Greece, because we were the Power which took steps that Greece should be heard before the Congress. Why did we do that? Because we have ever expressed our opinion that in the elevation of the Greek race—not merely the subjects of the King of Greece—one of the best chances of the improvement of Society under the Ottoman rule would be found, and that it was expedient that the rights of the Greek race should be advocated by that portion of it which enjoyed an independent political existence; and all this time, too, let it be recollected that my noble friend was unceasing in his efforts to obtain such a settlement of the claims, or rather, I should say, the desires of Greece with the Porte, as would conduce greatly to the advantage of that kingdom. And not without success. The proposition of Lord Salisbury for the rectification of the frontiers of Greece really includes all that moderate and sensible men could desire; and that was the plan that ultimately was adopted by the Congress, and which Greece might avail herself of if there be prudence and moderation in her councils. Let me here make one remark—which indeed is one that applies to other most interesting portions of this great question; it refers to the personal character of the Sultan. From the first the Sultan of Turkey has expressed his desire to deal with Greece in a spirit of friendliness and conciliation. He has been perfectly aware that in the union of the Turkish and Greek races the only balance could be obtained and secured against the Pan-Slavic monopoly which was fast invading the whole of his dominions. Therefore there was every disposition on his part to meet the proposals of the English Government with favour, and he did meet them with favour. Remember the position of that Prince. It is almost unprecedented. No prince, probably, that ever lived has gone through such a series of catastrophes. One of his predecessors commits suicide; his immediate predecessor is subject to a visitation more awful even than suicide. The moment he ascends the throne his Ministers are assassinated. A conspiracy breaks out in his own palace, and then he learns that his kingdom is invaded; his armies, however valiant, are defeated, and that the enemy is at his gates; yet, with all these trials, and during all this period, he has never swerved in the expression, and I believe the feeling, of a desire to deal with Greece in a spirit of friendship. Well, what happened?— What was the last expression of feeling on his part? He is evidently a man whose every impulse is good; however great the difficulties he has to encounter, however evil the influences that may sometimes control him, his impulses are good; and where impulses are good there is always hope. He is not a tyrant—he is not dissolute—he is not a bigot, or corrupt. What was his last decision? When my noble friend, not encouraged, I must say, by Greece, but still continuing his efforts, endeavoured to bring to some practical result this question of the frontiers, the Sultan said that what he was prepared to do he wished should be looked on as an act of grace on his part, and of the sense of the friendliness of Greece in not attacking him during his troubles; but as a Congress was now to meet, he should like to hear the result of the wisdom of the Congress on the subject. The Congress has now spoken; and though it declared that it did not feel justified in compelling the Sultan to adopt the steps it might think advantageous even for its own interests, the Congress expressed an opinion which, I doubt not, the Sultan is prepared to consider in the spirit of conciliation he has so often displayed. And this is the moment when a party for factious purposes, and a party unhappily not limited to England, is egging on Greece to violent courses! I may, perhaps, have touched at too much length on this topic; but the attacks made on Her Majesty's Government are nothing compared with the public mischief that may occur if misconception exists on this point.

There is one other point on which I would make a remark, and that is with regard to the Convention of Constantinople of the 4th of June. When I study the catalogue of congratulatory regrets with attention, this appears to be the ground on which a great assault is to be made on the Government. It is said that we have increased, and dangerously increased, our responsibilities by that Convention. In the first place, I deny that we have increased our responsibilities by that Convention. I maintain that by that Convention we have lessened our responsibilities. Suppose now, for example, the settlement of Europe had not included the Convention of Constantinople, and the occupation of the Isle of Cyprus? Suppose it had been limited to the mere Treaty of Berlin, what, under all probable circumstances, might then have occurred? In ten, fifteen, it might be in twenty years, the power and resources of Russia having revived, some quarrel would again have occurred, Bulgarian or otherwise, and in all probability the armies of Russia would have been assailing the Ottoman dominions both in Europe and Asia, and enveloping and enclosing the city of Constantinople and its all-powerful position. Well, what would be the probable conduct, under these circumstances, of the Government of this country, whoever the Ministers might be—whatever party might be in power? I fear there might be hesitation for a time—a want of decision—a want of firmness; but no one doubts that ultimately England would have said: "This will never do; we must prevent the conquest of Asia Minor; we must interfere in this matter and arrest the course of Russia." No one, I am sure, in this country who impartially considers this question can for a moment doubt what under any circumstances would have been the course of this country. Well, then, that being the case, I say it is extremely important that this country should take a step beforehand which should indicate what the policy of England would be; that you should not have your Ministers meeting in a Council-Chamber, hesitating and doubting, and considering contingencies, and then acting at last, but acting, perhaps, too late. I say, therefore, that the responsibilities of this country have not been increased; the responsibilities already existed, though I, for one, would never shrink from increasing the responsibilities of this country if they are responsibilities which ought to be undertaken. The responsibilities of this country are practically diminished by the course we have taken.

My Lords and Gentlemen, one of the results of my attending the Congress of Berlin has been to prove what I always considered to be an absolute fact, that neither the Crimean War nor this horrible devastating war which has just terminated would have taken place if England had spoken with the necessary firmness. Russia has complaints to make against this country that neither in the case of the Crimean War nor on this occasion—and I do not shrink from my share of the responsibility in this matter—was the voice of England so clear and decided as to exercise a due share in the guidance of European opinion. Well, Gentlemen, suppose my noble friend and myself had come back with the Treaty of Berlin, and had not taken the step which is to be questioned within the next eight-and-forty hours, could we with any self-respect have met our countrymen when they asked, What securities have you made for the peace of Europe?—How far have you diminished the chance of perpetually recurring war on this question of the East by the Treaty of Berlin? Why, they could say, all we have gained by the Treaty of Berlin is probably the peace of a few years, and at the end of that time the same phenomenon will arise, and the Ministers of England must patch up the affair as well as they could. That was not the idea of public duty entertained by my noble friend and myself. We thought the time had come when we should take steps which would produce some order out of the anarchy and chaos that had so long prevailed. We asked ourselves was it absolutely a necessity that the fairest provinces of the world should be the most devastated and most ill-used, and for this reason, that there is no security for life or property so long as that country is in perpetual fear of invasion and aggression?

It was under these circumstances that we recommended the course we have taken, and I believe that the consequence of that policy will tend to and even secure peace and order in a portion of the globe which hitherto has seldom been blessed by these celestial visitants. I hold that we have laid the foundation of a state of affairs which may open a new Continent to the civilisation of Europe, and that the welfare of the world and the wealth of the world may be increased by availing ourselves of that tranquillity and order which the more intimate connection of England with that country will now produce. But I am sorry to say that, though we taxed our brains and our thought to establish a policy which might be beneficial to the country, we have not satisfied those who are our critics. I was astonished to learn that the Convention of the 4th June has been described as an "insane" Convention. It is a strong epithet. I do not myself pretend to be as competent a judge of insanity as my right hon. opponent (Mr Gladstone). I will not say to the right hon. gentleman *Naviget Anticyram*, but I would put this issue to an English jury— Which do you believe most likely to enter into an insane Convention, a body of English gentlemen, honoured by the favour and the confidence of their fellow-subjects, managing your affairs for five years, I hope with prudence and not altogether without success, or a sophisticated rhetorician, inebriated with the exuberance of his own verbosity, and gifted with an egotistical imagination that can at all times command an interminable and inconsistent series of arguments to malign an opponent and to glorify himself?

My Lords and Gentlemen, I leave the decision upon that Convention to the Parliament and people of England. I believe that in that policy are deeply laid the seeds of future welfare, not merely to England, but to Europe and to Asia; and confident that the policy we have recommended is one that will be supported by the country, I and those that act with me can endure these attacks. My Lords and Gentlemen, let me thank you once more for the manner in which you have welcomed me to-day. These are the rewards of public life that never pall the sympathy of those who have known you long, who have worked with you long, who have the same opinions upon the policy that ought to be pursued in this great and ancient Empire. These are sentiments which no language can efficiently appreciate which are a consolation under all circumstances and the highest reward that a public man can attain. The generous feeling that has prompted you to welcome my colleague and myself on our return to England will inspire and strengthen our efforts to serve our country; and it is not merely that in this welcome you encourage those who are doing their best for what they conceive to be the public interests, but to tell to Europe also that England is a grateful country, and knows how to appreciate the efforts of her public servants, who are resolved to maintain to their utmost the Empire of Great Britain.

JOSEPH COWEN ON THE FOREIGN POLICY OF ENGLAND.

NEWCASTLE-ON-TYNE, JANUARY 31ST, 1880.

[ANTICIPATING the Dissolution of Parliament and a General Election, MR COWEN addressed a monster meeting of his constituents in the Town Hall, Councillor H. W. NEWTON presiding.]

MR CHAIRMAN, LADIES, AND GENTLEMEN,—I have rarely addressed a meeting with more misgivings than I do this one. My hesitation does not arise from any doubt I entertain as to the correctness of the statements I am about to make, of the strength of the argument I propose sustaining, or of the soundness of the deductions I intend to draw. On all these points I am thoroughly persuaded in my own mind. My reluctance to speaking springs from the conviction I entertain that anything I can say will be valueless, and may be locally mischievous. International problems of great intricacy and importance have come up for settlement since the last general election. Many of the issues started are old ones, some of them centuries old, but they were not then before the electors. The Liberals, as a body, have assumed towards them an altered attitude. They have abandoned, no doubt for reasons which appeared to them good, the historic policy of the country, if not the traditional principles of the party. There is necessarily difficulty in fixing with precision the position of a complex party in a state of change. But no injustice will, I think, be done to anyone by saying that many Liberals, on foreign questions, have espoused in spirit, if not in substance, the doctrines which were held with such tenacity and expounded with such earnestness by that band of capable men who made the world their debtors by their labours for Free Trade.

I have not been able to become a convert to this new faith. I am not, and never was, an adherent of what is popularly known as the "Manchester School." On this subject there is between myself and some of my friends a distinct divergency, which I have no desire either to minimise or ignore. I am in favour of an European and national, as against an insular and —I use the word in no offensive sense—a parochial policy. It may seem somewhat hard to dismiss a member because, in the course of a Parliament, he has not been able to change his creed. I recognise, however, the right of the constituency to demand uniformity of view from their representatives. I also feel that in my present position I am a source of embarrassment to many and of annoyance to some; and I have repeatedly expressed my willingness, and I do it again to-night, to solve all difficulties by quietly retiring. It has not been thought desirable that an election should take place in Newcastle at this time; and although my immediate retirement might meet with the approval of some, I understand that it would not meet with the general approval of the electors. Such being the case, in my judgment it would have been wise not to have re-opened troublesome topics, which may add possible irritation to honest difference by promoting a discussion that can be fruitful of no good results. I do not object, without further hearing, to be tried, condemned, and, if you decree it, dismissed.

There is nothing that I have said on this question that I wish either to modify or retract. There is nothing that I have done which I regret. I may be mistaken; I am not infallible; but I believe that the course of policy I have supported has been the best for England and the best for liberty. I fear my convictions are too strongly fixed to be shaken. I am not either so sanguine or so egotistical as to suppose that anything I can say will turn my friends from the faith they have accepted with so much devotion. Apart from political considerations, party passions and personal predilections and prejudices have been imported into the controversy, and in some instances these have been intensified by religious animosities. It is hopeless to reason against such a combination of active and angry sentiments. But the blast that blows loudest is soon overblown; and having lodged an earnest protest in support of my opinions, I am willing to bend to the storm and wait for the sobering effects of experience and the modifying influence of time to wear out the asperity of the political jehad which is now being preached against doctrines that, to my mind, have the semblance at least of truth and justice to sustain them. But if I am to speak I will do so frankly, without reservation or equivocation. In a country where unfortunately speech is so much controlled by, and so much based on, party interest, little favour is shown to the politician who ignores its consideration and ventures upon the dangerous practice of striving to be impartial. If he speak the unbiassed sentiments of his own mind he secures the opposition of his former supporters, the slanders of his atrabilarious opponents, and the sneers, if not the suspicions, of some of his associates. But sincerity of utterance is the only channel of truth, and I believe that my fellow townsmen will listen to declarations of opinion which may involve opposition, and possibly censure of some of them, if these declarations are untainted, as I trust in my case they will be, with either levity or ignorance. I cannot cite a new fact, and no one can adduce a new argument either for or against the policy that this country has recently pursued. The subject has been written about and spoken of so often, and at such length, that every argumentative thread is worn thin and bare. The literature on the interminable theme is a veritable kaleidoscope, in which every form of thought, every shade of opinion, is presented in all shapes of attraction and

But if what I say is not new, it will only be in keeping with the speeches of more distinguished persons. We are not philosophers speculating upon what might be, nor philanthropists dilating upon what ought to be, nor poets chanting the dirge of a brilliant but buried past. We are matter-of-fact politicians, talking of the prosaic present. And politics, I fear, are too often controlled more by self-interest than by sentiment. We are not dealing with an ideal State. If we were, the fragmentary and composite Empire of Britain would not realise my Utopia. Greece, whose name has been for centuries a watchword upon earth, whose fame will never fade, from whose history mankind have derived inspiration and guidance, and which still rises upon our intellectual sight like a mountain-top gilded with sunshine, amidst the devastations of a flood— Greece, I say, rather than law-giving, conquering, Imperial, splendid, but savage Rome, would be my model. I would have a State in which every man is free, and where every man is fortified against superstition by education, and against oppression by arms; where the arts and graces of Athens, and the martial independence of Sparta, would commingle with the mercantile and industrial enterprise and the naval prowess of Britain; and in which, while influence and authority are won by intellectual strength and moral worth, a proud defiance could be bid to despotism's banded myriads.

But these are the dreams of the idealists. We belong to the real and the active, and not the imaginary world. We are to deal with things as they are, and not as we can sketch them in our fancy. We are the inheritors of a Colonial Empire, the most widespread, scattered, and extensive ever known. It reaches to every region, and has its feelers and its feeders in every corner of the globe. Some of these possessions came to us in a questionable shape, and by means that no one can justify, and that I, at least, have no desire either to palliate or excuse. But the present generation of Englishmen are guiltless of the crime attending their acquisition. Our Colonies cover an area of three millions of square miles, and have a population fourteen million persons following diverse pursuits, but all animated by one mind, aim, and tradition. In India we have a frontier of twelve thousand miles, an area of one and a half million square miles, and 240,000,000 of people under our sway. Our insular position frees us from many of the dangers which surround Continental States, but our external Empire makes us at the same time one of the most sensitive and assailable of nations. No serious movement can take place in any part of the earth without our feeling its influence. No country ever occupied such a peculiar position as Britain and her daughter empires now hold. It is not egotism to say that, notwithstanding all our shortcomings, power so vast was never wielded with so sincere a desire to use it beneficially. Every tribe we touch acknowledges our supremacy, and looks to us either in conscious fear of weakness, or with brightening hope of participating in our elevation. To secure the existence, to rivet the cohesion of this vast dominion, blest with one of the highest forms of freedom that the world has ever seen, to carry to distant countries and succeeding ages the loftiest form of civilisation, is our mission. To abandon the opportunity of usefulness thus conferred, to throw aside the hope of securing equal rights and impartial freedom, to destroy the means of establishing a feeling of fraternity and consciousness of common material interests amongst so many millions of our fellow-beings, would be a narrow, a niggardly, a short-sighted, and a foolish policy for a great nation to pursue.

If we left South Africa, what would be the result? There are 250,000 British born men and women—our own kith and kin living there. Without some protection from the Home Government, the homesteads they have erected by years of patient toil, the centres of civilisation and of commerce that they have created by their enterprise, would be endangered, if not destroyed. Their assailants would not be the natives of the soil, who are friendly and inoffensive, but savage invaders from the North, who are as much alien and aggressors as the Dutch. If we abandoned India, a like, but more disastrous result would ensue. The scores of different races and nations into which the population of that country is divided would fly at each other's throats. In the earliest encounters probably the fierce, courageous, unteachable, and intractable Mahommedans, who are forty millions strong, would re-assert their supremacy, but after years of internecine war and social disorder the country would eventually fall a prey to a foreign invader—possibly Russia. The 8,000 miles of railway, the 18,000 miles of telegraph, the canals, and other creations of English capital, would be destroyed. The machinery for the administration of justice, and the protection of life and property, which England has created, and which has assured to the common people of India more security and greater personal freedom than they ever enjoyed under former rulers, would be upset. This country would suffer equally with the Indian people; the £128,000,000 of Indian debt would have to be provided for; civil servants and officers whose careers would be destroyed would require their pensions, and compensation would possibly be demanded by traders who would be ruined by our change of policy. India, England, and the world would all be injured. No Englishman could contemplate such a contingency with approval, or acquiesce in it with satisfaction. Now that we possess it, we are bound to protect and defend India—to hold it against any enemy as stoutly as we would hold Cornwall or Caithness.

England is not so many square roods of land, but a nation whose people are united in love of soil and race, by mutual sympathy and tradition, by character and institutions. It is not a fortuitous concourse of individuals merely bound over to keep the peace towards each other, and, for the rest, following their own selfish objects, and crying outside their own cottage, counting-house, or country, let everything "take its course." Our country is something more than the mere workshop of the world, a manufactory for flashy clothing, and a market for cheap goods. We are pledged to each other as citizens of a great nationality, and by solidarity of life. We owe a duty to ourselves, to our families, and to our country, and also to our generation and to the future. We have grown great, not merely by the extent of our possessions and the fertility of our soil, but by the preservation of our liberties and the energy and enterprise of our people. The present generation is the outcome of centuries of effort. The history of England is woven and interwoven, laced and interlaced with the history of Europe and the world for a thousand years. Wherever liberty has struggled successfully, or wherever it has suffered in vain, there our sympathies have gone. There is nothing in human affairs that can be foreign to us. Wealth almost beyond the dreams of avarice, territorial possessions, and education bring with them heavy responsibilities. Power, to the very last particle of it, is duty. Unto whom much is given, of him much will be required.

As we have inherited, so we have to transmit. No one can look slightingly on the results which rest upon our national resolves. But if ever a nation, drunk with the fumes of power and wealth, makes an apotheosis of gold and material pleasure, prefers riches to duty, comfort to courage, selfish enjoyment to heroic effort and sacrifice, it sinks in the respect of others, and loses the first and strongest incentive to human effort. Great work demands great effort, and great effort is the life and soul both of individuals and nations. I contend, therefore, for these two principles the integrity of the Empire, and the interest, the right, and the duty of England to play her part in the great battle of the world, as did our illustrious ancestors, the forerunners of European freedom.

Let me apply these principles to the recent controversies in the East and the action that has been taken by this country. India is one of our most distant, as it is one of our most important dependencies. We hold it more as conquerors than colonists. There are urgent and obvious reasons why our communication with it should be rapid, easy, and expeditious. Mechanical science, and commercial enterprise, have led to make the best route to it through the Isthmus which unites the continents of Asia and Africa. The Egyptians, the Phœnicians, and the Carthagenians, before the Christian era, travelled to India this way. In the Middle Ages the Genoese and Venetian merchants went by the same road. The first envoy whom England ever sent to India also journeyed by this path—Bishop Sherborne, who was deputed by good King Alfred to undertake a mission to the people on the coast of Coromandel and Malabar. As before the Christian era, so to-day—the most direct route to the East is by the Isthmus of Suez and Asia Minor. The Suez Canal is the link which unites our Eastern and Western Empires. Through it we not only reach India but our dependencies in the Chinese Seas, our Australian colonies, the Mauritius, and the British settlements on the East Coast of Africa. It is the neck which connects the head with the extremities of our Empire. It has been suggested that if we lost it we could resume our old road by the Cape of Good Hope. It is quite true that this could be done. It is equally true that we might return to pack-horses and stage waggons as a means of transit, but it is not likely that we shall do so; it would be contrary to the genius of civilisation and the spirit of our times thus to recede. We have got the Canal, and in the interests of ourselves and of the world we will hold it free for everyone at all hazards. If Russia were to obtain political supremacy on either side of the Bosphorus, she could stop the Canal or intercept our way to India by the Euphrates Valley. North of the Danube she is comparatively harmless; but with the Black Sea, the Sea of Marmora, and the Straits, she would have at her command a position unequalled in the world for commerce and for war. She could barricade the Dardanelles, and behind it she would have two inland seas, which would be at one and the same time harbour, arsenal, dockyard, and naval station. She could there with security and ease equip and arm her ships, and train her sailors, and manœuvre her fleet. In the numberless islands and roadsteads of the Archipelago she would have protection for conducting either offensive or defensive warfare, such as is to be found in no other part of the globe in equal space. This position is the key to Europe—one of its life-arteries. Its occupation by a conquering, ambitious, and despotic Power would be a danger to England, to Europe, and to liberty.

The aspirations of the Russian peasant are southward. He yearns to be clear of the Boreal regions of snow and solitude in which he is enveloped for the greater part of the year. As naturally as the sap rises in the vine, so naturally does the desire of the Russian rise to reach more genial regions, and to burst the political and frozen cerements which rob him of life and of development. It is only the force of the iron yoke that makes him a labourer. By choice and by taste he would be a wanderer, a boatman, a pedlar, or a travelling mechanic. Russia is not a nation like France, or Italy, or Spain; it is not a dynastic aggregation of States like Austria; but it is a crushing and devouring political mechanism, which has annihilated full fifty distinct nationalities. It kills every spring of independence; it intercepts and has covered whole continents with the melancholy monuments of nations. Poland, the Niobe of nations, whose gallant sons have been the knight-errants of liberty the world over, has been all but interred by her in Siberia. Circassia, the cradle of the human race, whose people are the manliest and handsomest in the world, has been converted into a tomb. And she is now seeking to engulph the desert steppes, the briny waters, and the shifting burning sands that lie between the Caucasus, the Caspian, and the Afghan Table Land The interest, the instinct, and, to some extent, the necessity, of the Russian people, urge them to seek "fresh fields and pastures new" away from their biting north winds, their icy frosts, their bleak and limitless plains. The government, which is Asiatic rule, bastardized by German beaucracy, with appropriating frenzy has striven to annex territory in all directions; while the Emperors, animated by an ambition akin to that of "Macedonia's Madman and the Swede," have been dazzled by a dream of universal empire. To find a foothold for their power in the unrivalled natural resources which Turkey affords, has been their aim. The defeat of Russia in the Crimea modified for a time her external and internal policy. To soften the discontent created by the surrender of Sebastopol liberal legal changes were instituted, and a decree emancipating the serfs was promulgated. The benefits conferred by this instrument are more apparent than real. By it the peasants were relieved from some claims to the landlords, but they were charged with equivalent burdens for the national revenue; and the Imperial functionary is often a harder taskmaster than the local lord of the soil. M. Walewski calculated that the emancipation of the serfs doubled the direct taxes of the Empire. Repulsed in the south and west, Russia sought an outlet for her stream of conquest in Central Asia. Unnoticed, to a large extent unknown, she has, in that quarter of the globe, during recent years absorbed a territory nearly equal in extent to Continental Europe, and she has now a bristling array of bayonets in threatening proximity to our Indian Empire.

Although popular feeling and historical recollection have always favoured a campaign for supplanting the Crescent by the Cross, there is a small but intelligent and influential party in Russia who are adverse to this tempting and treacherous cry of "To Constantinople!" They contend that if the seat of Government were removed from the banks of the cold and misty Neva to those of the brilliant Bosphorus, the Empire would perish through the effeminacy generated by residence in the sunny and seductive South. Hardy Northmen would be replaced in the councils of the Czar by the intrigues of Greeks and Bulgars. This would lead to divisions in which the unwieldy dominions would be split in twain through the struggles for supremacy that would ensue between the genuine Slav and the idle mongrels that would flutter round the Court of the new Byzantium. This view has been maintained not only by authors like Gurowski, and by soldiers like Fadeof, but by many Russian Liberals. Three of the most remarkable men that the revolutions in the East sent into Western Europe were Bakunin, whom the Emperor Nicholas, after an interview with him, described as a "noble but dangerous madman"; Mr Alexander Herzen, one of the most fascinating of men, who combined the philosophy of Germany, the politics of Republican France, and the practical good sense of Englishmen, with the native Russian character; and Mieroslowski, the brilliant and eloquent Polish leader. I have heard all of these gentlemen contend that Europe would not see for many years—probably not for generations—another effort made by Russia to obtain Constantinople. They held this opinion not because they all approved of it— Bakunin certainly did not—but their belief was that the German party in Russia had so realised the hopelessness of a struggle with the Western Powers that they would not resume it. The nervous, hesitating, indolent, but kindly man who is now at the head of the Russian people, has always, until recently, been credited with a settled determination not to renew the enterprise that ended so disastrously for his father. The idea was general that India and China, rather than Turkey, would be threatened by Russian advance. I own that I largely shared that opinion. But events have shown that this was an error, and that the passion for accomplishing what the people of Russia believed to be their manifest destiny was not dead but only slumbered—the leopard had not changed his spots nor the Tartar his skin.

The first pronounced intimation of the retention of this old faith was seen in the course pursued by Russia during the Franco-German war. Immediately our friend and ally France was worsted in that disastrous conflict, the Czar intimated that he intended no longer to comply with the clauses of the Treaty of Paris that neutralised the Black Sea. He did not invite the other Powers of Europe who, along with himself, were parties to that Treaty to meet and discuss the reasonableness of his request for an alteration, but, with autocratic pride and despotic imperiousness, he proclaimed his determination to look upon a portion of that Treaty as null and void. He had observed that while France was in a position to unite with England for his resistance, but when she was temporarily disabled, he seized the opportunity to break an engagement which he had solemnly entered upon. This was the first sign of the change, the effects of which Europe has just witnessed. Russia, in her attacks upon neighbouring States, follows an uniform and unvarying plan. She begins usually by professing an interest in their welfare. At one time she is moved by sympathy for her brethren in bonds as if there were no person in bonds in Russia. At another time she is roused to fervour for her co-religionists, as if there were no persons suffering for their religious opinions within her own borders. She knows how to lure adjoining rulers to destruction by encouraging them in every frivolous expense, every private vice, and every public iniquity, as she did Abdul Aziz and many an unfortunate Asiatic Khan. She can compass the destruction of popular liberty by Jesuitical intrigue, as she did in Poland. She can engage in plots and conspiracies, as she did more recently in Bulgaria. Ignorance, ambition, corruption, are all made in turn to minister to her designs. The cupidity of Turkish pashas, who too often obtained their positions by bribery, and held them by oppression and extortion, and the hopeless confusion into which the ministers of the Sultan had allowed affairs to drift at Constantinople, formed a favourable field for the work of Russian emissaries. The stereotyped process was followed. There was first complaint, then suggestion, and then the inevitable conference, and the equally inevitable war. The Turkish people, both Mahommedan and Christian, suffered under solid and serious grievances. They had been oppressed and outraged by a system of administration that was outrageous and indefensible; but they sought redress of their grievances at the hands of their own rulers, and not from a foreign Power. This was shown by the stubborn resistance that was made to the advance of the Austrian troops into Bosnia and Herzegovina. The Hungarians are the truest friends the Turks had in Europe, and if they fought so stoutly to oppose their entrance to their provinces they would have fought with greater resolution against the admission of the troops of any other country.

... the Russian diplomatists and generals succeeded ... of trembling palace pachas around them at ... when they abstracted a Treaty that unmasked ... and placed them in a broad and startling light ... world.

... been any doubt before as to the aim Russia ... in the war, there could be none then. ... started on the campaign the Czar declared—first, ... did not intend to enter Constantinople; second, ... did not seek territorial acquisition; and third, that ... was to ensure the freedom of the oppressed ... He kept the word of promise to the ear, but ... to the hope. He did not enter Constantinople, true, but he surrounded it, and his troops would have ... it, if the English fleet had not been in the Sea of Marmora, and the English soldiers within call at Malta. ... the second engagement by annexing Bessarabia ... territory around Batoum, Ardahan, and Kars. By ... San Stefano he proposed the creation of what he ... described as a "big Bulgaria," in other words, ... province was to be created, whose borders ... extended to the shores of the Ægean. If the Treaty ... as drawn by Russia, she would have had a ... in the south, she would have had another ... at Antivari, and she would have been left ... of two thirds of the shores of the Black Sea ... to five miles north of Constantinople, round ... and Batoum. There would have been ... a few acres of ground, little more ... of the County of Durham; then the new ... like a wedge, would intervene; and beyond ... would have been Macedonia, Albania, and the ... provinces. Turkey, left without frontiers and ... would have fallen a ready and easy prey to ... whenever he felt herself strong enough and Europe ... to allow her to resume her crusade.

By this treaty Russia not only took territory in Armenia and Bessarabia, but she proposed also to subject the entire Balkan peninsula to her authority. She kept her third engagement by ignoring the nationality of the Roumanian inhabitants of Bessarabia, separating them from a free and uniting them to a despotic State. She despised the religious and race leanings of the Mahommedans near Batoum, and treated with contempt the nationality of Mahommedans living in the southern provinces of Turkey. She in this way either broke or evaded every engagement she made. To have allowed Russia to retain the position she projected for herself at San Stefano would have destroyed the balance of power in Europe, to have put the fate of Asia in her hand, and placed in her grasp the virtual dictatorship of two continents.

The main purpose of international arrangement is to secure the freedom and safety of smaller States, and to enable them to live their own lives while surrounded by Powers which could annihilate them without such protection. The law of nations prevents grasping, greedy Governments crushing weaker ones. If it were not sustained, the marauders of the earth would be let loose to prey upon their poor and feeble neighbours. It is no childish dislike of Russia that leads me to contend for the maintenance of this law and this policy. National enmity is no sound or permanent ground of either duty or policy. It is the defence of England and of Europe, the assertion and maintenance of the principles of free government as against a despotism—England and the Western Powers representing the one and Russia the other—that leads me to resist the advance of the Muscovites to the Bosphorus. In what way has the recent policy of this country contributed to the defence of the Empire, the maintenance of the way to India, and the upholding of the authority of this country in the councils of Europe? Let us look fairly at the facts as they are, and not as they are painted by rival partisans. To the jaundiced eye everything is yellow. By the fortunes of war—a hypocritical war, it is true, but still by the fortunes of war—Russia had Turkey at her mercy. She had fought and she had won. She did not occupy Constantinople, but she commanded it, and to the victors belong the spoil. It is true, as I have just explained, she made certain promises before commencing the conflict which she either evaded or broke. But that is not remarkable. It would have been more remarkable if she had kept them. The Treaty of San Stefano did not fully express her desires, but it did express the extent to which she believed she could with safety go in the presence of the indifference of other Powers, and the assumed incapacity and unwillingness of England to oppose her. The Treaty of Berlin did not fully express what this country wanted, but it did express the extent of the concessions that it was possible to obtain. A comparison of what was dictated by Russia at San Stefano, and what was accepted by her at Berlin, will show the measure of change made mainly at the instance of this country. The Russian troops have evacuated Turkish territory. This may appear a simple statement, but it is not unimportant. Every effort was made by her to retain possession of the provinces she had conquered. She strove to promote discord between the Mussulman and Christian inhabitants, hoping that that discord could be made a pretext for her remaining. Failing in that, she propounded the Jesuitical plan of a joint occupation of Eastern Roumelia by herself and other Powers. These schemes, however, were baffled; and there is now not a single Cossack trooper west of the Pruth. If the Treaty of San Stefano had stood as it was drawn, Turkey would not only have been dismembered but destroyed. She has now the opportunity of making a fresh start in national life. She can, if her rulers choose, rehabilitate herself in the estimation of Europe and of the world.

There is little evidence as yet, I am bound to say, of this disposition. The incorrigible pashas who control her policy seem to have learned nothing and forgotten nothing by the rude experience of the last three years. The Government is as rotten as the portals of the Porte are worm-eaten. These men have most of the vices of both Eastern and Western peoples, and few of their virtues. There are persons high in the confidence of the Sultan who are as completely under the control of the enemies of their country as Faust was under the control of Mephistopheles. But though the Porte perishes Turkey will remain. The Empire vanished, but France was left. There is, and has been for years, an active and patriotic party in Turkey, who have been striving to adapt their institutions to Western modes of life and to European requirements. The simple programme of this party is the fusion of the various races in the peninsula into an united State, based upon the equality, religious and political, of all. Fuad Pasha and Ali Pasha laboured long and earnestly for these principles, and they are advocated with equal sincerity by Midhat and his supporters. Men of all creeds and all races will be placed on a common level. This programme has the support of Christians and Mahommedans alike. One of the most painful and regrettable incidents of this controversy was the disparaging way in which the honest efforts of these Turkish reformers were spoken of by Liberal politicians in England. Whoever else cared to sneer at the Turkish Constitution, it certainly was no part of the duty of professed advocates of Liberal government to take up their parable against it. It is certainly not impossible to conceive of the establishment of a Government in which both Mahommedans and Christians may be united, and the pernicious influence which now predominates at Constantinople be exorcised from Turkish political life. By the Treaty of San Stefano injustice would not only have been done to the Greeks, but that country would have been condemned to sustain an exhausting conflict for its bare existence. By the extension of a Slav State to the Ægean, Greece would have been denied development. With resources limited and population scanty she would have been stripped of the elements of growth. She might have been an independent State truly, but so weak that she would have been unable to fulfil the purpose of her founation. She has now the opportunity of working out her redemption—she is the nucleus, the preparatory agency for the enfranchisement of a Hellenic State. Greece has a lofty mission to fulfil, and, despite present unfavourable signs, I do not despair of seeing her accomplish it. She is something more and better than when Byron mournfully described her as "Greece, but living Greece no more." She *does* live; she has sustained a soul almost "within the ribs of death"—

> "The Spartan blood that in her veins yet throbs at freedom's call:
> Every stone of old Greece—had it not its hero-tale?
> Where they fought, where they fell, 'twas on every hill and dale.
> The dead are but the hero seed that will spring to life again."

By the Treaty of Berlin, Greece gained but little, but at least she was not by it "cribbed, cabined, and confined" to the narrow limits of her too restricted territory. The idea of most European Liberals has been that Russian aggression could be stayed only by the creation of a belt of free States between the Danube and the Balkans. The different nationalities would be there grouped in distinct organizations, and, combined, they would be a more effective barrier to Muscovite progress than an effete and receding empire like Turkey. Many Liberals who agreed with this principle saw difficulties to its practical realisation. The inhabitants of this region are chiefly members of the Greek Church. The Czar is the head of that Church, and he holds them in a state of political as well as theological tutelage. Russia has often professed to assist at the birth of a new nation, but she always managed to keep her thumb upon its throat, so that it could be destroyed if it became troublesome. It was a common saying of the Russian troops in Bulgaria, "We have now got these Bulgar pigs, and we will drive them." Apart, however, from these speculative objections to the project of distinct nationalities—the oft-declared policy of the Czars—when the Emperor Nicholas proposed to Sir Hamilton Seymour that England and Russia should divide between them the possessions of the Sick Man, he said there were many points in his proposed scheme which he was willing to yield to the wishes of England, but there was one point on which he would never yield. Whatever else he consented to, he would never consent to the establishment of a number of small and independent States on the Russian frontier. These would be, he said, nothing but nurseries in which a perpetual crop of Mazzinis and Kossuths would be raised ; their opinions would penetrate into his dominions and endanger the necessary authority of his government.

This was then the settled policy of Russia, and has been authoritatively expressed repeatedly since. Bulgaria, as created by the Treaty of San Stefano, would have been little more than a Russian Principality; but by the Treaty of Berlin the Bulgarian people had had afforded to them the opportunity of winning for themselves an independent national life. Some few years ago the Bulgarians were held up in this country as models of Christian meekness. Recently they have been condemned with almost equal vigour, and their character has certainly developed some not very lovable attributes. They profess to be Christians, but they have scarcely acted upon the Christian principle of doing unto others as they would like to be done by. They complained loudly and justly of the oppression they suffered from the Turkish pashas ; but now, when they have the power, they have manifested toward their Mussulman neighbours a more arbitrary and tyrannical spirit than these Mussulmans ever showed towards them. But I have no wish to judge them harshly. A nation that has for generations been sunk in ignorance and vice cannot be expected all at once to realize the enlightened magnanimity of philosophers. People who have been trampled on will remember it ; those who have been injured will retaliate, and those who have been oppressed will not all at once forget. But the Bulgarians in time will take their place amongst the European family of nations, and shake off some of the offensive characteristics that have recently distinguished them. The most gratifying and encouraging intelligence that has come from the East of Europe recently is that these independent

States had realised their position. They have learned that Russia's interest in their behalf was certainly not disinterested. The Roumanians remember with bitterness that although they came to the assistance of their big neighbours when they were in sad straits before Plevna, their reward has been the loss of one of their most important provinces. The entire tone of feeling throughout these regions is a determination on the part of these States to assert their independence and shake themselves clear of Russian influence and direction. But the most important event that has taken place in Turkey has been the occupation of Bosnia by Austria. This action cannot be justified on the grounds of national right or justice. I certainly have no wish to extenuate or defend it. It is understood that the clause in the Treaty of Berlin, which assured these provinces to Austria, owed its authorship to Prince Bismarck and Count Andrassy. Germany contends that the Danube is a German stream—that as she controls its source so should she command its mouth. German colonists are planted along its banks, and their statesmen are unwilling to allow it to pass under the control of Russia. Austria objects to the creation of an independent Slav State on the west, as she has already on her eastern borders. For these dynastic and State reasons, the occupation, or rather the annexation, of these provinces by Austria has been assured. I am not justifying what has been done, and am dealing only with the facts as they are.

The occupation of Bosnia by Austria renders the advance of Russia to Constantinople all but impossible. Both political and military reasons combine to prevent her achieving her designs on the great city of the East. The case may be put in a sentence. The design of Russia, as revealed by the Treaty of San Stefano, was to obtain a preponderating influence in the Balkan peninsula. The object of England was to prevent her doing this. The result is that Russia is now further from the Bosphorus and less likely to get there, than she has ever been; and this has been accomplished chiefly by the action taken by this country. It has been achieved, too, without the loss of a single English life, or without our setting a single regiment in line of battle. Of all the strange things that I have heard during this controversy, the strangest is that Russia has achieved a victory, while England has sustained a defeat. We were told this in varying forms almost daily. I do not think anyone else in Europe says so except some English politicians. It is a fact beyond dispute, that the military and aggressive party in Russia are loudly proclaiming that the victories they won with so much difficulty in the field have been abstracted from them in the Council-Chamber. They were dissatisfied with the mode in which the war was commenced and for some time conducted, but the advance of the troops to the neighbourhood of Constantinople consoled them for a season. The Treaty of San Stefano, objectionable as it was regarded by England, was considered by the active party in Russia as incomplete and unsatisfactory. Their complaints against it, however, were mollified by the assurance held out to them that it was only temporary. But when even that unsatisfactory treaty had to be subjected to the revision and alteration of the other European States at Berlin, their discontent assumed an active and threatening attitude. The promulgation of the Treaty of Berlin corresponds with the recommencement of a period of political assassinations and plots. This reveals popular discontent, while the marching and counter-marching of Russian troops, and the massing of such numbers on the German and Austrian frontiers, reveal the state of feeling which pervades the governing class. It is indisputable that, in the estimation of men familiar with Russian society, the Treaty of Berlin has shaken the system of government to its foundation; while the war which Englishmen are so fond of regarding as a triumph for Russia and a discomfiture for this country, is looked upon by Russians as having entailed upon their country a harvest of discontent and disappointment. To balance the territorial advantages gained by other Powers, we have obtained a more assured position in the Levant.

O

I will not enter into the rather pitiful squabble about Cyprus—whether that island is what the poets of the past have painted it, "the blest, the beautiful, the salubrious, the happy, the dream and the desire of man," or, as it is drawn by partisan politicians in this country, "a fever bed and charnel-house." That it is advantageously situated for guarding the Suez Canal from any danger from the North, and that it affords a favourable starting point for advancing to the East through the Euphrates Valley, will scarcely be denied by anyone who has impartially examined the subject. Military and naval men maintain that it can be made not only a watch-tower but a depot for arms and a safe naval station. It is only twenty-four hours from Port Said, nine from Acre, and six from Beyrout. It is near enough to watch, and close enough to strike, if we required to strike, in defence of our road to the Red Sea and to the Persian Gulf. By the Anglo-Turkish Convention, England has taken upon herself heavy responsibilities. But if we had not effected that arrangement, the Sultan, like Shere Ali, despairing of help from England, would have thrown himself—reluctantly, no doubt, but still he would have thrown himself—into the arms of Russia; and whatever the result of such a bargain would have been to the people, the greedy pashas would have been secured in their pleasures and possessions. We had, therefore, either to accept the position or permit it to pass into the possession of a rival who, with such a leverage in the centre of two continents, could not only have imperilled our Empire in India, but our authority in Europe. We have often entered into Treaties with other nations entailing equally onerous obligations. We are bound to defend Greece against Turkey; Portugal against Spain; Belgium against France and Germany. We were bound to defend Denmark, and with culpable cowardice we evaded the responsibility. Under a stringent Treaty we are bound to maintain the independence of Sweden and Norway. If Russia should attempt to lease the fisheries in Swedish waters or the pasturage on Norwegian soil, this country is to be informed of the fact, and any attempt on her part to infringe upon the Scandinavian territory we are under engagement to resist by force of arms.

We are parties to other Treaties, many of them quite as risky as the one we have recently entered into with Turkey; and few of them offer such prospect of achieving such beneficial results as may spring from the Anglo-Turkish Convention. In Asia Minor there are 700,000 square miles of some of the finest land in the world, washed by three seas, watered by large rivers, and possessing spacious ports and harbours. The soil is capable of producing grain, fruit, and cotton in abundance, while the hills and the valleys abound in copper, lead, iron, and silver. Much of this fair and fruitful region on which the seasons have lavished all their beauty, and nature all its fragrance, is given over to malaria and to wild beasts—is the gathering-ground of predatory Kurds, and the camping-place of wandering Arabs. The spot from which the first enterprise of man started—the land around which such a wealth of the romance, the poetry, and the mystery fastens, which has influenced the destinies and formed the characters of not one, but many people—is now, from causes partly local and partly foreign, doomed to endure a system of rule which is little less than organised anarchy. We send our surplus population across the Atlantic or to the Antipodes. There is no reason why they should not find a field for their labours, and an outlet for their skill in a luxuriant land, rich with golden grain and an infinite variety of plants and fruit and minerals, within a few hours of our own shores. What has hitherto been wanted is security for life and property. Under the protection that might be, that ought to be, and I trust will be, given by this Treaty, these obstacles to colonisation would be removed.

English capitalists and the English Government have always refused seriously to consider the project of a railway through the Euphrates Valley, because they declined to risk such large investments in a country over which they had not sufficient control. This Treaty ought to, and I think will, dispense with this difficulty. The railway scheme is described by partisans as Utopian and visionary, but that is a kind of position which has grown stale and obsolete. It is not many years ago since the construction of the Suez Canal was, with the approval of English engineers, demonstrated by our townsman, Mr Robert Stephenson, to be an impossibility, and it was laughed at in the House of Commons by Lord Palmerston as the dream of a crack-brained Frenchman. But the Canal is, nevertheless, a great fact. Last year there passed through it between sixteen and seventeen hundred ships with a tonnage of nearly three million tons, and thirteen hundred out of the sixteen were English vessels — a proof of the importance of this waterway to this country. When the scheme of making a railway across the American Continent was first promulgated, it was met with characteristic derision, and yet now the line between the Atlantic and Pacific Oceans, a distance of nearly 2,800 miles, carries thousands of people in the course of a year. Russians in these matters are somewhat bolder and more enterprising than some Englishmen are. By the combined effect of river and railway, canal and lake, they have nearly united the basins of the Baltic, the Black Sea, and the Caspian. They have revived the old project of diverting the course of the Oxus, and by their system of land and water carriage, commencing at Riga and Warsaw, and terminating not far from our Indian frontier, they hope to secure a preponderating influence in Central Asia. The Euphrates Valley Railway would be 1,200 miles long, and the cost of its construction is estimated at £12,000,000 — a comparatively small sum when the amounts invested in railways in this country are considered. I know no more of the future than a prophet, but I think it would be no great venture to hazard the prediction that the railway will be made, and made, too, through English enterprise; that this work will not only act as a breakwater to Northern aggression, and a bulwark for the Indian Empire, it will be made the fulcrum for raising politically and socially an unfortunate people, and making the early seat of arts and refinement, the theatre of some of the most momentous events in history, once more bloom and blossom as the rose. My contention, in a sentence, is that our external Empire should be maintained and defended, as much in the interests of freedom and civilisation as in the interests of England and its distant dependencies; that we cannot honourably and without danger shrink from the responsibilities that our history and our position as the oldest, and one of the chief of free States in the world, entail upon us; that the security of our dominions in the East and the equilibrium of Europe were threatened by the advance of Russia on Constantinople; that the action this country took, although it was open to objection in its details, was necessary, and in the main judicious; that it largely contributed to thwart the dangerous, the aggressive designs of Russia; has protected our present, and made provision for our obtaining an improved way to India; may help to secure better government for Turkey; and has strengthened the influence of England in the councils of Europe.

It is impossible now to discuss at length the policy pursued in Afghanistan, but I wish to express shortly the views I entertain on the action that has been taken in that country. Our Indian possessions are encircled by the ocean on the south, the south-east, and south-west. On the east they are protected by high ranges of mountains and all but impenetrable forests. These mountains and these forests are occupied by savage tribes, who, although capable of great annoyance, as the Nagas are now, are incapable of inflicting any real political or military injury upon us. On the north and north-west our frontiers are the bases of the Himalaya and the Sulieman Mountains. It is an accepted canon in military science that a Power which holds the mountains and possesses what in soldiers' parlance is called the "issues of the frontier," has an enormous advantage over the Power which occupies the plains. This is an opinion which will scarcely be contested. These mountains are peopled by fierce, warlike, and turbulent tribes, who have no special love for England, but have just as much dislike to each other. They live partly by pasturage, partly by plunder. They fight for their own hand. The only State that has an organised Government of any strength is Afghanistan. As long as these passes and mountains, and the country generally, were occupied by tribes of this character, no danger to India was to be anticipated. Partly brigands, partly soldiers, they could annoy us, and levy blackmail on the adjoining inhabitants, yet they could not seriously disturb or threaten our authority. But it is the accepted opinion of men of all parties—statesmen and soldiers alike—that should this strong military position ever pass into the hands of a powerful Government, our exposed frontier would lay us open to serious danger. For years Afghanistan, if not friendly, has at least been neutral; and there was an understanding between Russia and England that that country should be considered as outside of their mutual interest and influence—that it should be regarded as a neutral territory, both being concerned in upholding its independence and neutrality. The advance of Russia, however, to the East so alarmed the late Ameer that he urged, some years ago, the English Government to enter into closer alliance with him than then existed. He pointed out that Russia was advancing, and did not conceal his fear that, unless he were protected by England, the same fate would overtake him that had overtaken many another Asiatic ruler. Our Government at that time did not share Shere Ali's fears, and refused to comply with the requests that he preferred. He became discontented; and from having a friendly leaning towards England, he now began to lean towards Russia, and to open negotiations with the Russian commanders in the adjacent provinces.

When Russia's objects in Turkey were thwarted by this country, she retaliated by striving to set our Indian frontiers in a blaze. No one can complain of her doing so; it is what we would have done, probably, in like circumstances. She objected to our fleet being in the Sea of Marmora, and she thought she would disturb us and distract our attention by assuming a threatening attitude in Afghanistan. A Russian mission was sent. It was received with ostentatious displays of sympathy by the Ameer, and, as far as he was able, he proclaimed that in future he would be the firm friend and ally of Russia, and if not the enemy, at least not the friend, of this country. If not in words, the substance of his declaration and his action at the reception of the Russian mission amounted to this. Our Government required that, as he had received a mission from Russia, he should also accept one from England. He refused to do it, and we attempted to force the mission upon him. It is unnecessary to repeat the facts which are in the recollection, no doubt, of all present. Shere Ali's refusal led to war, and after a small show of resistance he fled from Cabul, and shortly afterwards died. With his son, who was made his successor, we concluded peace, and entered into a Treaty. By that Treaty England got the right of sending agents to certain specified districts in Afghanistan, and also obtained an important frontier. Instead of having the base of the mountains as a border, we had the mountains themselves. By that Treaty the country should stand. The frontier secured to us by it should be maintained. A most lamentable, melancholy, and disastrous incident occurred in the autumn—the murder of Sir Louis Cavagnari and his suite. But that ought not to divert us from the settled policy that was developed and expressed by the Treaty of Gandamuk. I am in favour of holding the possessions we have, but we want no more. We have provinces plenty and to spare. Even if we possessed Afghanistan, it would be only a perplexing acquisition; but supposing it were a profitable one, it would be contrary to the wishes and feelings of the Afghans to come under British rule, and I am altogether opposed to enforcing it upon them. The Treaty that Yakoob Khan entered into embodies the policy of the country, and it should be upheld.

I have discussed principles and not personalities. I am

not interested either in defending or in decrying any body of men. All I have been concerned for is to state the grounds on which I have been led to support the assertion of what I believe to be Liberal principles and the maintenance of a national policy. It is easy to find fault, and easier still to impute bad motives to your opponents—

> "A man must serve his time to every trade
> Save censure. Critics all are ready made."

The shortcomings of the Government are as apparent to me as to the fiercest opponents of their foreign policy. They have often been weak, sometimes vacillating, not unfrequently wrong; but I wish to judge them as I would like them to judge me, or the party with which I am identified, under like circumstances. They have been beset by a succession of difficulties and dangers such as never before encompassed an Administration in our times. Apart from the inherent intricacies of the questions they have had to deal with, they have had to contend with the rival interests of other Powers, a strong opposition at home, and some divisions in their own party. It is not generosity, it is simply justice, to remember this. We should also recollect that, in dealing with foreign affairs, there are always some matters that cannot be explained. All Ministries are called upon at times to act upon information that they cannot make public—

> "What's done we partly may compute,
> But know not what's resisted."

It is possible, even in party warfare, to drive your attacks too far. Unqualified denunciation usually provokes reaction. The Government, which has had the support of large majorities in both Houses of Parliament, is accused of not only being wrong, but of being criminal; not only of being mischievous and mistaken, but of being malevolent and malicious. They are charged with having roamed round the world with incendiary designs, bent upon turning our frontiers into blazing bastions fringed with fire. The accusation is, in my judgment, not only incorrect but foolish. The indictment I would prefer against them would be of the very opposite character. I think they have acted with tameness and timidity. They have been six years in office, and the first half of that time presented them in their normal and natural character. An entire absence of political legislation, some mild but useful social measures, a free and easy administration, were their characteristics. Taking warning by their predecessors, their great effort was to avoid needlessly offending anyone. Events that they could not foresee, circumstances which they could not control, have driven them into warlike action. People are easily misled by a cry, but no man who has examined the facts for himself can contend that the English Government started the conflict in Eastern Europe. Whoever else began it—whether it was the Russian emissaries or the Turkish people themselves—certainly Lord Derby, who was then the Foreign Minister of this country, did not do so. He pressed the Sultan to settle the dispute with his subjects, and if that could not be done, he urged him, with somewhat cynical indifference, to suppress the insurrection. When that failed, he strove to localise the war. It might be said that England should have obeyed the three Emperors, and signed the ukase which the Imperial league issued from Berlin, and if Turkey refused to comply with their demands she should have been coerced—in other words, that we should have gone to war against her. It is a matter of opinion, but, in the judgment of men familiar with the East, had such a course been pursued, the Turks would have turned their backs to the wall, and with all the disciplined fanaticism of their race, they would have fought against Christians and coalesced Europe for their country and their faith. The resistance that was given in Bosnia to the advance of a friendly Hungarian army strengthens this view.

But 'if the Berlin Memorandum was refused, England assented and took part in the Conference of Constantinople. However we may condemn the course taken by the Government on the Eastern difficulties, no man can fairly say that they caused them. The Afghan war, for which they are more directly responsible, was the outcome of the action of Russia in Turkey. We may fairly criticise the policy of the Government, but no one, I think, can say that they sought a cause of quarrel. I do not contend that foreign politics are outside the domain of popular and Parliamentary criticism. On the contrary, I regret that for many years the English people have given so little and such fluctuating heed to foreign questions. But I do say that such delicate topics should not be made the battlefield of party. There are two modes of conducting a discussion—one to elicit information, to sustain, to direct and guide the Executive; another to win a party victory out of Government troubles. If the Government of the country is in difficulties abroad, the nation is in difficulties, and it grates as much against my national pride as against my sense of justice to go hunting for arguments against my political opponents amongst the stiffening corpses of your fellow-countrymen. On this subject I will quote the opinion of the late M. Thiers, when discussing the attitude taken in France by the Orleanists and the Legitimists during the Crimean War. The veteran French statesman, speaking to Mr Nassau, Senior, said—

"The rules of party warfare allow me to call my opponent a villain, though I know him to be honest; to abuse his measures though I know them to be useful; to attack his arguments with sophistry and even with falsehood—all this my opponent may do to me, and therefore it is fair that I should do it to him. But we must both of us abstain from using as our weapons to hold the foreign relations of our country. In these relations an error may be fatal. We may quarrel amongst ourselves; we must be united against the foreigner."

I am not insensible to the benefits of party government. English liberty, in a large measure, owes its stability to such organisation. Successes won by serious and prolonged struggles have been retained by party vigilance. The education gained in party struggles has made the victories permanent. It would be difficult, too, to replace a system that has become so acclimatised to our constitutional life. But party spirit, pushed too far, crushes individuality of thought, and cripples independent energy. It impairs the disciplinary value of the suffrage by destroying the voter's sense of responsibility. It lowers the character of the Parliament by converting independent representatives into political automatons, whose value consists in the unreflecting vigour with which they shout the party shibboleth. On points of procedure and of detail, a member may obey the party managers without injury or disadvantage; but when great national issues are at stake, a man forfeits his own respect, and becomes a recreant to his own country who ignores his convictions, and submits to think by deputy or to act by order. Some of our friends, I think, act somewhat inconsistently on this subject. One of their chief causes of complaint against the present Parliament is its want of independence. They charge it with being an unthinking party machine, and they applauded the action of Lord Derby and Lord Carnarvon when they separated themselves from their colleagues and announced their dissent from their policy. But when Liberals on the other side, acting from equally high motives, separate themselves from their leaders, they are censured, and in some instances ostracised. What is accounted as commendable independence on the one side is condemned as an exhibition of fractious self-will on the other.

There are in the House of Commons some thirty or forty members who, more or less, had supported the policy the Government had pursued on foreign questions. But their numbers possibly would have been larger if vote by ballot had been in operation in the House. Their action, however, in this Parliament is only in keeping with the action of other sections of the Liberal party in previous Parliaments. In the last Parliament the Nonconformists and Radicals were dissatisfied with the way the Government dealt with elementary education. The Irish members were discontented with the manner in which they dealt with university education. The hostility of Irish representatives to the Irish University the scheme of the Ministry led to their defeat in Parliament. The opposition of Nonconformists did not cause the defeat, but it certainly contributed to it at the poll. Yet the Ministers who were responsible for this educational legislation are to-day amongst the trusted leaders of the party. In the Parliament before that stronger differences were developed. Lord Russell introduced a Reform Bill, proposing to give a vote to every man who lived in a house of the value of £7. This moderate proposal was objected to by a section of Liberals, who denounced it as revolutionary. Their opposition led to the defeat of Earl Russell's Government, and the subsequent resignation of his Government. Lord Russell himself describes this party as consisting of three gangs—the timid, the selfish, and those who were both timid and selfish. For the first, he said, he had pity; for the second indignation; for the third contempt. During all his long career, he declared that he never encountered a body of politicians so little influenced by principle or animated by a patriotic spirit. The leader of the party he described as a man "sagacious, bold, and turbulent of wit." Yet this same leader was Chancellor of the Exchequer in the last Ministry, and is now one of the ablest of the Liberal leaders in the House of Commons. Another difference took place in the same Parliament which had more beneficial results. The Conservative Government proposed that household suffrage should be made the basis of the Reform Bill. This was objected to by the official Liberals of the day, who wished to have a rate-paying franchise instead of a household. A number of Radicals met in the tea-room of the Parliament House, declared that they approved of the principle of the Government Bill, and resolved that if the Ministry would give them an assurance that they would stand by that principle they (the Radicals) would support them. The Ministry *did* give the assurance, the Radicals *did* stand to the arrangement; and the result was that household suffrage became the law notwithstanding the opposition of the official Liberals of the time. The Adullamite defection drove the Liberal Government from office, and the tea-room defection succeeded in making a household suffrage the law of the land. There has never been a Parliament since the Reform Bill where instances of the kind have not occurred.

The policy on foreign questions that I and others in the House of Commons have defended is the old policy of this country. I have no wish to shelter myself behind big names or to shake myself clear of the slightest responsibility. I have too often been in a minority to be afraid of being in that position again. I know what it is to be in the right with two or three. But the policy I have expounded to-night, and which I have supported in Parliament, is the policy that was advocated by Mackintosh and Brougham, Horner and Lord Durham; it is a policy that received the approval of the philosophic Liberals, Molesworth, Mill, Grote, and Buller. It is the old Radical policy that was expounded by Major Cartwright, Lord Dundonald, William Cobbett, and General Thompson; and it was the common faith of Radicals when I first became interested in political affairs. It is not the faith, I know, of the "Manchester School"; but it is certainly of the early Radicals. I would quote from the speeches and writings of the men whose names I have cited numerous extracts to confirm my statement; but I will content myself with citing, in support of my position, a few words from a statesman whose name will, in every Liberal assembly, be received with favour. Earl Russell for fifty years played a leading and important part in the history of this country. No one has rendered the Liberal cause more effective service than he has done. He has not boxed the political compass and served all sides in turn. He ended as he began—a moderate and consistent advocate of Liberal principles. In his last work Lord Russell expressed the strong regret he felt at having retired, as he did, from the leadership after the defeat of the party in 1867. The reason why he regretted having retired was the policy the party was led to pursue on foreign matters. The policy that the present Opposition has supported is the policy of the late

Government. Lord Russell commended their domestic legislation, but censured in very strong and very emphatic terms their action in foreign matters. These are his words—

> "I had no reason to suppose, when I surrendered the leadership of the party, that he (the Liberal Prime Minister) was less attached than I was to the national honour, less proud than I was of the achievements of our armies by sea and land, that he disliked the extension of our Colonies, and that the measures he promoted would tend to reduce the great and glorious Empire of which he was put in charge to a manufactory of cotton and cloth, and a market for cheap goods, that the army and navy would be reduced by paltry savings to a standard of weakness and inefficiency. By his foreign policy he has tarnished the national honour, injured the national interests, and lowered the national character."

These are not my words. I never used language anything like so strong, but they are the words of the honoured and trusted leader of the Liberal party for the better part of half a century. I am not a conventional adherent of the fashionable Liberalism of the hour, but I am a life-long Radical by conviction, sympathy, training, and taste. I am concerned for something more and higher than the transference of the offices of State from one set of men to another. I will not trim my political faith to catch the passing breeze, however pleasant. "Unplaced, unpensioned, no man's heir or slave," I neither look for nor care for the honours, the favours, or the patronising approval lisped "in liquid lines mellifluously bland" of any party. There is only one consolation for a public man, and that is the approval of his conscience and a sense of duty done. I will not knowingly or consciously offend any man by either word or speech, but if I am placed in a position where I must speak, I will speak what I believe to be the truth, temperately, kindly, but plainly. Whatever my lot in life may be, whether I may be a member of the British Parliament again or not, I will labour for the advancement of Radical principles, and serve the Liberal cause according to my lights and to the best of my ability. But while I wear the party uniform I will never wear its plush. I will take any position, however humble, in the ranks, but it will be as a volunteer and not as a lackey. With me the people's welfare is the supreme law, and our country's honour and safety the first consideration. But I prefer national interests to the triumph of a faction. I am weak enough to own that I believe in the now derided obligation of patriotism and the duty of the individual to the State, as one of the first principles planted in the human breast. I know my country's defects, but I cannot join with those who exaggerate and parade them. The land of Michael Angelo and of Dante was not destitute of energy; but when she persistently proclaimed herself to be miserable and infamous through the mouth of Machiavelli, the world took her at her word and trod upon her. Englishmen disposed to decry their native land may remember with advantage the experience of Italy. It is ours to hand down to posterity, undimmed and undiminished, the priceless heritage of a free State, the imperceptible aggregations of centuries, won by the struggles of a heroic national life. It was planted, has been reared and watered by the sweat, the tears, the blood of some of the noblest of men. She has carried liberty and laws, art and thought, in triumph round the globe. If England is old, she is not decrepit, and has still within her daring and elasticity.

THE RIGHT HON. W. E. GLADSTONE ON THE BEACONSFIELD MINISTRY.

Edinburgh, March 17th, 1880.

[Previous to this date Mr Gladstone had already addressed the electors of Midlothian on three great occasions. He now opened his famous Midlothian Campaign in earnest, taking the Government to task with such tremendous energy as to force his convictions upon the people. The place of meeting on this occasion was the Music Hall, Mr Duncan M'Laren, M.P., presiding.]

Gentlemen,—When I last had the honour of addressing you in this Hall, I endeavoured, in some degree, to open the great case which I was in hopes would, in conformity with what I may call constitutional usage, then have been brought at once before you. The arguments which we made for a dissolution were received with the usual contempt, and the Parliament was summoned to attempt, for the first time in our history, the regular business of a seventh session. I am not going now to argue on the propriety of this course, because, meeting you here in the capital of the county and of Scotland, I am anxious to go straight to the very heart of the matter, and, amidst the crowd of topics that rush upon the mind, to touch upon some of those which you will judge to be most closely and most intimately connected with the true merits of the great issue that is before us.

At last the dissolution has come, and I postpone the consideration of the question why it has come, the question how it has come, on which there are many things to be said. It has come, and you are about to give your votes upon an occasion which, allow me to tell you, entails not only upon me, but upon you, a responsibility greater than you ever had to undergo. I believe that I have the honour of addressing a mixed meeting, a meeting principally and very largely composed of freeholders of the county, but in which warm and decided friends are freely mingled with those who have not declared in our favour, or even with those who may intend to vote against us.

Now, Gentlemen, let me say a word in the first place to those whom I must for the moment call opponents. I am not going to address them in the language of flattery. I am not going to supplicate them for the conferring of a favour. I am not going to appeal to them on any secondary or any social ground. I am going to speak to them as Scotchmen and as citizens; I am going to speak to them of the duty that they owe to the Empire at this moment; I am going to speak to them of the condition of the Empire, of the strength of the Empire, and of the honour of the Empire; and it is upon these issues that I respectfully ask for their support. I am glad that, notwithstanding my Scotch blood, and notwithstanding the association of my father and my grandfather with this country, it is open to our opponents, if they like, to describe me as a stranger; because I am free to admit that I stand here in consequence of an invitation, and in consequence of treatment the most generous and the most gratifying that ever was accorded to man. And I venture to assure every one of my opponents, that if I beg respectfully to have some credit for upright motives, that credit I at once accord to them. I know very well they are not accustomed to hear it given me; I know very well that in the newspapers which they read they will find that violent passion, that outrageous hatred, that sordid greed for office, are the motives, and the only motives, by which I am governed. Many of these papers constitute, in some sense, their daily

P

f od: but I have such faith in their intelligence, and in the healthiness of their constitution as Scotchmen, that I believe that many of them will, by the inherent vigour of that constitution, correct and neutralise the poison thus administered; will consent to meet me upon equal grounds, and will listen to the appeal which I make.

The appeal which I make to them is this: If my position here is a serious one, their position is serious too. My allegations have been before you for a length of time. I will not now again read to a Midlothian audience the letter in which I first accepted this candidature. By every word of that letter I abide; in support of every allegation which that letter contains, I am ready to bring detailed and conclusive proof. These allegations—I say to you, Gentlemen, to that portion of my audience—these allegations are of the most serious character. I admit, as freely as you can urge, that if they be unfounded, then my responsibility—nay, my culpability—before my country cannot be exaggerated. But, on the other hand, if these allegations be true—if it be true that the resources of Great Britain have been misused; if it be true that the international law of Europe has been broken; if it be true that the law of this country has been broken; if it be true that the good name of this land has been tarnished and defaced; if it be true that its condition has been needlessly aggravated by measures both useless, and wanton, and mischievous in themselves—then your responsibility is as great as mine. For I fully admit that in 1874 you incurred no great or special responsibility. You were tired of the Liberal Government; you were dissatisfied with them. [*Cries of* "No, no!"] Oh, I pardon; I am addressing my opponents. Scotchmen, I believe, as much as Englishmen, like plain speaking, and I hope I have given you some proof that if that be your taste I endeavour to meet it as well as I can; and I thank you — y for the manner in which, by your kindly attention, have enabled me to say what I think is the truth, whether it be — table or whether it be not.

Now the great question which we have been debating for the last three or four years—for I do not carry back the pith of what I have principally to say to the six years of the Government—is the question of the policy which has been pursued during that time; most especially by far the policy of the last two years, and the effect of that policy upon the condition of the country, upon the legislation of the country, upon the strength of the Empire, and, above all, upon the honour of the Empire. I am now going to compare the conduct of the present Government, which is commended to you as masterly in forethought and sagacity, and truly English in spirit—I am going to compare it with the conduct of the last Government, and to lay before you the proceedings of the results. It so happens that their histories are a not inconvenient means of comparison. England, as you are aware, has been involved in many guarantees. I said England—do not be shocked; it is the shortest word—Great Britain or the United Kingdom is what one ought to say. The United Kingdom—the British Empire has been and is involved in many guarantees for the condition of other countries. Among others, we were involved, especially since the Peace of Paris, but also before the Peace of Paris, in a guarantee for Turkey, aiming to maintain its integrity and its independence; and we were involved in another guarantee for Belgium, aiming to maintain its integrity and its independence. In the time of the present Government the integrity and the independence of Turkey were menaced— menaced by the consequences of rank, festering corruption from within. In the time of the late Government the integrity and independence of Belgium were not less seriously menaced. We had been living in perfect harmony and friendship with two great Military States of Europe—with Prussia and with France. France and Prussia came into conflict, and at the moment of their coming into conflict a document was revealed to us which the Ministers of those two States had had in their hands. Whoever was its author, whoever was its promoter, that is no affair of mine—it is due to Prince Bismarck to say that he was the person who brought it to light—but they had in their hands an instrument of a formal character, touching a subject that was considered and entertained. And that bad instrument was an instrument for the destruction of the freedom, independence, and integrity of Belgium. Could there be a graver danger to Europe than that?

Here was a State—not like Turkey, the scandal of the world, and the danger of the world from misgovernment, and from the terrible degradation it inflicted upon its subject races—but a country which was a marvel to all Europe for the peaceful exercise of the rights of freedom, and for progress in all the arts and all pursuits that tend to make mankind good and happy. And this country, having nothing but its weakness that could be urged against it, with its four or five millions of people, was deliberately pointed out by somebody and indicated to be destroyed, to be offered up as a sacrifice to territorial lust by one or other of those Ministers of Powers with whom we were living in close friendship and affection. We felt called upon to enlist ourselves on the part of the British nation as advocates and as champions of the integrity and independence of Belgium. And if we had gone to war, we should have gone to war for freedom, we should have gone to war for public right, we should have gone to war to save human happiness from being invaded by tyrannous and lawless power. This is what I call a good cause, Gentlemen. And though I hate war, and there are no epithets too strong, if you could supply me with them, that I will not endeavour to heap upon its head—in such a war as that, while the breath in my body is continued to me, I am ready to engage. I am ready to support it, I am ready to give all the help and aid I can to those who carry this country into it. Well, Gentlemen, pledged to support the integrity and independence of Belgium, what did we do? We proposed to Prussia to enter into a new and separate Treaty with us to resist the French Empire, if the French Empire attempted to violate the sanctity of freedom in Belgium; and we proposed to France to enter into a similar

Treaty with us to pursue exactly the same measures against Prussia, if Prussia should make the like nefarious attempt. And we undertook that, in concert with the one, or in concert with the other, whichever the case might be, we would pledge all the resources of this Empire, and carry it into war, for the purpose of resisting mischief and maintaining the principles of European law and peace.

I ask you whether it is not ridiculous to apply the doctrine or the imputation, if it be an imputation, that we belong to the "Manchester School," or to a Peace Party—we who made these engagements to go to war with France if necessary, or to go to war with Prussia, if necessary, for the sake of the independence of Belgium? But now I want you to observe the upshot. I must say that, in one respect, we were very inferior to the present Government—very inferior indeed. Our ciphers, our figures, were perfectly contemptible. We took nothing except two millions of money. We knew perfectly well that what was required was an indication, and that that indication would be quite intelligible when it was read in the light of the new treaty engagement which we were contracting; and consequently we asked Parliament to give us two millions of money for the sake of somewhat enlarging the numbers of available soldiers, and we were quite prepared to meet that contingency had it arrived. The great man who directs the Councils of the German Empire (Bismarck) acted with his usual promptitude. Our proposal went to him by telegraph, and he answered by telegraph, "Yes," the same afternoon. We were not quite so fortunate with France, for at that time the Councils of France were under the domination of some evil genius which it is difficult to trace, and needless to attempt to trace. There was some delay in France—a little unnecessary haggling—but after two or three days France also came into this engagement, and from that moment the peace of Belgium was perfectly secured. When we had our integrity and our independence to protect, we took the measures which we believed to be necessary and sufficient for that protection; and in every year since those measures, Belgium, not unharmed only, but strengthened by having been carried safely and unhurt through a terrible danger, has pursued her peaceful career, rising continually in her prosperity and happiness, and still holding out an example before all Europe to teach the nations how to live.

Well, Gentlemen, as that occasion came to us with respect to Belgium, so it came to our successors with respect to Turkey. How did they manage it? They thought themselves bound to maintain the integrity and independence of Turkey, and they were undoubtedly bound conditionally to maintain it. I am not now going into the question of right, but into the question of the adaptation of the means to an end. These are the gentlemen who are set before you as the people whose continuance in office it is necessary to maintain to attract the confidence of Europe; these are the gentlemen whom patriotic associations laud to the skies as if they had a monopoly of human intelligence; these are the gentlemen who bring you "Peace with Honour"; these are the gentlemen who go in special trains to attend august assemblies, and receive the compliments of august statesmen; these are the gentlemen who for all these years have been calling upon you to pay any number of millions that might be required as a very cheap and insignificant consideration for the immense advantages that you derive from their administration.

Therefore I want you to know, and I have shown you, how we set about to maintain integrity and independence, and how it was maintained then. I ask how they have set about it. But, Gentlemen, on their own showing, they have done wrong. We have it out of their own mouths. I won't go to Lord Derby; I will go to the only man whose authority is higher for this purpose than Lord Derby's, namely, Lord Beaconsfield. He tells you plainly that what the Government ought to have done was to have said to Russia, "You shall not invade Turkey." Gentlemen, that course is intelligible. It is a course, in my opinion, to have taken up arms for maintaining the integrity of Turkey against her subject races, or to take up arms against what the Emperor of Russia believed to be a great honour to humanity in going to apply a remedy to these mischiefs. But Lord Beaconsfield has confessed in a public speech that the proper course for the Government to have taken was to have planted their foot, and to have said to the Emperor of Russia: "Cross not the Danube; if you cross the Danube, expect to confront the power of England on the southern shore." Now, Gentlemen, that course is intelligible, perfectly intelligible; and if you are prepared for the responsibility of maintaining such an integrity, and such an independence, irrespectively of other considerations against the Christian races in Turkey, that was the course for you to pursue. It was not pursued, because the agitation, which is called the Bulgarian agitation, was too inconvenient to allow the Government to pursue it, because they saw that if they did that which Lord Beaconsfield now tells us it would have been right to do, the sentiment of the country would not have permitted them to continue to hold their office; and hence came that vacillation, hence came that ineptitude of policy which they now endeavour to cover by hectoring and by boasting, and which, within the last year or two, they have striven, and not quite unsuccessfully, to hide from the eyes of many by carrying measures of violence into other lands, if not against Russia, if not against the strong, yet against the weak, and endeavouring to attract to themselves the credit and glory of maintaining the power and influence of England.

Well, Gentlemen, they were to maintain the integrity and independence of Turkey. How did they set about it? They were not satisfied with asking for our humble two millions; they asked for six millions. What did they do, first of all? First of all they encouraged Turkey to go to war. They did not counsel Turkey's submission to superior force; they neither would advise her to submit, nor would they assist her to resist. They were the great causes of her plunging into that deplorable and ruinous war, from the consequences of which Her Majesty's Speech states this year, Turkey has not yet recovered, and there is not the smallest appearance of hope that she will ever recover. But afterwards, and when the war had taken place, they came and asked you for a vote of six millions. What did they do with the six millions? They flourished it in the face of the world. What did they gain for Turkey? In the first place, they sent a fleet to the Dardanelles and the Bosphorus. Are you aware that in sending that fleet they broke the law of Europe? They applied for a firman to the Sultan. The Sultan refused, and they had no right to send that fleet. But, however that may be, what was the use of sending that fleet? The consequence was that the Russian army, which had been at a considerable distance from Constantinople, marched close up to Constantinople. Is it possible to conceive an idea more absurd than that which I really believe was entertained by many of our friends—I do not say our friends in Midlothian, but in places where the intelligence is high that the presence of certain British ironclads in the Sea of Marmora prevented the victorious Russian armies from entering Constantinople? What could these ironclads do? They could have battered down Constantinople, no doubt; but what consolation would that have been to Turkey, or how would it have prevented Russian armies from entering? That part of the pretext set is too thin and threadbare to require any confutation. But they may say that that vote of six millions was an indication of the intention of England to act in case of need; and when it was first proposed, it was to strengthen the hands of England at the Congress. But did it strengthen the hands of England; and if so, to what purpose was that strength used? The Treaty of San Stefano had been signed between Russia and Turkey; the Treaty of Berlin was substituted for it. What was the grand difference between the Treaty of Berlin and the Treaty of San Stefano? There was a portion of Bessarabia which, down to the time of the Treaty of Berlin, enjoyed free institutions, and by the Treaty of Berlin, and mainly through the agency of the British Government, which had pledged itself beforehand by what is called the Salisbury-Schouvaloff Memorandum, to support Russia in her demand for that territory if Russia adhered to that demand, England, with the vote of six millions given to strengthen her influence, made herself specially responsible for handing back that territory, which enjoyed free institutions, to be governed despotically by the Russian Empire.

That is the first purpose for which, as I have shown you, your vote of six millions was available. What was the second? It was to draw a line along the Balkan Mountains, by means of which Northern Bulgaria was separated from Southern Bulgaria, and Southern Bulgaria was re-named Eastern Roumelia. The Sultan has not marched, and cannot march, a man into Eastern Roumelia. If he did, the consequences would be that the whole of that population, who are determined to fight for their rights, would rise against him and his troops, and would be supported by other forces that could be drawn to it under the resistless influences of sympathy with freedom. You may remember that three or four years ago utter scorn was poured upon what was called the "bag-and-baggage policy." Are you aware that that policy is at this moment the basis upon which are regulated the whole of the civil state of things in Bulgaria and Eastern Roumelia? What that policy asked was that every Turkish authority should be marched out of Bulgaria, and every Turkish authority has gone out of Bulgaria. There is not a Turk at this moment who, as a Turk, holds office under the Sultan either in Bulgaria or in Southern Bulgaria, which is called Eastern Roumelia—no, not one. The despised "bag-and-baggage policy" is at this moment the law of Europe, and that is the result of it; and it is for that, Gentlemen, that the humble individual who stands before you was held up and reviled as a visionary enthusiast and a verbose —I forget what—rhetorician, although I believe myself there was not much verbosity in that particular phrase. It appeared to me the people of England understood it pretty well—nay, more, the Congress of Berlin seemed to have understood it, and the state of things which I recommended was irresistible, and now, I thank God, is irreversibly established in those once unhappy provinces. Gentlemen, we have got one more thing to do in regard to these provinces, and that is this—I urged it at the same time when I produced this monstrous conception of the "bag-and-baggage policy"—it is this, to take great care that the majority of the inhabitants of these provinces, who are Christians, do not oppress either the Mohammedans, or the Jewish, or any other minority. That is a sacred duty; I don't believe it to be a difficult duty; it is a sacred duty. I stated to you just now that there was not a Turk holding office, as a Turk, in these provinces. I believe there are Turks holding office—and I rejoice to hear it—holding office through the free suffrage of their countrymen, and by degrees I hope that they, when they are once rid of all the pestilent and poisonous associations, and the recollections of the old ascendency, will become good and peaceful citizens like other people. I believe the people of Turkey have in them many fine qualities, whatever the Governors may be, capable under proper education, Gentlemen, of bringing them to a state of capacity and competency for every civil duty.

Gentlemen, it still remains for me to ask you how this great and powerful Government has performed its duty of maintaining the integrity and independence of Turkey. It has had great and extraordinary advantages. It has had the advantage of disciplined support from its majority in the House of Commons. Though I am not making any complaint, as my friend in the Chair knows, it was not exactly the same as happened in the days of recent Liberal Governments. It had had unflinching and incessant support from the large majority of the Lords. That was very far from being our case in our day. There is no reason why I should not say so. I say freely it is an historical fact—that the House of Lords, when the people's representatives are backed by a strong national feeling, when it would be dangerous to oppose, obstruct, or resist, then the House of Lords pass our measures.

So they passed the Disestablishment of the Irish Church, and so they passed the Irish Land Act; and I have no doubt that, if it pleases the Almighty, they will pass many more good measures. But the moment the people go to sleep — and they cannot be always awake — when public opinion flags and ceases to take a strong and decided interest in public questions, that moment the majority of the House of Lords grows. They mangle, they postpone, they reject the good measures that go up to them.

I will show you another advantage which the present Administration possesses. They are supported by several foreign Governments. Did you read in the London papers within the last few weeks an account of the energetic support they derived from the Emperor of Austria? Did you see that the Emperor of Austria sent for the British Ambassador, Sir Henry Elliot, and told him that a pestilent person, a certain individual named Mr Gladstone, was a man who did not approve the foreign policy of Austria, and how anxious he was —so the Emperor of Austria was pleased complacently to say —for the guidance of the British people and of the electors of Midlothian—how anxious he was that you should, all of you, give your votes in a way to maintain the Ministry of Lord Beaconsfield.[1] Well, Gentlemen, if you approve the foreign policy of Austria, the foreign policy that Austria has usually pursued, I advise you to do that very thing; if you want to have an Austrian foreign policy dominant in the Councils of this country, give your votes as the Emperor of Austria recommends. What has that foreign policy of Austria been? I do not say that Austria is incurable. I hope it will yet be cured, because it has got better institutions at home, and I heartily wish it well if it makes honest attempts to confront its difficulties. Yet I must look to what that policy has been. Austria has ever been the unflinching foe of freedom in every country of Europe. Austria trampled under foot, Austria

---

[1] Subsequent disclosures proved that this was not strictly correct, and Mr Gladstone apologetically withdrew the statement.

resisted the unity of Germany. Russia, I am sorry to say, has been the foe of freedom too; but in Russia there is an exception—Russia has been the friend of Slavonic freedom; but Austria has never been the friend even of Slavonic freedom. Austria did all she could to prevent the creation of Belgium. Austria never lifted a finger for the regeneration and constitution of Greece. There is not an instance—there is not a spot upon the whole map where you can lay your finger and say, "There Austria did good." I speak of its general policy; I speak of its general tendency. I do not abandon the hope of improvement in the future, but we must look to the past and to the present for the guidance of our judgments at this moment. And in the Congress of Berlin Austria resisted the extension of freedom, and did not promote it; and therefore, I say, if you want the spirit of Austria to inspire the Councils of this country, in Heaven's name take the Emperor's counsel; and I advise you to lift the Austrian flag when you go about your purposes of canvass or of public meetings. It will best express the purpose you have in view, and I, for one, cannot complain of your consistency, whatever, in that case, I might think of the tendency of your views in respect of principle, of justice, of the happiness of mankind, or of the greatness, the dignity, and the honour of this great Empire.

But, Gentlemen, still one word more, because I have not spoken of what has been the upshot of all this. There are a great many persons in this country, I am afraid, as well as in other countries, who are what is called Worshippers of Success, and at the time of the famous "Peace with Honour" demonstration there was a very great appearance of success. I was not myself at that time particularly safe when I walked in the streets of London.[1] I have walked with my wife from my own house, I have walked owing my protection to the police; but

---

[1] At the time of the "Jingo" Excitement, Mr and Mrs Gladstone were hustled by a gang of rowdies in Cavendish Square, and saved only from violence by taking refuge in the house of Dr, afterwards Sir, Andrew Clark.

that was the time, Gentlemen, when all those curious methods of maintaining British honour and British dignity were supposed to have been wonderfully successful. And now I want to ask you, as I have shown you the way we went about maintaining the independence and integrity of Belgium—what has become of the independence and integrity of Turkey? I have shown that they neither knew in the first instance the ends towards which they should first have directed their efforts, nor, when they have chosen ends, have they been able rationally to adapt their means to the attainment of those ends. I am not speaking of the moral character of the means, but how they are adapted to the end. And what did the vote of six millions achieve for Turkey? I will tell you what it achieved. It did achieve one result, and I want you well to consider whether you are satisfied with it or not, especially those of you who are Conservatives. It undoubtedly cut down largely the division of Bulgaria, established by the Treaty of San Stefano. Now, I am not going to maintain that that division was a right one, for that depends on a knowledge more minute than I possess; but the effect of it was to cut it down, as is perfectly well known—that is, put back under the direct rule of the Sultan of Turkey, and in the exact condition in which all European Turkey, except the Principalities, had been before the war, the population inhabiting the country of Macedonia, and about a million of people, the vast majority of them Christians. Two substantive and definite results, the two most definite results, produced were these—first of all, that Bessarabia, that had been a country with free institutions, was handed back to despotism; and secondly, a million and a half of people inhabiting Macedonia, to whom free institutions had been promised by the Treaty of San Stefano, are now again placed under the Turkish Pashas, and have not received one grain of benefit of importance as compared with their condition before the war.

But how as regards Turkey? I have shown results bad enough in regard to freedom. What did the British Plenipotentiaries say at Berlin? They said that some people seemed to suppose we had come to cut and carve Turkey. That is quite a mistake, said the Plenipotentiaries; we have come to consolidate Turkey. Some of the scribes of the Foreign Office coined a new word, and said it was to "rejuvenate" Turkey. How did they rejuvenate this unfortunate Empire, this miserable Empire, this unhappy Government which they have lured into war and allowed and encouraged to pass into war because they allowed their Ambassadors at Constantinople, Sir Henry Elliot and Sir Austen Layard, to whisper into the ear of the Turk that British interests would compel us to interfere and help her? What has been the result to Turkey? Now, I will say, much as the Christian populations have the right to complain, the Sultan of Turkey has a right to complain very little less. How has the Sultan been treated? We condescended to obtain from him the island of Cyprus, at a time when Austria was pulling at him on one side and freedom on the other. We condescended to take from him that miserable paltry share of the spoil. That is not all. What is the condition of Turkey in Europe? It is neither integrity nor independence. The Sultan is liable to interference at any moment, at every point of his territory from every one that signed the Treaty of Berlin. He has lost ten millions of subjects altogether, ten millions more are in some kind of dependence or other—in a condition that the Sultan does not know whether they will be his subjects to-morrow or the next day. Albania is possessed by a League. Macedonia, as you read in the papers, is traversed by brigands. Thessaly and Epirus, according to the Treaty of Berlin, should be given to Greece. The treasury of Turkey is perfectly empty, disturbances have spread through Turkey in Asia, and the condition of that Government whose integrity and independence you were told that "Peace with Honour" had secured, is more miserable than at any previous period of its history; and wise and merciful indeed would be the man that would devise some method of improving it.

To those gentlemen who talk of the great vigour and determination and success of the Tory Government, I ask you to compare the case of Belgium and Turkey. Try them by principles, or try them by results, I care not which, we knew what we were about and what was to be done when we had integrity and independence to support. When they had integrity and independence to protect, they talked, indeed, loud enough about supporting Turkey, and you would suppose they were prepared to spend their whole resources upon it; but all their measures have ended in nothing except that they have reduced Turkey to a state of greater weakness than at any portion of her history, whereas, on the other hand, in regard to the twelve or thirteen millions of Slavs and Roumanian population, they have made the name of England odious throughout the whole population, and done everything in their power to throw that population into the arms of Russia, to be the tool of Russia in its plans and schemes, unless indeed, as I hope and am inclined to believe, the virtue of free institutions they have obtained will make them too wise to become the tools of any foreign Power whatever, will make them intent upon maintaining their own liberties, as becomes a free people playing a noble part in the history of Europe.

I have detained you too long, and I will not, though I would, pursue this subject further. I have shown you what I think the miserable failure of the policy of the Government. Remember we have a fixed point from which to draw our measurements. Remember what in 1876 the proposal of those who approved of the Bulgarian agitation and who were denounced as the enemies of Turkey, remember what that proposal would have done. It would have given Autonomy to Bulgaria, which has now got Autonomy; but it would have saved all the remainder at less detriment to the rest of the Turkish Empire. Turkey would have had a fair chance. Turkey would not have suffered the territorial losses which she has elsewhere suffered, and which she has suffered, I must say, in consequence of her being betrayed into the false and mischievous, the tempting and seductive, but unreal and unwise policy of the present Administration.

There are other matters which must be reserved for other times. We are told about the Crimean War. Sir Stafford Northcote tells us the Crimean War, made by the Liberal Government, cost the country 40 millions of debt, and an income tax of 1s. 4d. per pound. Now what is the use of telling us that? I will discuss the Crimean War on some future occasion, but not now. If the Liberal Government were so clever, that they contrived to burden the country with 40 millions of debt for this Crimean War, why does he not go back to the war before that, and tell us what the Tory Government did with the Revolutionary War, when they left a debt on the country of some 900 millions, of which 650 millions they had made in the Revolutionary War, and not only so, but left the blessing and legacy of the Corn Laws, and of a high protective system, an impoverished country, and a discontented population—so much so that for years that followed that great Revolutionary War, no man could say whether the Constitution of this country was or was not worth five years' purchase. They might even go further back than the Revolutionary War. They have been talking loudly of the Colonies, and say that, forsooth, the Liberal party do nothing for the Colonies. What did the Tory party do for the Colonies? I can tell you. Go to the war that preceded the Revolutionary War. They made war against the American Continent. They added to the debt of the country 200 millions in order to destroy freedom in America. They alienated it and drove it from this country. They were compelled to bring this country to make an ignominious peace; and, as far as I know, that attempt to put down freedom in America, with its results to this country, is the only one great fact which has ever distinguished the relations between a Tory Government and the Colonies.

But, Gentlemen, these must be matters postponed for another occasion. I thank you very cordially, both friends and opponents if opponents you be, for the extreme kindness with which you have heard me. I have spoken, and I must speak in very strong terms of the acts done by my opponents. I will never say that they did it from vindictiveness, I will never say that they did it from passion, I will never say that they did it from a sordid love of office; I have no right to use such words; I have no right to entertain such sentiments; I repudiate and abjure them. I give them credit for patriotic motives—I give them credit for those patriotic motives, which are incessantly and gratuitously denied to us. I believe we are all united in a fond attachment to the great country to which we belong, to the great Empire which has committed to it a trust and function from Providence, as special and remarkable as was ever entrusted to any portion of the family of man. When I speak of that trust and that function I feel that words fail. I cannot tell you what I think of the nobleness of the inheritance which has descended upon us, of the sacredness of the duty of maintaining it. I will not condescend to make it a part of controversial politics. It is a part of my being, of my flesh and blood, of my heart and soul. For those ends I have laboured through my youth and manhood, and, more than that, till my hairs are grey. In that faith and practice I have lived, and in that faith and practice I shall die.

CHARLES BRADLAUGH AT THE BAR OF THE HOUSE OF COMMONS.

SECOND SPEECH, APRIL 26TH, 1881.

[MR BRADLAUGH'S first attempt to take his seat in the House as the Member for Northampton, May 21st, 1880, was frustrated on the ground that he claimed the right to affirm instead of subscribing the oath in the usual way. His second appearance in the House, on the above date, after having been in the meantime re-elected by his constituents, gave rise to the following impassioned speech.]

MR SPEAKER, — I have again to ask the indulgence of the House, while I submit to it a few words in favour of my claim to do that which the law requires me to do. Perhaps the House will pardon me if I supply an omission, I feel unintentionally made, on the part of the hon. member for Chatham (Mr John Gorst). In some words which have just fallen from him, I understood him to say that he would use a formal statement made by me to the Committee against what the Chancellor of the Duchy had said I had said. I am sure the hon. and learned member for Chatham, who has evidently read the proceedings of the Committee with care, would, if he had thought it fair, have stated to the House that the statement only came from me after an objection made by me — a positive objection on the ground that it related to matters outside this House, and that the House in the course of its history had never inquired into such matters; but I can hardly understand what the member for Chatham meant, when he said that he contrasted what I did say with what the Chancellor of the Duchy said I said; for it is not a matter of memory, it is on the proceedings of this House, that, being examined formally before the Committee, I stated: "That the essential part of the oath is in the fullest and most complete degree binding upon my honour and conscience, and that the repeating of the words of asseveration does not in the slightest degree weaken the binding of the allegiance on me." I now say I would not go through any form—much as I value the right to sit in this House, much as I desire and believe that this House will accord me that right—that I did not mean to be binding upon me without mental reservation, without equivocation. I would go through no form unless it were fully and completely and thoroughly binding upon me, as to what it expressed or promised. Mine has been no easy position for the last twelve months. I have been elected by the free votes of a free constituency. My return is untainted. There is no charge of bribery, no charge of corruption, nor of inducing men to come drunken to the polling-booth. I come here with a pure untainted return —not won by accident. For thirteen long years have I fought for this right—through five contested elections, including this. It is now proposed to prevent me from fulfilling the duty my constituents have placed upon me. You have force: on my side is the law. The hon. and learned member for Plymouth (Mr, afterwards Sir, Edward Clarke) spoke the truth when he said he did not ask the House to treat the matter as a question of law; but the constituencies ask me to treat it as a question of law. I, for them, ask you to treat it as a question of law. I could understand the feeling that seems to have been manifested were I some great and powerful personage. I could understand it had I a large influence behind me. I am only one of the people, and you propose to teach them that, on a mere technical question, you will put a barrier in the way of my doing my duty which you have never put in the way of anybody else. The question is, Has my return on the 9th of April 1881 anything whatever to impeach it? There is no legal disqualification involved. If there were, it could be raised by petition.

The hon. member for Plymouth says the dignity of this House is in question. Do you mean that I can injure the dignity of this House? This House which has stood unrivalled for centuries? This House, supreme among the assemblies of the world? This House, which represents the traditions of liberty? I should not have so libelled you. How is the dignity of this House to be hurt? If what happened before the 9th of April is less than a legal disqualification, it is a matter for the judgment of the constituency and not for you. The constituency has judged me; it has elected me; I stand here with no legal disqualification upon me. The right of the constituency to return me is an unimpeachable right. I know some gentlemen make light of constituencies; yet without the constituencies you are nothing. It is from them you derive your whole and sole authority. The hon. and learned member for Plymouth treats lightly the legal question. It is dangerous to make light of the law—dangerous, because if you are only going to rely on your strength of force to override the law, you give a bad lesson to men whose morality you impeach as to what should be their duty if emergence ever came. Always outside the House I have advocated strenuous obedience to the law, and it is under that law that I claim my right. It is said by the right hon. baronet (Sir Stafford Northcote), who interposes between me and my duty, that this House has passed some Resolution. First, I submit that that Resolution does not affect the return of the 9th of April. The conditions are entirely different; there is nothing since the date of that return. I submit next, that, if it did affect it, the Resolution was illegal from the beginning. In the words of George Grenville, spoken in this House in 1769, I say, if your Resolution goes in the teeth of the law—if against the Statute—your Resolution is null and void. No word have I uttered outside these walls which has been lacking in respect to the House. I believe the House will do me justice, and I ask it to look at what it is I claim.

I claim to do that which the law says I must. Frankly, I

would rather have affirmed. When I came to the table of the House I deemed I had a legal right to do it. The courts have decided against me, and I am bound by their decision. I have the legal right to do what I propose to do. No Resolution of yours can take away that legal right. You may act illegally and hinder me; and unfortunately, I have no appeal against you. "Unfortunately," perhaps, I should not say. Perhaps it is better that the Chamber that makes the law should never be in conflict with the courts which administer the laws that the Chamber makes. I think the word "unfortunately" was not the word I ought to have used in tnis argument. But the force that you invoke against the law to-day may to-morrow be used against you, and the use will be justified by your example. It is a fact that I have no remedy if you rely on your force. I can only be driven into a contest, wearying even to a strong man well supported, ruinous and killing to one man standing by himself—a contest in which, if I succeed, it will be injurious to you as well as to me. Injurious to me, because I can only win by lessening your repute, which I desire to maintain. The only court I have the power of appealing to is the court of public opinion, which I have no doubt in the end will do me justice. The hon. member for Plymouth said I had the manliness on a former occasion to make an avowal of opinions to this House. I did nothing of the kind. I have never, directly or indirectly, said one word about my opinions, and this House has no right to inquire what opinions I may hold outside its walls. The only right is that which the Statute gives you; my opinions there is no right to inquire into. I shelter myself under the laws of my country. This is a political assembly, met to decide on the policy of the nation, and not on the religious opinions of the citizens. While I had the honour of occupying a seat in the House, when questions were raised which touched upon religious matters I abstained from uttering one word. I did not desire to say one word which might hurt the feeling of even the most tender.

But it is said, Why not have taken the oath quietly? I did not take it then, because I thought I had the right to do something else, and I have paid the penalty. I have been plunged in litigation fostered by men who had not the courage to put themselves forward. I, a penniless man, should have been ruined if it had not been that the men in workshop, pit, and factory had enabled me to fight this battle. [*An interruption.*] I am sorry that hon. members cannot have patience with one pleading as I plead here. It is no light task, even if you put it on the lowest personal grounds, to risk the ambition of a life on such an issue. It is a right ambition to desire to take part in the councils of the nation, if you bring no store of wisdom with you, and can only learn from the great intellects that we have. What will you inquire into? The right hon. baronet would inquire into my opinions. Will you inquire into my conduct, or is it only my opinions you will try here? The hon. member for Plymouth frankly puts it, opinions. If opinions, why not conduct? Why not examine into members' conduct when they come to the table, and see if there be no members in whose way you can put a barrier? Are members, whose conduct may be obnoxious, to vote my exclusion because to them my opinions are obnoxious? As to any obnoxious views supposed to be held by me, there is no duty imposed upon me to say a word. The right hon. baronet has said there has been no word of recantation. You have no right to ask me for any recantation. Since the 9th of April you have no right to ask me for anything. If you have a legal disqualification, petition, lay it before the judges. When you ask me to make a statement, you are guilty of impertinence to me, of treason to the traditions of this House, and of impeachment of the liberties of the people. My difficulty is that those who have made the most bitter attacks upon me only made them when I was not here to deal with them.

One hon. and gallant member recently told his constituents that this would be made a Party question, but that the Conservative members had not the courage to speak out against me. I should have thought, from reading *Hansard*, not that they wanted courage, but that they had cultivated a reticence that was more just. I wish to say a word or two on the attempt which has been made to put on the Government of the day, complicity in my views. The Liberal Party has never aided me in any way to this House. Never. I have fought by myself. I have fought by my own hand. I have been hindered in every way that it was possible to hinder me; and it is only by the help of the people, by the pence of toilers in mine and factory, that I am here to-day, after these five struggles right through thirteen years. I have won my way with them, for I have won their hearts, and now I come to you. Will you send me back from here? Then how? You have the right, but it is the right of force, and not of law. When I am once seated on these benches, then I am under your jurisdiction. At present I am under the protection of the writ from those who sent me here. I do not want to quote what has happened before; but if there be one lesson which the House has recorded more solemnly than another, it is that there should be no interference with the judgment of a constituency in sending a man to this House against whom there is no Statutory disqualification. Let me appeal to the generosity of the House as well as to its strength. It has traditions of liberty on both sides. I do not complain that members on that (the Conservative) try to keep me out. They act according to their lights, and think my poor services may be injurious to them. [*Cries of* "No!"] Then why not let me in? It must be either a political or a religious question.

I must apologise to the House for trespassing upon its patience. I apologise because I know how generous in its listening it has been from the time of my first speech in it till now. But I ask you now, do not plunge with me into a struggle I would shun. The law gives me no remedy if the House decides against me. Do not mock at the constituencies. If you place yourselves above the law, you leave me no course save lawless agitation instead of reasonable pleading. It is easy to begin such a strife, but none knows how it would end. I have no court, no tribunal to appeal to: you have the strength of your votes at the moment. You think I am an obnoxious man, and that I have no one on my side. If that be so, then the more reason that this House, grand in the strength of its centuries of liberty, should have now that generosity in dealing with one who to-morrow may be forced into a struggle for public opinion against it.

JUSTIN M'CARTHY
IN DEFENCE OF HIS COLLEAGUES.

House of Commons, February 23rd, 1883.

[In the adjourned Debate on the Amendment proposed on the Main Question affecting Irish Affairs in the Queen's Speech, Mr W. E. Forster charged Mr Justin M'Carthy and his Colleagues with complicity in the recent outrages and crimes in Ireland.]

The fate of the Amendment now before the House gives me very little concern. Neither its fate, nor its purport, nor its wording is of much account to me, or to those with whom I have the honour to act. One thing is clear, that the Amendment is directed not against the Irish members, but against Her Majesty's Ministers. I care not whether it is rejected or passed, and I do not propose to make my business either the arraignment or the defence of the Government as regards its general policy. I shall confine myself to two speeches delivered in the course of this debate—that of the right hon. gentleman the member for Bradford (Mr Forster), and that of the right hon. gentleman the Chief Secretary for Ireland. Now the speech of the right hon. gentleman the member for Bradford was undoubtedly what writers in the newspapers sometimes call "a great effort." It was a tremendous effort. I always thought the right hon. gentleman had a good deal of theatrical talent, which he had not up to the present fully developed. Those who heard his remarkable speech will agree with me that it was mimetic as well as historic. It gave us that entertainment which is often described in the play-bills of theatres and music-halls as "imitations of popular performers." I wish I saw him in his place in the House at present. I am hardly mistaken in thinking that he favoured the House with what he believed to be imitations of the voices and manners of some hon. members of the Irish Party. I am content that he shall have all the favour which his familiar attacks upon some members of that Party, and his erudition in American newspapers, can win him for a time from this House and the public. I know, too, that his motive was not merely, although it was mainly, to discredit the Irish members. He had his mind fixed also upon discrediting and damaging the Government from which he has been discarded; and I am convinced that there are members of that Government—aye, members who are at this moment sitting on the Treasury Bench—whom he had in his mind with a wish to discredit my hon. friend the member for the City of Cork (Mr Parnell). Whatever his speech was made up from— from American newspapers, from reports of meetings in the country, from hints, and more than hints, in the passionate press of London—there was one quality of that speech which was all the right hon. gentleman's own, and that was its envenomed malignity. I never heard in this House a speech more entirely inspired with the purpose of deliberate defamation. I believe it was the right hon. gentleman's intention to do all the damage he could to the characters of some members of the House by a process of systematic calumny. He accused some of my hon. friends, and with them of course myself, of conniving at outrage and assassination. He talked of offering us an alternative; but he gave none. He made it clear that his charge was nothing short of deliberate connivance with outrage and assassination. Here is the sort of alternative the right hon. gentleman offered us—

"I give the hon. member an alternative, that either he connived at outrages, or, when warned by facts and statements, he determined to remain in ignorance; that he took no trouble to test the truth of whether outrages had been committed or not, but that he was willing to gain the advantage of them."

I point out that this is no alternative; that men who are informed that outrage and assassination are going on, and who determine to remain in ignorance, and are willing to gain the benefit of outrage and assassination, are distinctly conniving at those crimes. Therefore, I tell the right hon. gentleman that when he pretended to give us an alternative he did nothing of the kind; and that as he had made up his mind to charge us by implication with conniving at murder, he ought to have stood boldly up and said so. He ought to have said so in those plain words he sometimes is able to use, and ought not to have shielded himself behind the pretence of an alternative. I should have thought that the right hon. gentleman would be the member of this House least inclined, owing to certain memories he must have, to fling accusations of sympathy with murder recklessly at other men. When charging us with these crimes, he must have recalled a time when a newspaper, then far more influential than it now is—*The Times*—charged him with sympathy with secret assassination. I do not charge the right hon. gentleman with having sympathy with crime; but for the reason I have stated he ought to have felt a sentiment which would have prevented him from recklessly hurling similar charges in the faces of men as honourable as himself, and who feel as little thirst for blood as he does. On the 14th of March 1864, one who was then a member of this House, and is now high in Her Majesty's Colonial Service—Sir John Pope Hennessy—brought forward certain statements in this House with regard to a right hon. friend of mine, for whom I have the highest respect, the member for Halifax (Mr Stansfeld), and who was accused by certain newspapers of sympathy with assassination because he had harboured Mazzini and some of his friends. This became the subject of debate in this House, and led to the right hon. gentleman the member for Halifax resigning his position in the Government. The right hon. gentleman the member for Bradford stood up for his friend. I do not blame him for that—he believed him to be innocent. But what were the evidences given, and the assassination theory held, by the man for whom the right hon. gentleman the member for Bradford stood up in this House? Extracts were then read from Mazzini's letter, "The Theory of the Dagger." Such passages as these were read—

"Blessed be the knife of Palafox: blessed be in your hands every weapon that can destroy the enemy and set you free. The weapon that slew Mincovich in the Arsenal initiated the insurrection in Venice. It was a weapon of irregular warfare like that which, three months before the Republic, destroyed the Minister Rossi in Rome. . . . Sacred be the stiletto that began the Silician Vespers."

The right hon. gentleman the member for Bradford rose and said—

"The hon. and learned gentleman has brought forward a charge against an absent man—Signor Mazzini—who, whatever his faults, was a man of high character."

Whatever his faults? What though he blessed the knife of one man and the dagger of another, and the system of "irregular warfare" which removed Count Rossi, the Minister of the late Pope Pius IX., who was murdered on the steps of the Capitol, he was "a man of high character"! The right hon. gentleman's Leader of the present day did not agree with his estimate of Signor Mazzini. The present Prime Minister had written in a preface to a translation of Signor Farini's "Roman States"—"The Satellites of Mazzini make common cause with assassins." After those extracts had been read and four days had passed, during which the right hon. member for Bradford had time for reflection, the subject was again raised, and the right hon. gentleman said—

"I should not be ashamed of being the friend of Mazzini." [*Irish cheers, and a cry of The Dagger!*] "I am not ashamed of being his acquaintance."

Well, I think that that incident is not without its interest and moral. The Irish members who brought forward that question at the time did not charge the right hon. gentleman, or think of charging him, with sympathy with assassination. The charge was that he and his companions showed a levity which disregarded what a man might do, so long as that man was a foreign patriot. *The Times* of March 15, 1864, had a leading article on the subject, which is not without its application to the present circumstances. The right hon. gentleman was not then in the flush and heyday of youth. He was able to judge whether Mazzini and his associates and satellites were what they were represented to be. *The Times* said—

> "Who, then, is this M. Mazzini, to whose innocence this gentleman (Mr Stansfeld) and Mr W. E. Forster pledge themselves? Let anyone read the passages quoted by Mr Hennessy last night, and say whether the friends of M. Mazzini have any right to indulge in high-flown indignation when it is alleged that he might possibly be engaged in a conspiracy against a Potentate's life."

I ask whether the right hon. member for Bradford was justified in seizing at the chance of high-flown indignation because the newspaper that accused him then of sympathy with assassination accuses some of us now of the same thing. I wonder that the memory of that episode in his career has not made him more generous — yes, I will say, more honest— towards men whom, in his heart, he no more believes to be guilty of that charge than honourable men then believed him to be. I pass from that not uninstructive incident to the right hon. gentleman's attack on Irish members, and the grounds on which that attack was made. He had something to say about myself in connection with *United Ireland*, a paper published in Dublin. He said much the same thing about a year ago. He then went over the story of some articles that he said appeared in that paper. I believe they were not articles, but headings of paragraphs; and he appealed to me, though I was not in my place at the time, to know whether I approved of all these various paragraphs and headings. Now, the right hon. gentleman must have known—at all events he might have known— that I could not have seen that newspaper then. He knew that I had been out of England the whole of that recess, from the end of one Session to the beginning of another. [An IRISH MEMBER.—"He did."] He did, and he said so himself in this House, for he indulged in some more or less graceful satire at my expense, and complained that, instead of helping to keep order in Ireland, I had been enjoying myself among the monuments of ancient Greece. But since I was so culpable as to be enjoying myself among the monuments of ancient Greece, and in countries much further off, he might have known that it was not likely that a Dublin paper followed me in all my wanderings. He knew that at the time he was speaking—at the time he was so playfully chiding me for the amusement of the House he must have known that that paper was prevented from coming into this country; and though I made strenuous efforts shortly after to get copies of it, and see if it contained the terrible things it was said to contain, I was unable to obtain a copy. However, I allow that to pass. It would not much matter if the right hon. gentleman could have sustained his charge. If he had not returned to it, I should not have cared to raise it. But I am quite willing to tell him, if it affords him the slightest interest, the history of my connection with that paper. It was started to get rid of a notorious print, which appears lately to have lived by the levying of blackmail in Dublin. It was founded by a Committee of gentlemen in whom I have the greatest trust; and the editorship was given to a man whom I regard and respect, and whom I know to be incapable of conducting a journal on the principles the right hon. gentleman described. Under these conditions I felt content, having no control over the paper, to go abroad among the monuments of ancient Greece, and to leave the paper in the hands of the able editor who has already shown his ability in this House. I did not inquire in my absence how he conducted it. I know he conducted it honourably and well; and we have learned that the only things the right hon. gentleman objects to are the paragraphs and headings which got into the paper while he had the responsible editor under lock and key in one of his prisons.

I have said enough on that point. I do not believe that any investigation would convict that editor of publishing any articles which men of honour would be ashamed to sanction. The right hon. gentleman went over many points with the object of associating me and others with plots and assassinations. For example, he spoke of a telegram sent by Mr Brennan, who was the correspondent of *The Irish World*, to that paper. The telegram is given variously in the different journals, but I would ask the right hon. gentleman, Is this which I am about to read the right version?—

"All sorts of theories are afloat concerning this explosion"—that is the Salford dynamite explosion—"but the truly loyal one is that Fenianism did it."

What is the plain and evident meaning of that? Is it not that the fashionable and loyal theory, as a matter of course, is that the Fenians did it? I ask the right hon. gentleman, Is not that the manifest meaning? [Mr W. E. FORSTER.—"I would ask the hon. member to read the remainder of the telegram."] I quote the whole of the printed version I have. The right hon. gentleman charged me with deliberate avoidance of reading articles in order that I might be able to say I do not know of the incitement to assassination they contained. Then he said—

"I expect, or suspect"—probably suspect, it is more in his line—"I suspect the hon. member (meaning myself) has been careful not to read the articles to which I refer."

The charge is, perhaps, hardly Parliamentary. There was a rude interruption last night, which we all regret, to an imputation which ought not to have been made; but the right hon. gentleman is allowed to say—

"I suspect the hon. member has been careful not to read the articles to which I refer."

The whole theory and purpose of his declamation and defamation was to make members of this House responsible for every violent act done, and every violent word said, by any supposed follower of his in this country or America. I should like to know how that theory would apply to the right hon. gentleman.

The right hon. gentleman has not forgotten the riots which occurred in the Reform years, nor the men who got up these riots. He has not forgotten the riot which led to the breaking down of the Hyde Park railings, and the maiming and wounding of many of the mob and some policemen. The right hon. gentleman and his friends came back to power on that smash of the Hyde Park railings. The right hon. gentleman was well acquainted with the leader of the Democratic Movement the late Mr Beales. [Mr W. E. FORSTER.—" I did not know him personally."] Neither do I know personally those who have uttered these violent words and done these violent acts in Ireland, for which I am sought to be made responsible. Mr Beales is dead. Mr Beales was a man of honour and courage. I knew him and I respected him. But he certainly got around him, and could not help getting around him, men of very odd character and very odd pretensions. Does the right hon. gentleman remember a certain Mr Joseph Leicester, a famous glass-blower? [Mr W. E. FORSTER.—"I do not remember him."] He does not remember him? As a famous actress said on one occasion, "What a candour; but what a memory!" At the time Mr Leicester's name used to appear in every London newspaper every morning. This distinguished supporter of the right hon. gentlemen's party went to a great meeting one day—a great Trades' Demonstration, held, I think, in Trafalgar Square—and this was part of the speech of Joseph Leicester. There was then, as there has been more lately, a kind of rush and raid on the House of Commons to force them to pass a certain Bill, and this was what this demagogue here said—

"The question is, were they to suffer those little-minded, decrepit, hump-backed, one-eyed scoundrels, who call themselves the House of Commons, to defraud them any longer of their rights?"

I was not a member of the House of Commons then, and did not come in for any part of that lively personal description; but I ask the right hon. gentleman if someone as nearly connected with the hon. member for the City of Cork as Mr Leicester was with the right hon. gentleman, had used words of that description to a meeting of Irishmen, what would he have said? The riots in Hyde Park took place, and people were wounded. ["Question!"] There was no cry of "Question" when the right hon. gentleman was defaming me and others, and went over land and sea and over years to find charges against us. It is quite to the question. I want to say to him and the House that it is impossible in any movement to hold the leaders responsible for every idle word and act said and done by their followers. Of this movement Mr Beales was the leader, and when the right hon. gentleman and his friends came into power, did they repudiate Mr Beales? They made him a County Court Judge. Did they at any time, while these proceedings were going on, repudiate the language of any man? No. There was a newspaper in London at the time, of which the right hon. gentleman sitting near him (Mr John Bright) knew something, in which a writer, not now living, had once called on the people, if a certain thing were not done, to destroy the House of Lords, and to strew the Thames with the wreck of their painted chamber. I ask the right hon. gentleman, who took in that paper, whether he read it or not? [*Cries of* "*Morning Star.*"] Yes, *The Morning Star*. [Mr W. E. FORSTER.—"I was not a shareholder."] The matter was brought to the notice of this House by an hon. member, and I am not aware that the right hon. gentleman said one single word in condemnation of that language. And remember, Mr Speaker, that the time of the Hyde Park riots was not a time of peace. We have heard, again and again, that things may be allowed in time of peace; but that was not a time of peace. Those were dangerous times. Troops were kept in readiness—the air was full of danger. During the whole of that time the right hon. gentleman never said, as far as I know, one word to dissociate himself or any of his friends from those acts or words. I should like to ask the right hon. gentleman another question. Did he never hear at that time that a famous Continental leader of revolution was over in London, and was in negotiation with some of the men concerned in these affairs, with the hope of assisting them in a Democratic revolution? [Mr W. E. FORSTER.—"No."] He never heard of it? He never read any of the papers published at that time? He never read histories published since that time? Over and over again in newspapers, magazines, and books—has the story of the foreign incendiary been told, and the right hon. gentleman never heard of it or read of it; and yet he supposes I read every copy of *The Irish World!*

I think I have sufficiently shown that the right hon. gentleman ought to be cautious how he makes charges against us of sympathy with assassination, or of having assisted or connived at crimes, and how he lays down the theory that a man is bound to know what is done by everybody else who is concerned with him in any popular movement. I will tell the right hon. gentleman and the House how outrages grew up in Ireland of late. The Land League was formed with the full and deliberate intent of drawing agitation above the surface. That was its motive. Its purpose was to maintain public platforms on which agitation might go on openly and in the face of day, by which men would be withdrawn from that terrible system of conspiracy which has been the bane and curse of Ireland for so many years. That was the motive of the Land League. I saw that was its distinct purpose, and it was succeeding so manifestly in the purpose that I joined the League. The right hon. gentleman expects that everyone has read every letter written by everyone else. I should ask him if he did me the favour of reading a letter of mine which was published in all the papers in England in reference to my joining the Land League? [Mr W. E. FORSTER.—"No."] He did not. He only reads *The Irish World*, and I did not write to *The Irish World* to explain my intentions. In that letter I stated concisely and clearly my reasons for believing the Land League would do good, and why I thought it was the duty of every patriotic Irishman to join it. I believed it was doing good by helping to close the era of conspiracy. But there came upon Ireland one autumn and one winter three influences of evil together—famine, the House of Lords, and the right hon. gentleman. The country was miserably pinched with ——. The House of Lords rejected the poor little Compensation for Disturbance Bill, which might have stopped for a while the sufferings of the people ; and then, to improve the situation, the right hon. gentleman got his law for the arrest of suspicious men, under which he flung the leaders of the people into prison. Then it was that outrages began to increase. After the arrest of the hon. member for the City of Cork the movement drifted leaderless and hopeless, dropped from the high point to which it had risen in publicity and on the platform, into the seething ferment of the sea of conspiracy. The leaders of the land movement had nearly succeeded in raising Ireland out of conspiracy. That is what I fully and firmly believe, and thus History hereafter will I am certain write it out. The Chief Secretary to the Lord-Lieutenant made a serious mistake when he appealed to us to-night to justify all manner of executions simply on the ground that so many murders had been committed. It is not the theory of this country that for so many murders there shall be so many executions. That is the theory of certain Eastern States; but that is happily not yet the theory even in Ireland. Were the murders ten times more in number than the men put on trial for them, I should be at liberty still, if I thought I had reason, to examine into the justice of each trial and the way in which it had been conducted; and if it could be shown that there was anything like systematic jury-packing in even one trial, no matter how many murders had been committed, I should denounce it.

The right hon. gentleman seemed a little hopeful towards the end of his speech when he spoke of the great decrease of outrages, and when there was drawn from him the statement that there was also a decrease of evictions. In searching for the causes which had led to this decrease of outrages, the fact of the decrease of evictions must not be overlooked. The right hon. gentleman then became a little more ominous in saying that he feared that lately evictions had been on the increase. Was it not possible that with the increase of evictions might come an increase of outrages? It must be remembered that there is now no such thing as the right of public meeting or free speech in Ireland. A man may make a speech if he likes at his own risk: but the right hon. gentleman tells us that if he thinks there is anything in the speech which might lead to inflame the feelings of anyone, he will prevent or punish the making of such speeches, although he knows the speaker had no evil intention whatever. There is no free platform in Ireland; no free Press—no right to hold a public meeting. There is no way in which the sentiments and grievances of the people can be freely expressed. You are labouring in the dark. You are driving disaffection beneath the surface. You alone will be responsible for the consequences of the terrible and stringent measures you have adopted. As the hon. member for the City of Cork said, there is no longer any probability of the Irish Leaders or Irish Members of Parliament standing between you and the elements of conspiracy. I do not blame the right hon. gentleman the Chief Secretary so much for the change that has come about. The responsibility for that change I lay, as I have already said, on the shoulders of another man. I may say of him, as was said of another famous politician, that it has seldom been within the power of any human creature to do so much good as the right hon. gentleman for Bradford has prevented.

LORD RANDOLPH CHURCHILL ON THE EGYPTIAN CRISIS.

PRINCE'S HALL, PICCADILLY, FEBRUARY 16TH, 1884.

[THE fall of Sinkat and the massacre of its garrison excited the most bitter indignation in all Conservative minds. When the announcement was made in the House of Lords on the 12th inst., LORD SALISBURY moved a vote of censure on the Government, describing its policy pursued in Egypt as "vacillating and inconsistent," and also as "an act of blood-guiltiness." A similar vote was moved in the House of Commons by SIR STAFFORD NORTHCOTE. Indignation meetings were held everywhere, and the Liberal Government seemed tottering to its fall.]

MR ALGERNON BORTHWICK, MY LORDS AND GENTLEMEN,—I rise for the purpose of moving the first Resolution, and in order that we may consider that Resolution with advantage, I would beg all these gentlemen here, who do not altogether concur with the views which we are going to expound, to listen to the discussion with equanimity, and, if possible, to reply to the arguments we may urge. [A VOICE.—"They're for an Amendment."] It would conduce more to the dignity of a London meeting, it will conduce more to the maintenance of the high character of the citizens of this great Metropolis, if any gentlemen who have counter opinions to urge to those of the majority of the meeting, will come to the platform and address us. We have, Gentlemen, to-day to set an example to the country: let us first set an example of order. The Resolution which I have to propose is in these terms:—"That in the opinion of this meeting, Her Majesty's Government are solely responsible for the anarchy which prevails in Egypt, and the bloodshed which has occurred, and which is imminent in the Soudan, and that the vacillating and pusillanimous policy of the Ministers deserves the severest censure of the country."

We are gathered together this afternoon for a serious purpose; no other, indeed, than to pronounce, after due deliberation, the strongest and most resolute condemnation of Mr Gladstone's Egyptian Policy, and our detestation and abhorrence of the bloodshed and misery of which he has been the immediate and direct cause. I say Mr Gladstone's Egyptian Policy, because I utterly decline to recognise as responsible agents either his Ministerial colleagues or his Parliamentary supporters. Those parties have so wallowed in a stifling morass of the most degraded and servile worship of the Prime Minister that they have sunk below the level of slaves; they have become mere puppets, the objects of derision and contempt; they have lost all claim to the title of Englishmen, and I think they have lost all claim to the title of rational human beings. To give you an instance of the abject imbecility which has struck down the Liberal Party, I would mention what occurred in the House of Commons on Thursday night. Mr Forster in that great speech which he made that evening—a speech in which he promised one vote to the Government in the House of Commons, and alienated a hundred thousand votes from the Government in the country—Mr Forster, I say, expressed the opinion that the Government ought to have rescued the garrison of Sinkat. "How?" cried out some importunate Liberals. "How?" was the plaintive cry they raised. "How?" shouted Mr Forster, turning upon them, so that they wished themselves a hundred leagues under the sea, "How? why, by doing a fortnight earlier what they are doing now, sending British soldiers to the garrison's rescue." There is a good instance of the hopeless and incurable mental alienation to which the once free and independent Liberal Party have been reduced by Mr Gladstone! It was indeed a melancholy spectacle.

I said that our purpose this afternoon was a serious one, and it is so. It is a serious thing for Englishmen to meet together in open day for the purpose of doing all they can to destroy a Government. But we are not alone. Thousands of your countrymen have already met, and thousands more will meet, animated by the same feelings as yourselves, and, like yourselves, resolved to exhaust their energies in a supreme effort to avert further disgrace from our names, future defeat from our army, and ultimate ruin from our country, by dashing from his pride of place the evil and moonstruck Minister who has brought England into grievous peril. Perilous, I say, is our condition, for it is perilous for a country to shed human blood in vain; it is perilous for a country to assume responsibilities which it is too cowardly to discharge; it is perilous for a country to permit its foreign interests to be in such a condition that any morning we may awake to hear Europe demanding reparation and even vengeance. Once again, for the fourth time in four years, do the Ministry, whose programme was peace, and whose component parts were Quakers, call upon you to give them authority to wage a bloody war. Of their former wars the results have been either infamous or futile— infamy in the south of Africa; futility in the north of Africa. Will you, I ask, with these memories still fresh in your minds, permit these false guides again to direct your course? There can be but one answer. If war is again to be urged; if British blood and British treasure are again to be poured forth; if the regeneration of Egypt and the East is once more to be taken in hand, then other heads must do the work, and other policies must be pursued. A Parliament which has long ceased to represent England must be dissolved, and a Ministry, for a parallel to which you must go back to the days of Shaftesbury or Lord North, must be placed on its trial by the people. We have to provide for the safety of the hero Gordon; for the safety of the 4,000 British soldiers sent to Suakim; for the safety of the garrisons of the Soudan, 30,000 souls in all, whose one and only hope is now reposed in you. Above all, we have to provide for the safety of our position in the Delta of the Nile. Shall labours such as these, interests so tremendous and so vital, be committed to the hands of Mr Gladstone and his colleagues, men who have on their souls the blood of the massacre of Maiwand, the blood of the massacre of Lang's Nek, the blood of George Colley, the blood of Lord Frederick Cavendish and Mr Burke, and many other true and loyal subjects of the Crown in Ireland, the blood of Hicks Pasha and his 10,000 soldiers, the blood of the army of General Baker, the blood of Tewfik Bey and his 500 heroes? For four years this Ministry has literally waded in blood; their hands are literally dripping and reeking with blood. From massacre to massacre they march, and their course is ineffaceably stamped upon the history of the world by an overflowing stream of blood. How many more of England's heroes—how many more of England's best and bravest, are to be sacrificed to the Moloch of Midlothian? This, too, is shocking and horrible—the heartless indifference and callousness of the Liberal Party to narratives of slaughter and unutterable woe. Fifteen times did Mr Gladstone on Tuesday night in his reply to the grave and measured accusations of Sir Stafford Northcote —fifteen times, I say, did he excite the laughter of his Liberal supporters with a frivolity which was too hideous to contemplate. Talk of Bulgarian atrocities! Add them together, and even multiply them if you will, and you will not exceed the total of the atrocities and the infamies which have distinguished with an awful reputation the most blood-stained and withal the most cowardly Government which England has ever seen.

Well, we are met together this afternoon as loyal subjects of the Queen and as lovers of our country for this purpose, and this purpose only—to put a stop to further wicked and wanton bloodshed. We know that great empires must sometimes fight great battles, and that empires which fear to fight battles will soon cease to be empires; but we are resolved that the battles which we have to fight shall be fought for definite objects and for noble ends, and that poltroons and traitors, in the garb of Ministers of the Crown, shall sacrifice no longer for worthless and degraded aims the life-blood of our country. The supporters of the present Government exclaim that the Tory Party, although prodigal of censure, is deficient in a policy of its own; and with many taunts they call upon us to disclose the direction in which our efforts would be turned in the event of a change in the Councils of the Crown. The demand cannot be considered unfair, and the reply is not so difficult as some people seem to think. We recognise to the very uttermost the immense responsibilities which this country has incurred towards Egypt, and towards the interests of Europe there, and to the discharge of these responsibilities we would be prepared to apply all the resources, if need be, of the Empire of the Queen; and till those responsibilities are satisfied we would neither stop nor stay. The history of the Tory Party in the past is, I fearlessly assent, an ample guarantee that the recognition of a responsibility and the full discharge of a responsibility are inseparable and consequential. I cannot claim to have the smallest share in the Councils of the leaders of the Tory Party, whoever they may be—and therefore, as far as they are concerned, I speak without authority. But having studied with some care the history of our Party in the past, possessing an unbounded faith in its future, and being not altogether ignorant of the state of public opinion, I will venture to say this much—that the policy of the Tory Party, should it be placed in power, will be the policy of calling things by their right names. The occupation of Egypt by the British forces will be called a Protectorate of Egypt by the British Empire, having for its object the establishment, in process of time, of a Government at Cairo, which shall be consonant with the legitimate and laudable aspirations of the Egyptian people, which shall be able to protect itself alike from internal tumult and from foreign intrigue, which, while it shall develop the undoubted resources of Egypt, shall faithfully discharge the equitable liabilities of its people, and which, as far as human governments can do, shall give promise of prosperity and happiness in the land of the Nile. We are now in Egypt by the sufferance of Europe, but we must endeavour to be in Egypt by the mandate of Europe. Our Protectorate, to be effective, and authoritative, and secure, should be acquiesced in by a European Congress, in which Turkey shall be adequately represented and the rights and powers of the Sultan loyally secured. Our Protectorate, if it is to be crowned with success, must not shrink from dealing comprehensively and boldly with the financial indebtedness of Egypt, even though such dealing should involve some pecuniary liability on ourselves. The work, if you undertake it, will be a work of time—perhaps a long time. It will be a work of difficulty, and perhaps a work of danger; but it would also be a work of duty and a work of honour; and from work of that kind Britain has never yet recoiled. It is a work which, if courageously persisted in, will bind more closely to us than heretofore the sympathies of the Mohammedan races, and will establish on deeper foundations our dominions in the East. Our aims are honour, peace, and freedom, and we should not shrink from prosecuting those aims, if need be, by force of arms. Conscious of their magnanimity, we would go boldly forward, knowing well that the results of our policy would surely be to undo the heavy burdens and to let the oppressed go free.

THE RT. HON. JOSEPH CHAMBERLAIN ON LIBERAL AIMS.

BIRMINGHAM, JUNE 3RD, 1885.

[ON this date a Deputation of the Council of the Western Division of Birmingham waited upon MR CHAMBERLAIN at the Forward Club, urging him to stand for that Division in Parliament in the forthcoming General Election. They asked him for no pledge, none being necessary.]

MR PAYTON AND GENTLEMEN,—I thank you very much for the cordiality with which you have invited me to be your representative in Parliament, and I take it as an earnest of the spirit and the genuine kindness with which I may hope to be received by the constituency itself. I think you will not be surprised when I say that I come before you to-day with mixed feelings. I am going, I hope, to be your member; but I cannot forget that I am, and that I have been, the representative of the whole of this great constituency, and being and having been member for Birmingham is really a very proud thing to reflect upon. It is not only that it is, I believe, the largest of the constituencies of the United Kingdom; at the time of the last general election we numbered, I think, something like 65,000 registered electors, and other towns of larger population, like Liverpool and Glasgow, could only muster a few over 60,000. It is not merely the size of the borough which has made it an honour to represent it, it is also the great influence which it has so continuously exercised upon the political life and the legislation of the country; and to represent in the future 10,000 of my fellow-townsmen after having represented 65,000, is like living in a cottage after having resided in a palace. [*Laughter.*] At the same time, I hope that the difference is more apparent than real, and that we shall continue to preserve the unity of this great constituency; and that although none of the seven members whom it will now enjoy will be entitled to speak authoritatively in the name of the whole, yet that as a body we shall speak with the one potent voice of Birmingham, united, as we have been of yore, in the pursuit of every Liberal measure.

Well, I may say that if the separation was to take place, there is no division of the town which it would be personally more gratifying to me to represent than this Western Division. Your Chairman has already alluded to the reasons which make me see a peculiar fitness in the invitation which you have been good enough to address to me. It is here that I made my first entry into public life. I believe my first political speech was made in a schoolroom in All Saints, under the presidency of my friend the Chairman, and in support of the candidature of Mr Dixon as one of the members for Birmingham. Afterwards I was connected with many of your leading citizens in establishing that undenominational school, also in All Saints, which gave a practical illustration of the scheme of the National Education League to which Mr Payton has referred, and which had so large a part in carrying the measure, of the advantages of which he has not said one word too much. As to St Paul's Ward, I am glad indeed to recollect that it was through the kindness of the electors of St Paul's Ward that I was introduced to local government and that I gained my experience of local life, which has been to me of the greatest possible value, and which has produced in my mind an enduring conviction of the importance and dignity of our local government, and an anxious desire to extend its functions and to increase the number of those on whom it may be conferred. Well, then, Gentlemen, I may say that I accept with gratitude the invitation which you have addressed to me. If there is to be opposition, I have no doubt that we shall give a good account of ourselves. And whether there be opposition or not, I have no doubt whatever that, if life is spared to me, somewhere about the end of November, I shall be the member for the Western Division of Birmingham.

I thank those who have already addressed you for the kindness with which they have said that from me they ask no profession of faith. Well, it is true that my public and political life has been all before you, and there is probably no subject of the slightest importance on which you do not already know my opinion, and with regard to which you do not know that I will not do all that in me lies to give force to that opinion. Of course, I do not expect that my opinion agrees with yours upon every subject or upon every detail. That would be to presuppose that you yourselves are entirely agreed, which is more, perhaps, than I have a right to expect, even from the constituency which I aspire to represent. No, Gentlemen, but though we may differ sometimes upon details, and sometimes upon methods, I believe that we are agreed upon the main lines of Liberal policy, and that we shall always be found shoulder to shoulder in endeavouring to secure their general acceptance. Now, this invitation, and the signs of activity which are everywhere around us, are proofs that we have arrived at a stage in our political history. The old order is passing away; the new order is beginning to make itself felt. I am not generally much inclined to indulge in political retrospect—I am more ready to say, "Let the dead past bury its dead; our business is with the present and with the future"; but standing here, as I do, at the turning of the ways, I will venture to assert that when the history of the last five years comes to be written, neither the Government of which I have the honour to be a member, nor the Parliament which was returned to power with such tremendous enthusiasm five years ago, will have any cause to fear its verdict. When that history comes to be written you know whose will be the central and prominent figure. You know that Mr Gladstone will stand out before posterity as the greatest man of his time—remarkable not only for his extraordinary eloquence, for his great ability, for his steadfastness of purpose, for his constructive skill, but more, perhaps, than all these, for his personal character, and for the high tone that he has introduced into our politics and public life. I sometimes think that great men are like great mountains, and that we do not appreciate their magnitude while we are close to them. You have to go to a distance to see which peak it is that towers above its fellows; and it may be that we shall have to put between us and Mr Gladstone a space of time before we shall see how much greater he has been than any of his competitors for fame and power. I am certain that justice will be done to him in the future, and I am not less certain that there will be a signal condemnation of those men who, moved by motives of Party spite in their eagerness for office, have not hesitated to load with insult and indignity the greatest statesman of our time, who had not allowed even his age, which should have commanded their reverence, or his experience, which entitled him to their respect, or his high personal character, or his long service to his Queen and to his country, to shield him from the vulgar affronts and lying accusations of which he has nightly been made the subject in the House of Commons. He, with his great magnanimity, can afford to forget and forgive these things; those whom he has served long it behoves to remember them, to resent them, and to punish them.

Now, I have said, Gentlemen, that I do not think that this Parliament will have any cause to fear the verdict of History. Just contrast it for a moment with the Parliament which preceded it. That was a Parliament and a Government which came into power under the most exceptionally favourable circumstances. Ireland was contented, there was peace all over the world, the finances were in the most admirable order. Never was there a better opportunity for a great and patriotic statesman to promote measures of urgent domestic importance, and yet I venture to say that during the whole existence of that Parliament, with the exception, perhaps, of the Artisans' Dwellings Act of Sir Richard Cross, which was, unfortunately, an unsuccessful, but which was, I believe, a well-meant attempt to grapple with a great social evil—with that exception there is not, I believe, one single Act to which the future historian will deem it necessary to make even a passing reference.

But now, when we came into power, everything was changed. There was trouble all over the world. South Africa was in a state of anarchy: there had been war, shortly to be renewed, in Afghanistan; Ireland was dissatisfied, and was on the eve of the greatest agitation which has ever convulsed that country since the Tithe War; the finances were in hopeless confusion; and yet, in spite of all these things, in spite of obstruction carried with the tacit approval of the leaders of the Tory Party up to the height of a science, and in spite of the most factious Opposition that, I believe, this country has ever known, there has not been a single Session which has passed without measures of important reform finding their place in the Statute Book, without grievances being redressed and wrongs being remedied. We have abolished flogging in the army, we have suspended the operation of the odious Acts called the Contagious Diseases Acts, we have amended the Game Laws, we have reformed the Burial Laws, we have introduced and carried our Employers' Liability Bill, we have had a Bankruptcy Act, a Patents Act, and a host of secondary measures, which, together, would have formed the stock-in-trade of a Tory Government for twenty years at least; and yet these are only the fringe, only the outside, of the more important legislation of our time, the chief elements in which have been the Irish Land Bill and the Reform Bill. The Irish Land Bill alone is a monument of Mr Gladstone's genius. He probably was the only man who could have successfully dealt with so gigantic, so complicated, and so difficult a subject. But he has passed two great measures dealing with that subject, giving to the Irish tenant full security of tenure, and now, at all events, he enjoys in their entirety all the improvements which he may make in his holding. And sometimes, Gentlemen, I cannot but wish that Liberals would have a little more faith in their principles, and a little more trust in the remedial legislation which they have assisted to pass. If Ireland is pacified at the present moment I do not attribute it to Coercion Bills; I attribute it to the reform of the Land Laws and to the removal of the deep-seated Agrarian grievance of the Irish peasant. Coercion may be necessary at times. Murder, and outrage, and assassination are things which no Government can tolerate, which no honest man will lift a finger to approve; and when these things stalk through the land, then they must be put down at all hazards and at all risk, by every means within the power of the Legislature and of the Government. But Coercion is for an emergency. It is nonsense to talk of a Constitutional system and Constitutional Government if the Constitution is always being suspended. When the emergency is over, then it is the duty of wise statesmen to seek out the causes of discontent and to endeavour to remedy them. Well, I believe that one of the greatest of Irish problems is still before us, and must wait for its solution until the new Parliament, whose advent we anticipate with so much interest and with such expectations. Mr Gladstone has removed two of the greatest grievances of Ireland. He has disestablished an alien Church and he has reformed the Land Laws. But there remains a question as important, possibly even more important, than both these two, and that is, to give in Mr Gladstone's own words, the widest possible self-government to Ireland which is consistent with the maintenance of the integrity of the Empire. What we have to do is to conciliate the national sentiment of Ireland. We have to find a safe means between separation on the one hand, which would be disastrous to Ireland and dangerous to England, and that excessive concentralisation on the other hand, which throws upon the English Parliament and upon English officials the duty and burden of supervising every petty detail of Irish local affairs, which stifles the national life, which destroys the sense of responsibility, which keeps the people in ignorance of the duties and functions of Government, and which produces a perpetual feeling of irritation, while it obstructs all necessary legislation. That is the problem, and I do not believe that the resources of statesmanship are exhausted, or that it will be impossible to find a solution.

We are going to have a new Parliament, when for the first time the whole people will be represented. We shall know what is the authoritative expression of the wishes of the majority of the people of Ireland. That is a great thing, and this authoritative expression of the wishes of the people of Ireland will be submitted to the judgment, not of classes, nor of those who are prejudiced by the existence of privileges or by separate and individual claims and rights, but to the whole people of England and Scotland. And when I think how much importance the English and the Scotch people attach to local Government, when I know how we in the towns prize it, when I know how Liberals in the country desire it, when I know how Liberals in the Metropolis are asking for it, I do not believe for a moment that they will hesitate before conceding to Ireland all the liberties and all the freedom which they will claim for themselves.

Well, now, Gentlemen, I do not think I need dilate upon the circumstances or the manner in which what has been called the greatest reform, the greatest Constitutional reform since the Revolution of 1688, has been carried through. The Tories opposed it, as they have opposed every measure of reform, as long as they dared, and until they saw the passions of the people were so aroused that it would be dangerous to resist any longer. They opposed it and attempted to delay it, attempted to minimise it, and now with characteristic effrontery, they are taking the credit for the passing of a measure, which, if their power had been equal to their will, we should never have seen up on the Statute-Book of the land. But though they have changed their language, they have not changed their tactics. We have had a taste of their spirit, even within the last few weeks. What the Tories have not dared to do in the House of Commons, they have put up their confederates in the House of Lords to do for them, and by making medical relief a disqualification for the franchise, they have taken away with the one hand what they gave with the other, and they have kept out from the enjoyment of their electoral rights probably one-fourth of those whom we sought to enfranchise.

Well, this is monstrous injustice. It is an intolerable thing that a poor labourer, with his 12/ or possibly 14/ a week, should be placed in time of sickness and trouble in his family between the alternative of either losing his electoral rights, or of leaving his family without the assistance which medical skill could afford. It is an iniquity which, if it be not set right in the present Parliament, it will be the first duty of the new Parliament to correct. In the meantime I do not doubt that the new electors, those of them to whom the Lords in their great mercy have still left their votes, will know how to judge between the two parties in the State, and will know what trust to place in the assurances which the leaders of that party are giving of their confidence in the people.

Well, Gentlemen, if I were to stop here, although I think I should have made out a pretty fair case for our domestic policy, I should lay myself open to the remark, "Oh, but you have said nothing about foreign policy; you confess then, that that at all events is a failure, and that there you have broken down." I am not going to confess anything of the kind; I am not going to make any such admission. I am going to claim your support for the main line of our foreign policy just as earnestly, and with as full a conviction of your assent as I have claimed your support for our domestic policy. I do not say that we have not made mistakes. I think it would be a very extraordinary Administration indeed which, dealing with such difficult and complicated business as has been placed before us recently, had not made any mistakes; it would be very wonderful if, looking back now with fuller knowledge, we were not able to put our finger on some point where we would wish to have acted differently from what we did; but I say, for the main line of our policy, I claim your approval, and of the main line of the policy of our opponents I ask you to mark your emphatic dissent. I am not content, however, to rest entirely upon the fact that if there were a change of Government the alternative which is presented to you by the Tories is not a very agreeable one. If words mean anything, and if the language of their leaders should be interpreted by the law of common sense, then in the last five years, if Lord Salisbury had been in office, we should have been at war with two at least of the Great Powers of Europe. I want you to consider the spirit in which the two parties have addressed themselves to foreign policy. I can well understand that there are some people, many perhaps in Birmingham, who are in favour of what is called absolute non-intervention in the affairs of other countries. But, Gentlemen, although, when I consider the difficulties in which intervention has frequently landed us, I can sympathise with such a feeling, I tell you plainly that it is impracticable, that it is impossible of realization. Our relations are so far spread, we have so many interests in so many different parts of the world, that we could not even if we would remain absolutely isolated in the midst of what is taking place around us, and the question is, In what spirit are we to address ourselves to the communications which we must necessarily have with foreign Powers? Now, if we may assume the leaders of the Tory party to speak for their followers, they would address themselves to any foreign nation with which we had matters of discussion in the spirit and tone of a superior dictating his will. They would state at the outset the demands which they make, and they would expect those demands to be instantly and entirely complied with. They would not abate one jot, they would yield nothing to the sensibility of others—

they would deal with all those questions in the spirit of those ... word should always be law.

Well, I do not think this is a tone which is becoming us, which it is right or which it is prudent for a Great Power to ... I believe, on the contrary, that the Government have ... justified in dealing with foreign nations, as with nations entitled to equal consideration with ourselves, and while endeavouring to maintain the honour and interests of this country, not on that account to ignore altogether the honour and the interests of the countries with which we have had to deal. Now, I should have liked to have said something at length upon the details of our recent negotiations with Russia; but as you have seen, those negotiations are not finally closed, and it would not, therefore, be permissible for me to deal fully with the communications which have already taken place. You are told that we have yielded basely to Russia, that we have compromised the interests of the country. Well, Gentlemen, all I will say is, that if it be found when the whole question is finally and happily settled—as I hope and believe it shortly will be—if it is then found that we have maintained the friendship and confidence of the Ameer of Afghanistan, that we have secured for our ally all that he himself has deemed of importance, that we have obtained everything that the Government of India has thought necessary for the security, order, and credit of the Empire, we shall not in that case be held to have failed, even though, in maintaining our position, we may have dealt with a great nation in a spirit of conciliation and of consideration, and, while anxious to maintain the dignity of this country, have been also ready to recognise the claims and the rights of the Power with which we have been dealing. Well now, it is in the same spirit that we have conducted all our negotiations and communications with our neighbours in France, and you will not doubt that we have had many difficult and complicated questions to discuss with the French Government.

It is said that here also we have truckled to the French, and that we have betrayed English interests and exhibited an unparalleled pusillanimity. Well, I would just say, in passing, that these are statements which I do not think it is very patriotic to make in times of great national difficulty and embarrassment. They are statements which are very apt to bring about their own fulfilment; because if a foreign Power learns from the leaders of a great party in this country that the Executive Government of the day is cowardly, weak, vacillating, and yielding, and that this foreign Government has only to demand in order that its utmost requirements may immediately be satisfied, I think you will say such a thing as that is very apt to increase the demands of the foreign Government, and that it is not at all likely to lead to a satisfactory settlement of our disputes. When I was in Paris the other day I was struck by a rather curious coincidence. When I left London the Tory Peers and some of the Tory speakers had been after their wont denouncing the Government in the language to which I have already referred, but when I got to France I found there were French politicians, French Ashmead-Bartletts and French Randolph Churchills, who were using precisely similar language concerning the Government of that country; only it was the other side of the shield that was thus presented to me; it was the French Government who was truckling to the arrogance of England, whose concessions knew no bounds, and who, if it had any care for the interests of France, would immediately issue its ultimatum to perfidious Albion. In the last article I read before I left, in *The Times*, I was told that the limits of concession on the part of the Government to France must, it supposed, at last have been reached. In the first article I read in the *Débats*, a most ably conducted journal in Paris, I found the French Government assailed most bitterly for the manner in which it had yielded everything to the insolence of England. Well, do not you think that when these things are being said on both sides, perhaps there is as little truth on one side as there is on the other, and that perhaps both Governments are wiser than these irresponsible writers in the Press, who risk sometimes a breach in the friendship which ought to exist between two great nations; wiser than the politicians whose recklessness endangered the peace of the world? Do not you think it possible that the two Governments may be each earnestly seeking to conciliate the interests and the honour of their respective countries?

I will not apologise for saying a few more words on this Egyptian question, because I attach the greatest possible importance to the French alliance. The friendship between France and this country has been slowly built up during a generation, it has done a great deal for civilisation, and it has helped on important occasions to secure the peace of Europe. I believe that near neighbours as we are, in our continued and cordial friendship lies the best guarantee for the future happiness of both our nations; and I would be sorry that any temporary misapprehension, any misrepresentation, should jeopardise the alliance to which I attach so great an importance. Now the Egyptian question has brought us face to face with great interests and a natural sensitiveness on the part of Frenchmen. To begin with, let me answer the question, "Why did you go to Egypt?" There are a great many people who think, in view of what has subsequently occurred, that it would have been wiser if we had kept away altogether; but then it should be borne in mind what the alternative would have been. We also have got interests in Egypt. I do not speak now of the sums of money which are invested there, whether in the Debt or in public works and national enterprises. I do not speak merely of the great trade with that country, of the cotton and corn which come from Egypt to England, and which are purchased with our manufactures. But Egypt is the highway to India and to our Colonial possessions; four-fifths of the ships that traverse the Canal are under the English flag, and probably a great deal more than one-half of all the merchandise which they bear is either going or coming between England and her own possessions. It is quite impossible that any Government with a sense of duty and responsibility should ignore these vast and important interests, and if we had allowed Egypt to become the prey of anarchy and disorder, and if subsequently some other Power had interfered and taken possession of the country, I do not believe that the Government would have been forgiven; I do not believe that it would have been held to have done its duty; and I do not believe that its action would have contributed in the long run to the peace of the world.

But if we have great interests, bear in mind that the French have interests of hardly lesser magnitude. Probably as a mere commercial speculation, they are less engaged in Egyptian affairs than we are; but then you will not forget that the Suez Canal itself we owe to the genius and enterprise of a great Frenchman, who, undeterred by ridicule, by opposition, I am afraid I must almost say by the hostility of England, so ably carried forward that great enterprise, which has done an immense deal for the civilisation and advantage of the world. It is not possible for Frenchmen to dissociate themselves from the honour and glory which attended upon the successful conduct of so great a matter; and we have to bear that in mind when we find that our neighbours are sensitive on the subject of our interference. Not only so; but, as you know, in past history the military annals of France have gained an added glory in connection with the enterprise which Napoleon successfully carried out in that country, so that we have to bear with Frenchmen when we find them, more perhaps than other nations, susceptible to the action we have found it our duty to take. We thought it our duty to consult and concert with them, and, as you know, in the first instance every step was taken in alliance with the French Government. At a certain period—at the time of the bombardment of Alexandria—the French Government broke off from that alliance. I am not complaining of their action; I am merely reciting facts. But it is well to bear in mind that it was they and not we who first severed the concert which up to that time had existed. Well, at that moment there were two courses which were open to us. We might if we had liked have taken possession of Egypt;

we might have announced a protectorate similar to the French protectorate of Tunis, or we might have annexed the country as the French have annexed Algiers. I suppose at that time such a course could have been pursued without immediate danger of war; but the Government thought it was assuming a responsibility altogether outside the proper sphere of English duty and of English interests. The Government thought that we had no right to destroy the independence of Egypt. They thought that we had no right to assume the immense responsibility which would follow upon our becoming, as we should have done, practically a European nation, and so losing the advantage which our insular position has hitherto given us; and, above all, we did not think it was worth our while, or desirable, or right, for such an object to risk the friendship of France, to which we attached so much value. Well, then, the alternative was this—the alternative was that we should remain in Egypt only so long as was necessary to restore order, and that then we should come away without having sought or obtained any territorial aggrandisement for ourselves. And when that policy was announced, what would you have said would have been the duty and the only natural course of a French patriotic statesman? I confess I should have said: "We are dealing with a Government which announces its intention in such a way as to afford us no just cause of offence. This Government has declared its willingness to evacuate Egypt as soon as order is re-established; it is our business to keep it to its pledges, and to make this policy as easy as possible to it." Well, I must confess I did not think that although it appears to me to be the obvious policy of French statesmen, it has always been the course which has been pursued by the French Government.

We have found great difficulties thrown in our way both in connection with the administration of Egypt and also in connection with the re-arrangement of its finances; and I cannot help pointing out to you, and through you to others, that one effect of this policy has been to delay the evacuation which both nations have equal reason to desire, to postpone it, to make it difficult, and perhaps even in the last resort to make it impossible. Now, Gentlemen, what are the objects with which we still remain in that country? In the first place we are bound to secure the independence of Egypt. It cannot be tolerated that after the sacrifices we have made, our going away should be the signal for another Power to take up a preponderating position there. We have a right to ask, we have a right to expect, that some guarantee will be given to us that other nations will be as self-denying as we intend to be ourselves before we can leave the country. But we have also something else to do. We have a duty which we owe to the Egyptians. We have to provide them with some form of government which is likely to be a settled one; we have to relieve the peasants from excessive or unjust taxation, which might be a cause of discontent and trouble in the future; and we have to create some kind of native or other army which may answer for the defence of the country against external enemies and against internal disorder. These are objects surely in which we may seek and obtain the cordial assistance of France, and which are not calculated to provoke jealousy or alarm among other nations of the Continent. I have dwelt upon this matter because, as I say, I believe that some of the unfriendliness, which I fear has sometimes prevailed, has been due to misunderstanding and to misapprehension, and because I believe that if that misapprehension could be removed, the reasons that should draw the two nations together are so strong that the clouds which have hitherto hung over our alliance will be entirely and speedily dispelled.

Gentlemen, I feel that I owe you an apology for addressing you at such length, and especially, perhaps, for speaking on subjects which are rather outside the ordinary scope and limit which I have fixed to my political addresses; but I have recently had more than one opportunity of speaking on the future domestic policy of the Liberal party, and I did not think that on this occasion it was necessary that I should repeat myself. I have nothing to add to what I have already said in reference to this matter; I have nothing to withdraw. I believe, and I rejoice to believe, that the reduction of the franchise will bring into prominence social questions which have been too long neglected, that it will force upon the consideration of thinking men of all parties the condition of our poor—aye, and the contrast which, unfortunately, exists between the great luxury and wealth which some enjoy, and the misery and poverty which prevails among large portions of the population. I do not believe that any Liberal policy, mine or any other, will ever take away the security which property rightly enjoys; that it will ever destroy the certainty that industry and thrift will meet with their due reward; but I do think that something may be done to enlarge the obligation and responsibility of the whole community towards its poorer and less fortunate members. In that great work, if I am permitted to take any part, I hope I may have, I am confident I shall have, your support and sympathy; and I hope that this great constituency of Birmingham will be as one man in carrying forward the Liberal measures from which in the past the country has derived such signal advantage. Gentlemen, I thank you very much for the cordiality with which you have conveyed to me your invitation. I hope that before long I may have an opportunity of addressing a larger meeting in the constituency, and I hope that the connection which has existed between us, first in the Town Council and in connection with local affairs, and then in Parliament, may not be broken during my lifetime.

C. S. PARNELL ON THE COERCION BILL.

HOUSE OF COMMONS, APRIL 18TH, 1887.

[IN the former part of this speech MR PARNELL denounced as a forgery the letter purporting to have been written by him, as giving countenance to the Phœnix Park Murders, and published in facsimile in *The Times* of this date. *See* APPENDIX.]

SIR,—The right hon. gentleman (Mr A. J. Balfour) refrained from answering the speech which I delivered on the first reading of this Bill, and the Government refused to allow the adjournment of the debate, in order that some other member of the Government should have an opportunity of answering it the next day; and now, upon the second reading of this Bill, he goes back to the speech, and he attempts an answer to it, at a time of the night when he knows perfectly well that no reply can be made to him; and, with characteristic unfairness—an unfairness which I suppose we may expect to be continued in the future—he has refused to me the ten or twelve minutes that I should have craved to refer to a villainous and barefaced forgery which appeared in *The Times* of this morning, obviously for the purpose of influencing the Division, and for no other purpose. I got up when the right hon. gentleman the member for Midlothian (Mr Gladstone) sat down. I had not intended to have made a speech at all upon the second stage of this Bill. I should not have said more than a very few words in reference to this forgery; but I think I was entitled to have had from the right hon. gentleman an opportunity of exposing this deliberate attempt to blacken my character at some time when there would have been some chance of what I stated reaching the outside world. I say there is no such chance now. I cannot suppose the right hon. gentleman, in refusing me the ten minutes which I crave, had not in his eye the design of practically preventing my denial of this unblushing calumny having that effect upon public opinion which it would otherwise have had if it had been spoken at a reasonable hour of the night. It appears that, in addition to the passage of this Coercion Act, the dice are to be loaded—that your great organs of public opinion in this country are to be permitted to pay miserable creatures for the purpose of producing these calumnies. Who will be safe in such circumstances and under such conditions? I do not envy the right hon. gentleman the Chief Secretary for Ireland, this first commencement of suppression of defence this first commencement of calumny and of forgery which has been made by his supporters. We have heard of the misdeeds of Mr Ford, the editor of *The Irish World*, but Mr Ford never did anything half so bad as this. [Mr A. J. BALFOUR.—I do not wish to interrupt the hon. member; but as he makes these accusations, I should like to explain that I intervened between the hon. gentleman and the House simply because I understood that it had been arranged that I should follow the right hon. member for Midlothian, and that the hon. member would follow me. No hint reached me that he was going to confine himself to an explanation of, or deal at all with the accusation in *The Times* to which he has referred. No hint of that kind reached me, and I conceive that the hon. member might have risen, had he wished, at any time earlier in the evening.] I was asked officially, at an early hour in the evening, whether I would speak after the right hon. member for Midlothian, and I replied that I would, and that I only intended to say a few words in reference to this calumny. I think I ought to have been given the opportunity which I desired.

Now, Sir, when I first heard of this precious concoction—I heard of it before I saw it, because I do not take in or even read *The Times* usually—when I heard that a letter of this description, bearing my signature, had been published in *The Times*, I supposed that some autograph of mine had fallen into the hands of some person for whom it had not been intended, and that it had been made use of in this way. I supposed that some blank sheet containing my signature, such as many members who are asked for their signature frequently send—I supposed that such a blank sheet had fallen into hands for which it had not been intended, and that it had been misused in this fashion, or that something of that kind had happened. But when I saw what purported to be my signature, I saw plainly that it was an audacious and unblushing fabrication. Why, Sir, many members of this House have seen my signature, and if they will compare it with what purports to be my signature in *The Times* of this morning, they will see that there are only two letters in the whole name which bear any resemblance to letters in my own signature as I write it. I cannot understand how the conductors of a responsible, and what used to be a respectable, Journal, could have been so hoodwinked, so hoaxed, so bamboozled, and that is the most charitable interpretation which I can place on it, as to publish such a production as that as my signature. My writing—its whole character —is entirely different. I unfortunately write a very cramped hand; my letters huddle into each other, and I write with very great difficulty and slowness. It is, in fact, a labour and a toil to me to write anything at all. But the signature in question is written by a ready penman, who has evidently covered as many leagues of letter-paper in his life as I have yards. Of course, this is not the time, as I have said, to enter into full details and minutiæ as to comparisons of handwriting; but if the House could see my signature, and the forged, the fabricated signature, they would see that, except as regards two letters, the whole signature bears no resemblance to mine

The same remark applies to the letter. The letter does not purport to be in my handwriting. We are not informed who has written it. It is not alleged even that it was written by anybody who was ever associated with me. The name of this anonymous letter-writer is not mentioned. I do not know who he can be. The writing is strange to me. I think I should insult myself if I said—I think however, that I perhaps ought to say it, in order that my denial may be full and complete—that I certainly never heard of the letter. I never directed such a letter to be written. I never saw such a letter before I saw it in *The Times* this morning. The subject-matter of the letter is preposterous on the surface. The phraseology of it is absurd—as absurd as any phraseology that could be attributed to me could possibly be. In every part of it, it bears absolute and irrefutable evidence of want of genuineness and want of authenticity. Politics are come to a pretty pass in this country when a leader of a party of eighty-six members has to stand up, at ten minutes past one, in the House of Commons, in order to defend himself from an anonymous fabrication, such as that which is contained in *The Times* of this morning. I have always held, with regard to the late Mr Forster, that his treatment of his political prisoners was a humane treatment, and a fair treatment; and I think for that reason alone, if for no other, he should have been shielded from such an attempt as was made on his life by the Invincible Association. I never had the slightest notion in the world that the life of the late Mr Forster was in danger, or that any conspiracy was on foot against him, or any other official in Ireland or elsewhere. I had no more notion than an unborn child that there was such a conspiracy as that of the Invincibles in existence, and no one was more surprised, more thunderstruck, and more astonished than I was when that bolt from the blue fell upon us in the Phœnix Park Murders. I know not in what direction to look for this calamity. It is no exaggeration to say that if I had been in the Park that day I would gladly have stood between Lord Frederick Cavendish and the daggers of the assassins, and, for the matter of that, between their daggers and Mr Burke too.

Now, Sir, I leave this subject. I have suffered more than any other man from that terrible deed in the Phœnix Park, and the Irish nation has suffered more than any other nation through it. I go for a moment to the noble Marquis the member for Rossendale (the Marquis of Hartington). The noble Marquis made a rather curious complaint of me. He said that, having denied point-blank a charge that had been made by him against me and the National League during the General Election last year, he was rather surprised that I did not again refer to the matter in the House of Commons. Well, I was rather surprised that the noble Marquis made a charge which he advanced without a particle of truth. He advanced that charge again to-night without a particle of proof, and I deny that charge, as I denied it before, in point-blank terms. I said it was absolutely untrue to say that the Irish National League or the Parliamentary Party had ever had any communication whatever, direct or indirect, with a Fenian organisation in America or this country. I further said that I did not know who the leaders of the Fenian organisation in this country or America were. I say that still. But the noble Marquis says he knows who they are, at least he tells us that Mr Alexander Sullivan—I believe that was the name mentioned —was president of the Clan-na-Gael, or Fenian organisation. When I asked him how he obtained his knowledge, he said that he obtained it from information he received as a member of Her Majesty's Government. That may be. But I am not in possession of the information with regard to the Clan-na-Gael which is possessed by the members of the present, or of the late Government. The Clan-na-Gael is a secret organisation; it is an oath-bound organisation; it gives no information with regard to its members to persons who are not members. I presume that the Government, if they obtained their information with regard to Alexander Sullivan, obtained it through their secret agents in America, through means which are not open to me in any capacity as a private person or a public politician. It is no answer to me to say that because the noble Marquis, a member of the late Government, with all the information obtainable by the wealth and resource of that Government at his disposal, believes Alexander Sullivan was a member and the leader of the Clan-na-Gael, or any secret organisation in America. I have never had any dealings with him, or any one else, either in Ireland or America, in respect to the doings or proceedings of any secret society whatsoever. All my doings on, and sayings and doings in Irish public life have been open and above board, and they have stood the test of the searching investigation of the three years' administration of the Crimes' Act by Lord Spencer, who has left it on record that neither any of my colleagues nor myself were in any way connected with the commission of, or approving of the commission of, any crime. Here are Lord Spencer's words spoken at Newcastle on the 21st of April 1886—

"Foremost among the many objections are these: It is said that you are going to hand over the government of Ireland to men who have encouraged—nay, some I have heard say even have directed—outrage and crime in Ireland. That is a very grave accusation. Now, I have been in a position in my official capacity to see and know nearly all the evidence that has been given in Ireland in regard to the murder and conspiracies to murder that took place in 1881 and 1882, and I can say, without doubt or hesitation, that I have neither heard nor seen any evidence of complicity with those crimes against any of the Irish representatives. It is right that I should clearly and distinctly express my condemnation of many of the methods by which they carried on their agitation. They often used language and arguments that were as unjustifiable as they were unfounded. They sometimes, perhaps from financial grounds, were silent when words would have been golden, when words might have had a great influence on the state of the country. They might even have employed men for their own legitimate purposes who had been employed in illegal acts by others; it is I must say, but, on the other hand, I believe those men to have an affection for, and a real interest in, the welfare of their country. Their ability has been shown and acknowledged in the House of Commons by all parties. I believe that, with full responsibility upon them, they will show that the only true way of obtaining the happiness and contentment of Ireland, is for the Government to maintain law and order, and defend the rights and privileges of every class and of every man in the country."

I cordially re-echo those words. I believe that that expresses the only real way of maintaining law and order in any country

—that you must obtain from the majority of the people of the country sympathy towards the law, without which the maintenance of the law is impossible; that you must show the majority of the community that the law is not only made, but that it is also administered for their benefit, and fairly and justly to all classes. In this way, and in this way only, can you ever obtain respect and sympathy for law and order in Ireland, or anywhere else. The present Bill may put down crime, or it may increase crime. If it puts it down, it will not put it down by instilling in the minds of the people a sympathy for law and order. Crime will die out only as the effect of sullen submission. You will be no farther, after you have been administering your Crimes Act, in the direction of the real maintenance of law and order than you were at the beginning; nay, not nearly so far. You are crushing by this iron Coercion Bill those beneficial symptoms in Ireland which a Government of wise statesmen and wise administrators would cherish and foster. You are preventing that budding of friendship between the two countries which this generation would never have witnessed in Ireland had it not been for the great exertions of the right hon. member for Midlothian. Who could have predicted, who would have ventured to predict, that the heat, the passion, the political antipathies engendered by the working of the Protection Act of 1881 and the Crimes Act of 1882 would have all disappeared in three or four short months, and that you would have had the English and the Irish people regarding each other as they did during that happy, that blessed period, and all this to be put an end to by the mad, the fatuous conduct of the present Government. You are going to plunge everything back into the seething cauldron of disaffection. You cannot see what the results of all this may be. We can only point to the experience of what has happened in past times. We anticipate nothing beneficial from this Bill, either to your country or to ours; and we should not be honest men if we did not warn you, with all the little force at our command, of the terrible dangers that may be before you.

T

I trust before this Bill goes into Committee, or at all events, before it leaves Committee, the great English people will make their voices heard, and impress upon their representatives that they must not go on any further with this coercive legislation. If this House and its majority have not sense enough to see this, the great heart of this country will see it, for I believe it is a great and generous heart, that can sympathise even when a question is concerned in reference to which there have been so many political antipathies. I am convinced, by what I have seen of the great meetings which have been held over the length and breadth of England and Scotland, that the heart of your nation has been reached—that it has been touched, and though our opponents may be in a majority to-day, that the real force of public opinion is not at their back. A Bill which is supported by men, many of whom are looking over their shoulders and behind them, like the soldiers of an army which a panic is beginning to reach, to see which is their readiest mode of retreat, is not likely to get through the difficult times before it emerges from Committee. The result will be modifications of the provisions of the most drastic of the Coercion Acts ever introduced against Ireland since 1833. Do not talk to me of comparing the suspension of the Habeas Corpus Act with the present Bill. We have suffered from both. We have suffered from some of the provisions of the present Bill, as well as from the Habeas Corpus Suspension Act, and we are able to compare the one with the other; and I tell you that the provisions of the Habeas Corpus Suspension Act empowered you to arrest and detain in prison those whom you suspected; but it guaranteed them humane treatment, which did much to soften the asperities that otherwise would have been bred between the two nations by that Act. Your prisoners under the Habeas Corpus Act were not starved and tortured as they will be under this. Your political prisoners were not put upon a plank bed, and fed on sixteen ounces of bread and water per day, and compelled to pick oakum, and perform hard labour, as they will be under this Bill. The Bill will be the means by which you will be enabled to subject your political prisoners to treatment in your gaols which you reserve in England for the worst of criminals, and it is idle to talk about comparison between the suspension of the Habeas Corpus Act, under which your prisoners were humanely and properly treated — although imprisonment is hard to bear under the best circumstances; but in the position in which this Bill will place them, your political prisoners will be deliberately starved with hunger and clammed with cold in your gaols. I trust in God, Sir, that this nation and this House may be saved from the degradation and the peril that the mistake of passing this Bill puts them in.

THE RIGHT HON. JOHN MORLEY ON HOME RULE.

Oxford, February 29th, 1888.

[On February 22nd, 1888, Lord Randolph Churchill, by the invitation of the Oxford Union Society, delivered a speech on Home Rule, opposing this Motion:—"That to satisfy the just aspirations of the Irish people, it is necessary that a Statutory Parliament be forthwith established in Dublin." On the Wednesday following Mr Morley treated the subject from the other side.]

Sir,—This is not my maiden speech to the Oxford Union, therefore it is not upon that ground that I venture to claim your indulgence. I was warned before I came here—and what I have heard since does not alter the weight of that warning—that I must be prepared to face a decisively hostile majority. But, in spite of that, I confess I felt in coming here none of those misgivings which the great Master of Romance made Louis XI. feel when he was infatuated enough to put himself in the hands of Charles the Bold of Burgundy. I feel perfectly confident that I shall receive from gentlemen present the courteous and kindly attention which Englishmen seldom refuse, even to their political opponents. It is quite true that at this moment party passion and political passion have reached a pitch of bitterness, and in some quarters I would almost say of ferocity, which has not been equalled in English history since the break-up of the Conservative party on the repeal of the Corn Laws forty-two years ago. In spite of that, I venture to commend the remarks which I shall intrude upon you to your favourable and indulgent consideration. I am accused very often of choosing to address what are called ignorant and credulous audiences. It cannot, at all events, be said that, in venturing to accept your very kind invitation to come here to-night, I have sought an audience which is ignorant, or an audience which is credulous. I suspect I shall find a scepticism in regard to my arguments the prevailing mood rather than credulity. An old Parliamentarian was once asked whether he had ever known a speech change opinions, and he answered: "Oh, yes, I have constantly known a speech to change opinions, but I have never known a speech to change votes." I do not aspire to-night to change votes; I content myself with the less arduous and more modest task of trying to change your opinions. I have listened with enormous interest and sincere pleasure to the debate which has proceeded since I entered the room. It has been animated and exhilarating, and if on one side I heard prejudices and sophisms to which I am accustomed, these prejudices and sophisms were expressed with very great ability, and with evident sincerity. The arguments on the other side—the side which I am here to press upon your attention—were admirably put, and I hope that they may have caused searching of hearts among some of those who are going to-night to vote against the Resolution before the House.

I am following to-night a very distinguished statesman whom you rightly welcomed last week. That noble Lord has shown himself to be a man of great shrewdness, some insight, and of very considerable liberality of mind. I am glad that you agree with me in that account. I hope you will go further with me when I say that, considering that he is a man of shrewdness, of insight, and of liberality of mind, it is no wonder that he has left Her Majesty's Government. But the noble Lord, in his speech, as far as practical issues were concerned, dealt mainly in the prophetic. Now the prophetic is a line in respect to Irish affairs in which the noble Lord does not at all excel. I remember very well in 1884, when the

Franchise Bill was before the House of Commons, that the noble Lord advocated and defended the enlargement of the franchise in Ireland, on the ground that the new voters whom that Bill would admit to political power would, on the whole, be a Conservative force, and would to some extent neutralise the Nationalist forces in the towns. The election of 1885 showed what foresight there was in that particular prophecy of the noble Lord; and I venture, with all respect, to warn you that the prophecies which he made to you last week, with respect to the probable course of events affecting self-government, will, within the next two or three years, be seen by you in this hall to have been as futile, as random, and as ill-founded as the prophecy which he made in 1885. You must not forget that the noble Lord himself was once a Home Ruler. [*A cry of "No, no!"*] Some gentleman says "No," but I assure him he is mistaken. Lord Randolph Churchill said in the House of Commons that he had been himself in Mr Butt's days inclined to look favourably upon Home Rule on Mr Butt's lines. It cannot be denied that Lord Randolph Churchill has been himself in his day a Home Ruler, and in his day he may be a Home Ruler again.

I will not detain you long in dealing with Lord Randolph Churchill's positions, but there are one or two of them so remarkable that I cannot allow them, considering the noble Lord's importance in the public eye, to pass without a word of remark. The noble Lord defined the Irish question, and I have no fault to find with that definition. He said that the Irish question arose from this fact, that we cannot obtain from Ireland, first of all, the same reverence for the law; secondly, the same material prosperity; and thirdly, the same contentment and tranquillity that we obtain in England and Scotland. I think that is a perfectly fair statement of the question. But then, does it not occur even to those who are going to vote against this Resolution to-night, that a statesman who admitted that we had obtained nothing better than a result so unsatisfactory, so discreditable, and so deplorable, would say: "Since the result has been such, we must change the system which has produced that result"? I think that is a fair way of answering the question as the noble Lord defines it. Did he so answer it? On the contrary, what he said was: "Since the result has been so discreditable, so deplorable, and so unsatisfactory, therefore I urge you, of the Oxford Union, to vote in favour practically of maintaining every jot and tittle of that system exactly as it now stands." I do not know how the school of logic goes in Oxford since my day; but I think if theoretic logic had been dealt with on the same principle as the noble Lord deals with questions of practical logic, he would have come away from the schools with no *testamur*.

And now I come to a more important part of the noble Lord's speech. What is the good of the policy which he pressed upon your attention? What is the bright and cheerful prospect that he holds out to you as the result of following that policy? It is so extraordinary and so remarkable from a man of the n ble Lord's shrewdness, that I really will beg your very close scrutiny of the position which he then took up, and of the very astonishing arguments to which he resorted. The noble Lord said that the Irish party is deeply divided into two sharply-opposed sections—one of them is the section which is content with Parliamentary, Constitutional, and peaceful methods; and the other is the party of violence and force. That is perfectly true. There have always been in Irish history these two opposed forces. It is a very old story; and one part of the story that I have always heard is that in the old days when the quarrel between the moral force party and the physical force party waxed very hot, it generally ended in the moral force party kicking the physical force party downstairs. The noble Lord reversed this. He said, depend upon it, as Home Rule receded in the distance, those who do not believe in the efficacy of Parliamentary methods would assert their superiority over those who do believe in Parliamentary methods. I will ask the House to put that proposition into rather plainer English. What it means is, that when Home Rule is put up n the shelf, the Fenian Movement—which the noble Lord truy remarked could scarcely be said to exist at the present m ment—would rise in undisputed triumph, and the Constitutional, peaceful, and Parliamentary movement would receive its quietus. And that is the noble Lord's argument in this House for opposing the Resolution now before it! I cannot imagine that the golden prospect which the noble Lord places before you is one that is really calculated to bring comfort or relief to British statesmen. I agree with him absolutely in his prediction. I have often said that if you do shelf Home Rule, if you once show the majority of the population of Ireland that they have nothing to hope for from the equity and common sense of Great Britain, then I firmly believe that you will have a revival of the old party of violence, of conspiracy, of sedition, and of treason. But the prospect that he regards with satisfaction and complacency—the prospect of the revival of the violent party and the depression of the peaceful party—that prospect fills me, and I hope fills all well-considering men here, whether they be Unionists or Home Rulers, with repugnance and horror. We shall regard the revival of such a state of things as most dishonouring to England, and as merciless t Ireland.

But I would ask, Gentlemen, to press the noble Lord's argument home, to test it and to probe it to the bottom from his ow speech. You are to force Home Rule back, in order to restore those halcyon days of which the noble Lord himself gave you an account when, as he said, and I daresay correctly said, half the population of Ireland were either sworn Fenians or else in close sympathy with Fenianism. That is extreme language. But what is still more extraordinary is the purpose and object with which you are to effect this most curious manœuvre. What was the purpose and the object of shelving Home Rule wit' the prospect of a revival of Fenianism? Pursue the noble Lord's train of thought. You are to raise Fenianism from the dead, you are to stamp out the Constitutional men, and to give new life to the men of violence and conspiracy; you are to fan into a glow all the sullen elements of insurgency in Ireland, in order, forsooth, that the Empire should be the better able to face all these troubles that are coming upon Europe, as the noble Lord thinks, and may truly think—to face all these troubles with concentrated strength and undivided resources! Surely of all extraordinary short cuts to concentrated strength and undivided resources, none can be more extraordinary than to take care to keep a disaffected province at your very gates. The moral charm of such a policy as that is only equalled by its practical common sense. Why, the other day, in the wilds of Donegal, there was occasion—or the Government thought there was occasion—to arrest a certain priest, and to carry this priest in the midst of his flock to the Court-house, where he was about to be tried, it required a force of horse, foot, and artillery of something like 500 or 600 of Her Majesty's troops. Now it does not need a very elaborate arithmetical calculation to satisfy ourselves if it takes 600 troops to safely look after one insignificant parish priest in the wilds of Donegal for trial, how many troops will it take to hold Ireland when half the population are sworn Fenians, or else in close sympathy with Fenianism.

So much for the noble Lord's argument, because that was the real argument of his speech. No, Sir, gentlemen here may depend upon it that, if the time ever comes, as it has come before, when this great and mighty realm shall be called once more by destiny or her duty to face a world in arms in some high cause and policy of State, she will only have her strength concentrated and her resources undivided on the condition that her statesmen and her people have plucked up the root of strife in Ireland, and turned the domestic enemy on our flank into our friend and our ally. But I think we may all agree to recognise the hollowness of the cause, when so able a man as the noble Lord, appealing to you in the name of the Empire and the strength of the Empire, argues for the perpetuation of a state of things which morally, and politically, and materially weakens, disables, and cripples the forces of the Empire. So much for the goal of the policy which the noble Lord pressed upon you. It is the same goal which Ministers—the same Lord is no longer a Minister—it is the same goal which Ministers are constantly alleging in the House of Commons that they place before themselves, and most paradoxical and extraordinary things they say in defence of the proposition that they are reaching the goal. What is the goal? The goal is to give to Ireland the same reverence for the laws, the same material prosperity, the same contentment and tranquillity, that we have in England and Scotland. Yes; but there are some very astonishing congratulations to be heard in the Ministerial camp as to the speed with which and as to the manner in which they are nearing that goal. For instance, the Attorney-General said the other day that they must be considered to be surmounting the difficulties that concerned English government in Ireland. Well, but why? The Attorney-General said that the Government were surmounting difficulties in Ireland, because meetings and movements which had once been open were now secret. I am sure that many of you, though you have other things to do than to follow very closely the history of Ireland, and of the good and bad movements in Ireland, must be well aware that the great bane of Ireland and of Scotland when they cross the seas—whether they go to the United States or the English Colonies—has been secret association. The great triumph, I will say, of the League and of the National Movement since the year 1880, has been that those associations which formerly were secret, and therefore dangerous, are now open, and will be open as long as this most reckless Government will allow them to be. Ask yourselves—I appeal to your candour—ask yourselves whether, if treason is taught, and if murder is hatched, is treason likely to be taught, is murder likely to be hatched, in open meetings? No, it is impossible. But what is possible? I am afraid that what is certain is, that if you repress public combination—if you go through that odious and ridiculous process which is called driving discontent beneath the surface—if you do that, you are taking the surest steps that can be taken to have treason taught and murder hatched.

Now, I ask gentlemen here before they vote to-night—or, at all events, to turn it over in their minds after they have voted whether the goal is being reached by the present policy, a policy which the rejection of this Resolution encourages and endorses. I am not talking away from the Resolution, because I am trying to call the attention of gentlemen to the alternative of the policy set out in the Resolution of the hon. mover. I hope, therefore, you will agree that I am keeping close to the point. The point is the alternative of the policy of Home Rule. We have had since the Session began a series of debates in the House of Commons upon the administration of the Coercion Act. Of course I am not an impartial witness, but I think that the subtle something which is called the impression of a great assembly, the impression of the House of Commons, is that the Government have not shown that they have attained any of the ends which they proposed to themselves when they passed this piece of legislation. All the tests that can be applied to the success of the operation of that Act appear to me to show that it has achieved none of the ends that were proposed. Have they put down the League? It is perfectly certain that the League is as strong as ever. I know that an attempt is made to make out the contrary case, but from any test that you can apply to the strength of the League, whether it be to the number of branches, to the copiousness of subscriptions, or to the numbers at the meetings—according to any of these tests, so far as I can make out, the League is not in the least degree weakened. Have they put down the Plan of Campaign? It is very clear that the Plan of Campaign has not been put down. It is true, to come to a third point, that there is a great decline in boycotting. That is quite true, but the point that you have got to make good is that the decline in boycotting is due to the Government policy. There are more explanations than one for the decline of boycotting. If you want my explanation, since you have been so very kind as to ask me to come here, and are so good as to listen to me so attentively, my explanation is that the decline of boycotting is due, first of all, to the fact that a great many of the boycotted persons have wisely, or unwisely, yielded to and joined the League; and, secondly, what is a far more important consideration, boycotting has declined because a great many landlords have under pressure, or from other motives, made those reductions which equity required and which the peace of the country demanded.

Now, I think it is very important that you should try and realise for yourselves what the policy of Coercion is in actual practice. I am not going to detain this House very long by reading extracts. One of the most respected lawyers in the North of England and a very old friend of mine, who is a very experienced man, was in the Court at Galway on the 13th of this month during a trial of twelve men for rioting. Now, this is what he says —

> "There was a great crowd to welcome Mr Blunt on the evening of January 7. When Mr Blunt was brought to the giol at Galway the people were orderly on the whole, but they cheered for Mr Blunt, and they pushed through the police at the station in their anxiety to see Mr Blunt."

Was there any harm in that? My friend goes on to say—

> "Orders were given to clear the station."

I will ask you to mark that I am not criticising what happened. I want to get you into Court. My friend goes on to say—

> "The station was cleared in half a minute, the police batoning the people and knocking them down. What attempt was made on February 13 to bring any offence home to the twelve accused persons? All that could be urged against them was that they had waited for and had cheered Mr Blunt."

And I think they had as much right to do so as if they had been in Oxford Station. To continue—

> "The charge was not dismissed, it was adjourned and resumed on February 14, the next day. The Crown then called four fresh policemen, of whose evidence no notice had been given to the accused, and these four fresh policemen told a new tale. The crowd, which, according to the evidence of the day before, was described as orderly, was now described as disorderly. It was now represented that the police had been interfered

with and were in actual peril. There was stone-throwing, but it was outside the station, and no attempt was made to connect the accused with anything that took place outside the station, or anything worse than shouting or cheering. The result was that eleven or twelve of the accused men were sentenced to a fortnight's or a month's imprisonment with hard labour; and one of them calling out that he would do the same again, the magistrate, with what I must call a truly contemptible vindictiveness, said, 'You shall have another week's imprisonment for saying that.' The upshot of the whole case was that these men—two of them, mind you, Town Commissioners, respected public men in the confidence of their fellow-citizens — were punished, not for concerting a riotous meeting, not for throwing stones, not for attacking the police, not for doing anything to alarm reasonable and courageous persons, but simply for waving their hats and caps in honour of Mr Blunt."

Now, I say that is, unfortunately, a typical case. [*Cries of* "No."] Yes, it is a typical case. If gentlemen who doubt that will take the trouble, as I have done, to read the reports from day to day of what goes on in these Courts, if they will take the trouble to hear evidence that Englishmen, not partisan Irishmen, have seen administered in these Courts, they will agree that this is a typical case, that men are treated violently, that they are then summoned for an offence which is not properly proved—[*A cry of* "No."]—what I say I hope to show in a moment—and for acts which are not in themselves an offence or a crime.

Somebody protested when I used the word "prove." I will ask him, and I will ask the House, to listen to a little extract which I am going to read to show the kind of evidence which in these Courts is thought good enough. It is the case of a certain Irish member, Mr Sheehy, who was convicted, and this is a very short passage from the cross-examination of the shorthand writer. Mr Sheehy was brought up for words spoken; it was vitally important to know what were the words spoken, for which he was about to have inflicted upon him a very severe punishment. This is, in a very few words, a passage from the cross-examination of the Government reporter—

"Did you ever study shorthand?"
"I did not. I might look over the book, but that is all. As far as I know, shorthand is not studied by any man in the barracks. There was no

c____l' to my knowledge, in Trench Park on the day of the meeting w__ knew shorthand. The meeting lasted from three o'clock till a quarter ____ Mr Sheehy was speaking the greater part of the time. When Mr Sheehy spoke a sentence or a sentence and a half, I took down all I c___ remember at the time. I took no note of what he would be saying w__le I was taking down the two sentences which I remembered at the time. I consider Mr Sheehy a slow speaker."

"While you would be writing a sentence, how many sentences would he __ ahead of you?"

"Well," said the constable or reporter, "he might get two or three."

"Then when you would complete your sentence, would you skim over what he had said in the meantime and then catch him up again?"

"Yes, I would try and remember what he would say in the meantime."

"When you say that you would try and remember, what do you mean?"

"I mean that when I heard a sentence or two I would take that down, __ I pay no attention to what he would say in the meantime."

How many gentlemen here must have been in English Courts, and heard the careful, austere, and impressive standards which the Judges of those Courts apply to evidence? I say, when you hear such evidence as that, do you not think you are listening to the proceedings of a Court in a Comic Opera? Pray remark that in a charge of this kind a phrase or a qualification of a phrase may be of vital importance. It may make all the difference in the construction and the interpretation that the Court would put upon a word spoken; and yet you see that the qualifying phrases and words might have been dropped out while the reporter was taking down the other sentences. It is a sheer caricature of evidence.

I must inflict one more story upon you—it is the last—because you must know it is no use using vague general words about Coercion. Realize what Coercion means. I ought to say that those words I have just read and that case was mentioned in the House of Commons. Those words were read out in the House of Commons. No answer was attempted to them by the Government. I am not going to use any case which has not been challenged in the House of Commons. Well, here is a case, of a certain Patrick Corcoran. Patrick Corcoran is the foreman printer of *The Cork Examiner*. He is therefore purely a mechanic. He was tried, his name being on the imprint of the newspaper, for publishing proceedings of the suppressed branches of the National League. On the hearing of the first summons the joint-editor and manager came forward and said he alone was responsible for everything that appeared in the paper, and that Corcoran was a mere mechanic, and had no power or control in any sense or degree over the matter published. Well, of course, as he had no control over the matter published, he could not have what the lawyers call that guilty mind which was necessary, according to the Act, for the commission of the offence; because the Act requires that this publication should be uttered with a view of promoting the objects of the incriminated association. Well, Corcoran, this mechanic, was sent to prison for a month. [*Cries of* "Shame!"] Yes, and mark the point. Most of you know that if a sentence is for more than a month, then there is a right of appeal. Corcoran's counsel implored the Bench to add a week to the sentence so that there might be this right of appeal, or else to state a case for a Superior Court, which would have been the same thing. The Magistrate refused even that. That is rather sharp; but that was not all. They took up another charge, in substance the same, for publishing reports of meetings number two, and on the footing of the second summons they gave Corcoran another month's imprisonment. I hope gentlemen see the point—that by this method of accumulated penalties they managed to give him a two months' sentence, and yet to deprive him of the right to appeal which he would have had from a single two months' sentence.

These are illustrations which I commend to the attention of gentlemen who oppose this Resolution, because they are inevitable features in the system which is the alternative to the system advocated in the Resolution. [*Cries of* "No, no!"] Well, I will have one word to say about that in one moment. But I ask you, in the meantime: Can you wonder that under such circumstances as those of which I have given you three actual illustrations—that Irishmen do not respect the law and do not revere the tribunals where that law is administered? Imagine how the existence of such a state of things would affect you who are Englishmen. Would you endure to be under exceptional repressive legislation of this kind so administered? I do not believe you would. Englishmen never have acquiesced in legislation and administration of that kind; they have fought against it from age to age, and Irishmen will rightly fight against it from age to age.

I listened with especial interest, and, if I may say so, with admiration to the speech of the gentleman who preceded me, in whom I am glad to recognise the germs of hereditary gifts; and, if it is not impertinent in me to say so, I hope he will continue to cultivate those remarkable gifts; and—forgive me for saying so—I hope he may one day use them in a better cause. The hon. gentlemen struck the keynote. I accept that note. He said, "Think of the sons and daughters of Ireland." Think of the sons and daughters of Ireland; it is for their sake as much as for our own, not more, but as much— it is for the sake of the sons and daughters of Ireland that I am and have been an advocate of giving Ireland responsibility and self-government. Can you wonder? Put yourselves in the place of the sons and daughters of Ireland. These transactions, of which I have given you a very inadequate specimen, fill their minds. They hear scarcely anything else in the speeches of their leaders and in the talk of those in whom they have confidence. They talk of these things when they meet at fairs, when they meet at chapel, when they meet at athletic sports. And they read scarcely anything else in the newspapers. And if they cannot read, then their children read these proceedings out to them. Now think of a generation growing up in this demoralising and poisoned atmosphere of defiance and suspicion and resentment, and think whether you are doing your duty; think how you are preparing for the growth of a generation in Ireland in whom the spirit of citizenship shall be wholesome and shall be strong. It is of no avail to tell me that a lawyer in his study has this or that objection to this or that section. What I see in Ireland is a population in whom you are doing your best to breed want of reverence for the law, distrust of the tribunals, and resentment against the British rule which fastens that yoke upon their necks.

When I said that the Government were pursuing a policy of pure repression, somebody objected. I should like him to be kind enough to tell me what other dish there is on the Ministerial table for Ireland, except repression. Let us go to the law and the testimony. We used to be told—I see old and respected friends of mine around me who are Liberal Unionists, and their party used to say that they would not assent to Home Rule, but that they would assent to an extension of local government in Ireland. [*A cheer.*] I am glad to hear that cheer, but it is a very forlorn cry. I will ask you for a single instant to listen to the history of the promise of the extension of local government in Ireland. In 1842, forty-six long years ago, a Commission reported in favour of amending the system of county government in Ireland. A Bill was brought in to carry out that recommendation in 1849. It was rejected. It was brought in in 1853, and it was rejected; again in 1856 it was rejected; again another in 1857, which also was rejected. Then there was a pause in the process of rejection until 1868, when a Parliament and the Government of the day resorted to the soothing and comforting plan of appointing a Select Committee. That, just like the previous Commission, issued a copious and an admirable report, but nothing more was done. In 1875 a Bill was brought in for County Reform in Ireland, and in 1879 another Bill was brought in which did not touch the evils that called for remedy. In 1881, in the time of the Gladstone Administration, and at a time when Ireland, remember, was in a thousand times worse condition than the most sinister narrator can say she is now, the Queen in her Speech was made to say that a Bill for the extension of local government of Ireland would be brought in; nothing was done. In 1886 the distinguished man whom you had here last week himself said—I heard him say it one afternoon—he made this promise in the name of the Government of which he was a leading and an important member—that it was the firm intention of the Government to bring in a measure with a view of placing all control of local government in Ireland in the hands of the Irish people. [*Cheers.*] Some of you cry, "Hear, hear," but that is all gone. Listen to what Lord Hartington, the Master of the Government, has since said. The noble Lord has said that no scheme for the extension of local government in Ireland can be entertained until there has been a definite repudiation of nationality by the Irish people. I do not want to press that too far, but at all events you will agree with me that it postpones the extension of local government in Ireland to a tolerably remote day. Do not let Liberal Unionists deceive themselves by the belief that there is going to be a moderate extension of local government for Ireland. Do not let them retain any such illusion. Proposals for local government will follow these Royal Commissions, Committees, Bills, Motions, into limbo, and we shall hear no more of extension of local government. This is only one illustration among many others, which, taken together, amount to a demonstration of the unfitness and incompetence of our Imperial Parliament for dealing with the political needs, the admitted and avowed political needs, of Ireland. One speaker said something about fisheries. There was a Select Committee appointed in 1884, and there was another Royal Commission reporting a few weeks ago, but I am not sanguine enough to think that more will be done in consequence of the recommendations of that Commission than has been done in consequence of the recommendation of others. Again, there are the Irish railways. I was wrong, by the way, that a Royal Commission was on fisheries—it was on Irish industries generally, fisheries included. On the question of railways there was a Royal Commission in 1867, and a small Committee was appointed in 1868. There were copious and admirable reports. There is another copious and admirable report laid on the table of the House of Commons this week. Nothing has been done, and I do not believe anything will be done. That is another field in which

Ireland abounds in requirements and necessities, and which the British Parliament has not the power, knowledge, or inclination to deal with or to touch.

One gentleman who spoke to-night with great ability—and if people think these things I do not know why they should not be said—reproduced to my regret the old talk about the Hottentots. I confess this is the most painful part of the present controversy—that there should be men (I am sure he is one of them) of generous minds, of public spirit and patriotism, who talk, and sincerely talk, of union, and the incorporation of Ireland with Britain, and yet think that this kind of language, and what is far more, this kind of feeling, is a way likely to produce incorporation and union. I have seen a good deal of Irishmen. I saw a great, a tremendous crowd of Irishmen the other day on their own soil. They comported themselves, many tens and scores of thousands of them, comported themselves with a good humour, a perfect order, a temper generally of which any capital in Europe—London, Paris, Berlin, or Vienna—might have been proud. I think you can do something better with such a people than alienate them by calling them and by thinking of them as Hottentots, or as in any way inferior to ourselves. That is not the way to have union and incorporation. That is not the way to make the Empire stronger. And I apply the same to the language that is used about the Irish members. I am not prepared to defend all that the Irish members have said and done. No, and I am not prepared to defend all that English members have done. But I ask here, as I asked in Dublin, is there to be no amnesty? Is there never to be an act of oblivion? These men, after all, have forced upon the British Legislature, and have extorted from the British Legislature, laws for the benefit of their own down-trodden and oppressed people. Those laws were either right or wrong. If they were wrong, the British Legislature ought not to have passed them. If they were right, you ought to be very much obliged to the Irish members for awakening your sense of equity and of right.

I return again—I am going to conclude in a moment—I return again to the point. You have the future in your hands, because what has been said is true; the future depends upon the opinions of the men between twenty and thirty, which, I take it, is the average of the audience I have the honour of addressing. What is the condition of Ireland? Here, too, I will repeat what I said in Dublin. In Ireland you have a beggared gentry; a bewildered peasantry; a random and harsh and aimless system of government; a population fevered by political power and not sobered by political responsibility. This is what you have to deal with; and I say here, with a full sense of important responsibility, that rather than go on in face of that distracted picture, with the present hard, incoherent, cruel system of government in Ireland, rather than do that I would assent to the proposal that has been made, if that were the only alternative, by a great representative of the Unionist party, by Lord Grey. And what does Lord Grey suggest? Lord Grey suggests that the Lord-Lieutenant should be appointed for ten years, and during those ten years—it is a strong order—during those ten years he is to make what laws he thinks fit without responsibility either to Ministers or to Parliament. It is a strong order, but I declare—and I believe that Mr Parnell has said that he agrees—that I would rather see Ireland made a Crown Colony to-morrow than go on in the present hypocritical and inefficient system of sham representation. You may then have the severity of paternal repression, but you will have the beneficence of paternal solicitude and supervision. What you now have is repression and neglect; and repression and neglect you will have until you call the Irish leaders into council and give to the majority of the Irish people that power in reality which now they have only in name.

One minute more and I will sit down. The Resolution raises very fairly the great issue that now divides and engages all serious minds in this country—the issue which has broken up a great political party, which has tried and tested more than one splendid reputation, and in which the Liberal party have embarked all their hopes and fortunes as resolutely and as ungrudgingly as their forefathers did in the case of Catholic Emancipation. The opponents of this Resolution ought to have told us, what no opponent to-night did tell us--for I listened very carefully—they ought to have told us what it is they mean. Merely to vote a blank and naked negative to this Resolution? It is not enough, it cannot be all, merely to say "No" to this Resolution. You are not going through the familiar process of rejecting an academic Motion or an abstract proposition. In refusing this proposition you are adopting an Amendment. I have taken the liberty to draft a Unionist Amendment. I will gladly place it in the hands of any Unionist Member who may think it expedient to move it. This is the alternative Amendment to the Resolution of the hon. mover—"That, inasmuch as Coercion, after being tried in every form and under all varieties, has failed to bring to Ireland that order and content we all earnestly desire, Coercion shall be made the permanent law of the land; That as perfect equality between England and Ireland is the key to a sound policy, Coercion shall be the law in Ireland and shall not be the law in England; That as decentralisation and local government have been long recognised and constantly promised as a necessary reform in Irish affairs, the time has at length arrived for definitely abandoning all reform in Irish local government; That since the backward condition, and the many admitted needs of Ireland urgently call for the earnest and unremitting attention of her rulers, the exclusive attention of this Parliament shall be devoted to the consideration of English, Scotch, and Welsh affairs; That, in view of the fact that representative institutions are the glory and strength of the United Kingdom, the Constitutional demands of the great majority of the Irish representatives shall be disregarded, and these representatives shall have no voice in Irish affairs and no share in Irish government; and, finally, That as Mr Pitt declared the great object of the Union to be to make the

Empire more secure by making Ireland more free and more happy, it is the duty of every true Unionist to make Ireland more miserable in order to prevent her from being free."

That, Sir, is the Amendment which you are, I fear, presently going to vote. [*Cries of* "No!"] Yes, you are. That is what you are going to vote, and I have failed in the speech which you have most kindly and indulgently listened to, if you do not see that that Amendment, with its stream of paradoxes and incoherencies, represents the Unionist policy. That is a policy which judgment condemns and which conscience forbids.

RICHARD COBDEN ON THE CORN LAWS.

HOUSE OF COMMONS, FEBRUARY 24TH, 1842.

[THE original motion for the total repeal of the Corn Laws, passed in 1815, was made in the House by the Hon. Chas. Pelham Villiers (now known as "the Father of the House of Commons"), February 18th, 1842, when he presented and read a numerously-signed petition from the three kingdoms praying that the Corn Laws be immediately repealed.]

SIR,—The right hon. gentleman who has just sat down (Sir Howard Douglas) would have given still greater satisfaction to the House if he had assured us that he would, when he spoke, always keep strictly to the subject-matter under discussion. I must be allowed to say that my hon. friend the member for Wolverhampton (the Hon. C. P. Villiers) has very just grounds for complaining that in all this discussion, to which I have been listening for seven nights, while there has been much talk of our trade with China, and of the war with Syria, while there has been much contest between parties and partisans, there has been very little said upon the question really in hand. I may safely say that, on the other side, not one speaker has grappled with the question so ably laid down by my hon. friend. That question simply is, how far it is just, honest, and expedient, that any tax whatever should be laid upon the food of the people. This is the question we have to decide; and when I heard the right hon. Baronet (Sir Robert Peel) so often express the deep sympathy he felt for the working classes, I did expect that he would not have finished his last speech without giving some little consideration to the case of the working man in connection with this question. I will venture to call the attention of the Committee to the question of the Bread Tax as connected with the labouring classes, as it bears upon the wages of labour; and I call upon you all to meet me upon neutral ground while we discuss the interests of those working people who have no representatives in this House. As I hear from the other side so many and such strong expressions of sympathy, I call upon them to give practical proof of the existence of that sympathy with the hard labouring population, and not to delay until they are reduced to that state when they can only receive the benefits of your legislation in the abject condition of pauperism.

Sir, in reading, which I have done with some attention, the reports of the debates which took place in 1815, prior to the passing of the Corn Bill of that year, I have been struck with the observation that all who took part in that discussion agreed on one point of the subject, namely, that the price of food regulated the rate of wages. That principle was not only laid down by one side of the House, but it met with the concurrence of both. Men the most opposite in political opinions I find agreeing upon that principle. Mr Horner, Mr Baring, Mr Frankland Lewis, Mr Philips, Mr Western, those who opposed the Corn Law, and those who strenuously advocated its principle, all alike agreed upon the same point, that the price of food regulated the price of labour. So completely did they agree, that one speaker laid down the principle mathematically, and framed a computation in figures to show the relative proportions in which the principle would work, and to what extent the payment of labour would rise or fall in ratio to the rise or fall of the price of food. The same delusion existed amongst the capitalists out of doors. There was a petition presented in 1815, signed by the most intelligent merchants and manufacturers in Manchester, praying that the Corn Law should not pass, because it would so raise the rate of wages that the British manufacturers would no longer be able to compete with those abroad, who had to pay wages so much less in amount. That delusion certainly did then exist; but I have been struck with the deepest sorrow to observe that the minds of many men who bear their part in the discussion now should still be labouring under the same erroneous impression. The great body of those who legislated in 1815 passed their Bill in the honest delusion that the operation of the law would be such as I have described. I believe that if the fact, if the true state of the case had been then known, if they had known what now we know, that law would never have been passed in 1815. Every party in the House, and many out of doors, were deceived; but there was one party which was not deluded—the party most interested in the question—namely, the working classes. They were not deluded, for they saw with instinctive sagacity, without the aids of learning and education, without the pretence of political wisdom, what would be the operation of the law upon the rate of wages. Therefore it was, that when that law was passed your House was surrounded by the excited populace of London, and you were compelled to keep back an enraged people from your doors by the point of the bayonet. When that law passed Murder ensued. Yes, I call it Murder, for a coroner's jury returned a verdict of Wilful Murder against the soldiers. The disturbances were not confined to London; but throughout the North of England, from 1815 to 1819, when the great meeting took place on Peter's-field, there never was a meeting in the north of England in which banners were not displayed with inscriptions of "No Corn Laws!" There was no mistake in the minds of the multitudes upon this question. It was always understood by them. Do not let hon. gentlemen suppose that there is any mistake in the minds of the working classes upon this topic. There never was, and there is not now. They may not indeed cry out exclusively for the repeal of the Corn Laws; they have looked beyond the question, and they have seen, at the same time, other evils greater than this which they are now calling upon you to remedy; and when they raise the cry of Universal Suffrage and The People's Charter, do not let hon. gentlemen opposite suppose, because the Anti-Corn Law League may, perchance, have run into collision with the masses upon some points, that the people are consequently favourable to the existence of the Corn Laws.

What has surprised me more than anything is to find that in this House, where lecturers are, of all men, so much decried, there exists on the other side such an ignorance upon this subject. [*Cries of* "Oh! Oh!"] Yes, I say, an ignorance upon this subject that I never saw equalled in any body of working men in the North of England. ["Oh! Oh!"] Do you think that the fallacy of 1815, which, to my astonishment, I heard put forth in the House last week, namely, that wages rise and fall with the price of food, can prevail with the minds of the working men after the experience of the last three years? Have you not had bread higher during that time than during any three years during the last twenty years? Yes. Yet during those three years the wages of labour in every branch of industry have suffered a greater decline than in any three years before. Still, hon. gentlemen opposite, with the reports of Committees before them, which, if they would take the trouble to consult them, would prove the decline of wages within those three years, are persisting in maintaining the doctrine that the price of food regulates the rate of wages under the belief that this new law will keep up the price of labour. Then I am told that the price of labour in this country is so much higher than the wages abroad, that the Corn Laws must be kept up in order to keep up labour to the proper level. Sir, I deny that labour in this country is higher paid than on the Continent. On the contrary, I am prepared to prove, from documents on the table of your own House, that the price of labour is cheaper here than in any other part of the globe. I hear an expression of dissent on the other side, but I say to hon. gentlemen, when they measure the labour of an Englishman against the labour of the foreigner, they measure a day's labour indeed with a day's labour, but they forget the relative quality of the labour. I maintain that if quality is to be the test, the labour of England is the cheapest in the world. The Committee which sat on Machinery in the last

Session but one, demonstrated by their Report that labour on the Continent is dearer than in England. You have proof of it. Were it not so, do you think you would find in Germany, France, or Belgium so many English workmen? Go into any city from Calais to Vienna, containing a population of more than 10,000 inhabitants, and will you not find numbers of English artisans working side by side with the natives of the place, and earning twice as much as they do, or even more? Yet the masters who employ them declare, notwithstanding the pay is higher, that the English labour is cheaper to them than the native labour. Yet we are told that the object of the manufacturers in repealing the Corn Laws is to lower wages to the level of the Continent. It was justly said by the hon. member for Kilmarnock that the manufacturers did not require to lower the rate of wages in order to gain high profits. If you want proof of the prosperity of manufacturers, you will find it when wages are high; but when wages drop, the profits of the manufacturer drop also. I think manufacturers take too intelligent and enlightened a view of their own position and interest to suppose that the impoverishment of the multitudes they employ can promote or increase manufacturing prosperity.

Sir, by deteriorating such a vast population as that employed in manufactures, you run the risk of spoiling not the animal man only, but the intellectual creature also. It is not from the wretched that great things can emanate; it is not a potato-fed population that ever led the world in arts or arms, in manufactures or commerce. If you want your people to be virtuous or happy, you must take care that they are well fed. Upon this assumption, then, that the manufacturers want to reduce wages, and upon the assumption that the Corn Laws keep up the price of labour, we are going to pass a law to tax the food of the hardworking, deserving population! What must be the result? You have heard, from the right hon. Baronet, Sir Robert Peel, an answer to the fallacy about our competing with foreign manufacturers. He has told you we export forty or fifty millions. We do then already compete with foreigners. You tax the bones and muscles of your people. You put a double weight upon their shoulders, and then you turn round upon them and tell them to run a race with Germany and France. I would ask, with Mr Deacon Hume, who has been before quoted in this House, "To whom do the energies of the British people belong? Are they theirs or are they yours?" Think you that these energies were given to the English people that they might struggle for a bare existence, whilst you take from them half of what they earn? Is this doing justice to the "high-mettled racer"? Why, you don't treat your horses so. You give your cattle food and rest in proportion to their toil, but men in England are now actually treated worse. Yes, tens of thousands of them were last winter treated worse than your dogs and your horses. What is the pretence upon which you tax the people's food? We have been told by the right hon. Baronet that the object of the law is to fix a certain price for corn. Since I have been listening to this debate, in which I heard it proposed by a Prime Minister to fix the price of corn, I doubted whether or not we had gone back to the days of our Edwards again, and whether we had or had not travelled back some three or four centuries, when they used to fix the price of a table-cloth or a pair of shoes. What an avocation for a legislator! To fix the price of corn! Why, that should be done in the open market by the dealers. You don't fix the price of cotton, or silk, or iron, or tin. But how are you going to fix this price of corn? Going back some ten years, the right hon. Baronet finds the average price of corn is 56s. 10d., and therefore, says he, I propose to keep up the price of wheat from 54s. to 58s. The right hon. Baronet's plan means that or nothing.

I have heard something about the prices which it has been proposed by legislation to affix to wheat. I remember that Lord Willoughby D'Eresby said the minimum price ought to be 58s., and I see by the newspapers that the Duke of Buckingham has just announced his opinion that 60s. ought to be the lowest. There is one hon. gentleman in this House who, I hope, will speak on this subject—for I have seen him endeavouring to catch the Speaker's eye—and who has gone a little more into particulars respecting the market price he intends to procure for commodities by Act of Parliament. I see in a useful little book called "The Parliamentary Pocket Companion," in which there are some nice little descriptions given of ourselves, under the head "Cayley," that that gentleman is described as being the advocate of " such a course of legislation with regard to agriculture as will keep wheat at 64s. a quarter, new milk cheese at 52s. to 60s. per cwt., wool and butter at 1s. per lb. each, and other produce in proportion." Now it might be very amusing that there were to be found some gentlemen still at large who advocated the principle of the interposition of Parliament to fix the price at which articles should be sold ; but when we find a Prime Minister coming down to Parliament to avow such principles, it really becomes anything but amusing. I ask the right hon. Baronet, and I pause for a reply : Is he prepared to carry out that principle in the articles of cotton and wool? [Sir ROBERT PEEL: It is impossible to fix the price of food by legislation.] Then on what are we legislating? I thank the right hon. Baronet for his avowal. Perhaps, then, he will oblige us by not trying to do so. Supposing, however, that he will make the attempt, I ask the right hon. gentleman, and again I pause for a reply : Will he try to legislate so as to keep up the prices of cotton, silk, and wool? No reply. Then we have come to this conclusion—that we are not legislating for the universal people. We are openly avowing that we are met here to legislate for a class against the people. When I consider this I don't marvel, although I have seen it with the deepest regret, and I may add indignation, that we have been surrounded during the course of the debates of the last week by an immense body of police. [*Cries of* "Oh! oh!" *and laughter from the Ministerial side.*]

I will not let this subject drop, even though I may be greeted with laughter. It is no laughing matter to those who have got no wheat to sell, nor money to purchase it from those who have. If the agriculturists are to have the benefit of a law founded on the calculation of ten years' average, to keep up their price at that average, I ask, are the manufacturers to have it too? Take the manufacturers of the Midland counties, the manufacturers of the very articles the agriculturists consume. Their goods have depreciated 30 per cent. in the last ten years. Are they to continue to exchange their commodities for the corn of the landlord, who has the benefit of a law keeping up his price on a calculation of a ten years' average, without the iron manufacturer having the benefit of the same calculation? I have great doubts whether this is legislation at all. I deny that it is honest legislation. It is no answer for the right hon. Baronet to say that he cannot, even if he wished, pass a law to keep up the price of manufactures. It is no satisfaction for being injured by a Prime Minister to be told that he has not the power, even if he has the will, to make amendment. I only ask him to abstain from doing that for which he cannot make atonement, and surely there is nothing unreasonable in that request. I have but touched upon the skirts of this subject. I ask the right hon. Baronet whether, while he fixes the scale of prices to secure the landowners 56s. a quarter, he has got also a sliding scale for wages? I know but of one class of labourers in this country whose interests are well secured by the sliding scale of corn duties, and that class is the clergy of the Established Church, whose tithes are calculated upon the averages. But I want to know what you will do with the hardworking classes of the community, the labouring artisans, if the price of bread is to be kept up by Act of Parliament. Will you give them a law to keep up their rate of wages? You will say that you cannot keep up the rate of wages; but that is no reason why you should pass a law to mulct the working man of one-third of the loaf he earns. I know well the way in which the petitions of the hand-loom weavers were received in this House. "Poor ignorant men," you said, "they know not what they ask, they are not political economists, they do not know that the price of labour, like other commodities, finds its own level by the ordinary law of supply and demand. We can do nothing for them." But I ask, then, why do you pass a law to keep up the price of corn, and at the same time say you cannot pass a law to keep up the price of the poor man's labour? This is the point of view in which the country are approaching this question; and the flimsy veil of sophistry you are throwing over the question, and the combination of figures put together and dovetailed to answer a particular purpose, will not satisfy the people of England, till you show them that you are legislating impartially for the advantage of all classes, and not for the exclusive benefit of one. What are the pretexts upon which this Corn Tax is justified? We have heard, in the first place, that there are exclusive burthens borne by the agriculturists. I heard one explanation given of those burthens by a facetious gentleman who sits near me. He said that the only exclusive burthens upon the land which he knew of were mortgages. I think the country has a right to know, and indeed I think it would have been no more than what was due to this House if those burthens of which we have heard so much had been named and enumerated. The answer I heard from the right hon. gentleman (Sir R. Peel) opposite was that there was a great variety of opinions on the subject of these burthens. That I could myself have told the right hon. Baronet. As a law is to be framed, founded expressly upon these alleged burthens, it would have been but fair at least to tell us what they are. I shall not enter upon the subject now; but this I will tell the right hon. gentleman, that for every particular burthen he can show me as pressing upon the land, I will show him ten exemptions. Yes, ten for his one.

There is one burthen that was referred to by the right hon. Member for Renfrewshire (Mr P. M. Stewart), which is the Land Tax. I am surprised we have not yet got the returns moved for many months since, relative to the Land Tax of other countries. What are our ambassadors and diplomatists about, that we cannot have the returns of the revenue and expenditure of foreign countries? Our own *bureaux* must be badly kept, or we ought to have this information already here in London. Being without official information, however, I will not run the risk of making a general statement, lest I should fall into error. I have, however, one document which is authentic, as it is on the authority of M. Humaun, the Finance Minister of France; and he states that the Land Tax in that country is 40 per cent. on the whole revenue, and 25 per cent. on the revenue of the proprietors of the soil; so that in France the landowner pays 5s. in the pound, while in this country you have a Land Tax of £1,900,000, not 5 per cent. of the income, and you call for a fresh tax upon the poor man's loaf to compensate you for the heavy burthen you bear. I will tell the Prime Minister that, in laying on this tax without first stating his views on this point, he is not treating the House and the country with proper respect. I have seen, with some satisfaction, that admissions have been made (and indeed it has not been denied) that the profits of the Bread Tax go to the landowners. Now in all the old Committees on agricultural concerns, it was alleged that it was a farmer's question—an agricultural labourer's question; and never till lately did I hear it admitted that the Bread Tax did contribute to the benefit of the landowners, on account of those exclusive burthens that are set up as a pretence for its continuance. Ought we not to know what these burthens were when this Corn Law was passed? Having patiently waited for twenty-five years, I think we are entitled at last to a clear explanation of the pretext upon which you tax the food of the people for the acknowledged benefit of the landowners.

The right hon. Baronet tells us we must not be dependent upon foreigners for our supply, or that that dependence must be supplementary, that certain years produce enough of corn for the demand, and that we must legislate for the introduction of corn only when it is wanted. Granted. On that point the right hon. Baronet and I are perfectly agreed. Let us only legislate, if you please, for the introduction of corn when it is wanted. Exclude it as much as you please when it is not wanted. But all I supplicate for on the part of the starving people is, that they and not you shall be the judges of when corn is wanted. By what right do you pretend to gauge the appetites and admeasure the wants of millions of people? Why, there is no despotism that ever dreamed of doing anything so monstrous as this; yet you sit here, and presume to judge when people want food, dole out your supply when you condescend to think they want it, and stop it when you choose to consider that they have had enough. Are you in a position to judge of the wants of artisans, of hand-loom weavers? you, who never knew the want of a meal in your lives, do you presume to know when the people want bread? Why, in the course of the present debate the right hon. Baronet said that from 1832 to 1836 sufficient corn was produced at home for the population; and yet in his last speech he told us that there were 800,000 hand-loom weavers who in 1836 were unable to supply themselves with the commonest wants and necessaries of existence, even though they worked sixteen and eighteen hours a day. Was it not also of that period that Mr Inglis, the traveller in Ireland, wrote, when he wound up his account of that country by the emphatic and startling declaration that one-third part of the population perished prematurely from diseases brought on by the want of the necessaries of life? Yet, in that state of things, the right hon. Baronet gravely comes forward, and tells us that the country produces a sufficiency of food!

I have heard other admissions too; one in particular by the right hon. Paymaster of the Forces (Sir E. Knatchbull), who said the landlords were entitled to the Corn Law to enable them to maintain a high station in the land. [Sir E. KNATCHBULL: To enable them to maintain their present station in Society.] A noble Lord, also (Lord Stanley), admitted that the price of food did keep up the rent of land, but did not raise wages. What does that mean, but that the rent of land is kept up at the expense of the working classes, who are unrepresented in this House? I say that the right hon. Paymaster of

X

the Forces and the noble Lord do not deal fairly with the people, for they are giving themselves an outdoor relief which they deny to the poor in the Union Workhouses. It is not merely an extension of the Pension List to the landed proprietors, as was said by *The Times* some years ago, when that paper stigmatised the Corn Laws as an extension of the Pension List to the whole of the landed aristocracy; it is the worst form of pauperism; it is the aristocracy submitting to be fed at the expense of the poorest of the poor. If this is to be so, if we are to bow our necks to a landed oligarchy, let things be as they were in ancient Venice; let the nobles inscribe their names in a golden book, and draw their money direct from the Exchequer. It would be better for the people thus to suffer our aristocracy than to circumscribe our trade, destroy our manufactures, and draw the money from the pockets of the poor by indirect and insidious means. Such a course would be more easy for us, and more honest for you. But have the hon. gentlemen who maintain a system like this considered that the people of this country are beginning to understand it a little better than they did? And do they think that the people, with a better understanding of the subject, will allow one class not only to tax the rest of the community for their own exclusive advantage, but to be living in a state of splendour upon means obtained by indirect taxation from the pockets of the poor? The right hon. Baronet (Sir R. Peel), I apprehend, knows more of the state of the country than most of his followers; and I would exhort him to bear in mind that there is a widespread feeling extending into every part of the country that upon him, and him alone, will rest the responsibility of the manner in which he shall legislate upon this subject. He has now been in the possession of a great power for many months; he had due warning when he took office of the course it would be necessary for him to pursue. He knows the existing state of commerce and manufactures. He has had ample opportunities of acquainting himself with the actual condition of the people. He is not legislating in the dark, and this I will venture to tell him, that bad as he finds trade now, he will live (if he follows out the course in which he purposes to embark) to find it much worse. I hope, sincerely hope, that he is prepared for the consequence. We have never heard of an honest English merchant coming forward to say that this law would give him a trade in corn. The corn traders alone have been appealed to. The right hon. Baronet tells us that we must force forward this discussion, that we must proceed at once to the settlement of this question, because, forsooth, he has heard from many corn traders that it is very important that the matter should remain no longer in abeyance. If the trade in corn is still to be left in the hands of a peculiar class of dealers, in the hands of a class who are habitual gamblers, will that be an alteration of the law calculated to amend the situation of those who are engaged in the general trade and commerce of the country? Why should there be corn merchants any more than tea merchants or sugar merchants? Why should not the general merchant be enabled to bring back corn in exchange for his exports, as well as cotton, tea, or sugar? Until you pass a law enabling the merchant to make a direct exchange for corn, as well as for other commodities of foreign production, you will give no substantial relief to commerce. Nor is your law calculated to lower the price of food. You will have people amongst you maintaining the same wolfish competition to raise the price of bread, and you will have capitalists day by day struggling against bankruptcy. For this state of things the right hon. Baronet, Sir Robert Peel, will be responsible. I own, indeed, that I heard in the right hon. Baronet's second speech something like an apologetic tone of reasoning; some deprecatory as to his present position, not being able to do all that he would do. That tone would be very well if the right hon. Baronet had been forced into the present position by the people, or summoned there by the Queen; then with some shadow of fairness he might resort to the plea that his position was a difficult one, and that he would do more if his party would permit him. But let me remind the right hon Baronet that he sought the position he now fills, and though I am no friend, no political partisan, of the noble Lord the member for London (Lord John Russ ll), though I have no desire to see him again in power, governed by his old opinions, this I must say, that the measure which the noble Lord proposed upon the Corn Law, though in itself not good, was still infinitely better than that of the right hon. Baronet. And I beg to call to the right hon. Baronet's mind, that if he is now placed in a situation of difficulty, that difficulty was sought by himself, and, consequently, cannot now be pleaded in extenuation of his present measure. He told us at Tamworth that for years and years, ay, even from the passing of the Reform Bill, he had been engaged in reconstructing his party. I presume he knew of what materials that party was composed. I presume he was not ignorant of the fact that it consisted of monopolists of every kind: of monopolists of religion, monopolists of the franchise, monopolists of sugar, monopolists of corn, monopolists of timber, monopolists of coffee. These were the parties that gathered around him, and out of which he was to construct his new Parliament. They were fully alive to the occasion. They set to work to revive the old system of corruption. They bribed and they bought. Yes, they bribed, they bought, and they intimidated, until they found themselves in office, and the right hon. Baronet at their head, as their leader and champion. Did he expect that this party had expended their funds and their labour in the Registration Courts— for there, as the right hon. Baronet himself has stated, I believe the Constitution will henceforth be fought—did he think that they had expended this labour and this money in order that they might come into office and assist him to take away their monopolies? The right hon. Baronet must have known the party he had to deal with, for he had a very old connection with them; and, therefore, I presume he was not disappointed when he came into office, having thrust out men who, with all their faults, were still far better than those who succeeded them. Having thrown those men out of office, and being unable to carry the measure which they proposed, and were ready to carry into effect, I say that he has now no right to set up the difficulty of his position as a bar to the universal condemnation which his proposition must receive in the estimation of every just politician in the country. He is the cause, yes, I say he is the cause, of our present position, and upon his shoulders will the people rest the whole of the responsibility.

I will now say a word to the gentlemen on this side of the House who have such great difficulties, such bogglings and startings, at the danger of giving their assent to the motion of my hon. friend the member for Wolverhampton (Hon. C. P. Villiers). I will say a word or two to the noble Lord the member for London (Lord John Russell), and to my noble and right hon. neighbours, as to the difficulties of conscience which they appear to entertain about a total and immediate repeal of the Corn Laws. I hear on this side of the House, in almost all directions, an acknowledgment of the principle for which I and others contend, that is, the principle of perfect freedom in the trade in corn. But there are some of my noble and right hon. neighbours who think there should be a duty on corn for the purpose of revenue. How can there be a duty for revenue unless it be a duty for Protection? I ask my noble and right hon. neighbours who entertain that view of the subject to reconsider it before they go to a division. With that word of advice to those who sit near me, I proceed to make a remark in reference to the little word "now," about which many gentlemen on this side of the House seem also to feel a considerable difficulty. There are gentlemen here who think that the Corn Laws ought to be repealed, but they cannot reconcile themselves to the immediate repeal of them. They do not like to repeal them *now*. "We admit," say they, "the injustice which these laws inflict upon twenty-five millions of the people for the advantage of a select few; but inasmuch as some thousands of persons have a beneficial interest in this wrong inflicted upon the millions, we cannot suddenly deprive them of the advantage they possess." Now, with all due deference to gentlemen who use that argument, I must be permitted to say that I think they are showing a very great sympathy for the few who are gaining, and vastly little sympathy indeed for the many who are suffering from the operation of these laws. I would put it to those gentlemen whether, if it had been in their power, immediately after the passing of the Corn Law in 1815, to repeal that law, they would have given any compensation to the landed interest in the shape of an eight or ten years' diminishing duty upon the importation of foreign grain? No; they would have repealed them at once. Then, I ask, do they think that twenty-seven years' possession of the wrong— twenty-seven years of exclusive advantage — twenty-seven years of injustice to the rest of the community,—entitles this interested and selfish party to increase its demand in the shape of compensation? I give the hon. gentlemen who are near me credit for being quite sincere in their scruples. I have heard such scruples very often expressed before; but I once heard them met at a public meeting of electors in what appeared to me to be a very satisfactory manner. There was great difficulty on the platform among the Whig gentlemen who were assembled there about the repeal of the Corn Laws, and they were arguing about the danger and hardship of an immediate repeal of them. They were at length interrupted by a sturdy labouring man in a fustian coat, who called out, "Whoi, mun! where's the trouble of taking them off? You put them on all of a ruck"; meaning that they had been put on all of a sudden. And so they were. The law was passed without notice in 1815, notwithstanding the remonstrances of the people.

Then, I say, let us abolish this law, and the sooner the better. I will not trespass further upon the patience of the House. I consider that this question is now drawn within such narrow limits as to depend upon these two points: "Are you, the landed interest, able to show that you are subjected to exclusive burthens?" If so, then the way to relieve you is not to put taxes on the rest of the community, but to remove your burthens. Secondly, "Are you prepared to carry out even-handed justice to the people?" If not, your law will not stand; nay, your House itself, i. based upon injustice, will not stand!

APPENDIX.

APPENDIX.

I.

THE TIMES ON "PARNELLISM AND CRIME."

MR PARNELL AND THE PHŒNIX PARK MURDERS.

A GREAT sensation was created on April 18th, 1887, by the publication in *The Times* of the following letter in *facsimile*, dated nine days after the Phœnix Park murders:—

"15/5/82.

"DEAR SIR,
"I am not surprised at your friend's anger, but he and you should know that to denounce the murders was the only course open to us. To do that promptly was plainly our best policy.

"But you can tell him, and all others concerned, that though I regret the accident of Lord F. Cavendish's death, I cannot refuse to admit that Burke got no more than his deserts.

"You are at liberty to show him this, and others whom you can trust also, but let not my address be known. He can write to House of Commons.
 "Yours very truly,
  "CHAS. S. PARNELL."

This was accompanied by the following letterpress:—

"In concluding our series of articles on 'Parnellism and Crime,' we intimated that, besides the damning facts which we there recorded, unpublished evidence existed which would bind still closer the links between the 'constitutional' chiefs and the contrivers of murder and outrage. In view of the unblushing denials of Mr Sexton and Mr Healy on Friday night, we do not think it right to withhold any longer from public knowledge the fact that we possess, and have had in our custody for some time, documentary evidence which has a most serious bearing on the Parnellite conspiracy, and which, after a most careful and minute scrutiny, is, we are satisfied, quite authentic. We produce one document in *facsimile* to-day by a process the accuracy of which cannot be impugned, and we invite Mr Parnell to explain how his signature has become attached to such a letter.

"It is requisite to point out that the body of the manuscript is apparently not in Mr Parnell's handwriting, but the signature and the 'Yours very truly' unquestionably are so; and if any Member of Parliament doubts the fact, he can easily satisfy himself on the matter by comparing the handwriting with that of Mr Parnell in the book containing the signatures of Members when they first take their seats in the House of Commons.

"We particularly direct attention to the erasure in the manuscript,[1] as undersigned evidence of authenticity; and should any questions be raised as to the body of the letter being in another handwriting, we shall be prepared to adduce proof that this peculiarity is quite consistent with its genuine character.

"The body of the letter occupies the whole of the first page of an ordinary sheet of stout white note-paper, leaving no room in the same page for the signature, which is placed on the fourth page near the top right-hand corner. It was an obvious precaution to sign upon the back instead of upon the second page, so that the half-sheet might, if necessary, be torn off, and the letter disclaimed.

"It is right and necessary to explain that the 'Dear Sir' is believed to be Egan, and that the letter was addressed to him in order to pacify the wrath of his subordinate instruments in the Phœnix Park murders—then (on May 15th, nine days after the tragedy) still at large and undetected. The anxiety of the writer to keep his address unknown will be noted, and is curious in connection with a belief prevailing at the time that Mr Parnell was so impressed by the danger he had incurred by denouncing the

---

[1] After the word "plainly" in the first paragraph, the words "the only course" had been written and crossed through.

assassinations, as to have applied for the protection of the police on the plea that his life was in peril.

"Mr Parnell in his letter describes Lord F. Cavendish's death as an 'accident,' but he 'cannot refuse to admit that Burke got no more than his deserts.' That is his language to the 'Inner Circle'; but before Parliament, yielding to what he considered 'the only course,' or, as it stands amended in the text, 'our best policy,' he spoke on Monday, May 8th, two days after the murders, as follows :—

"'MR PARNELL said he wished to be permitted to express, on the part of his hon. friends, on his own part, and, he believed, on the part of every Irishman in whatever portion of the world he might live, their most unqualified detestation of the horrible crime which had been committed in Ireland. (Hear, hear.) He could not now refer to the steps which the Government proposed to take. He did not deny that it might be impossible for the Government to resist taking measures such as had been mentioned by the Prime Minister. But he wished to express his belief that the crime had been committed by men who absolutely detested the cause with which he had been associated—(hear, hear)—and who had devised that crime, and carried it out as the deadliest blow in their power against the hopes and the new course which the new Government had resolved upon.'

"Particular attention may now be drawn to the wicked suggestion here made that the Phœnix Park murders had been the work of the enemies of Parnellism and the League, 'devised and carried out as the deadliest blow in their power against the hopes and the new course' which the Government had resolved upon. Has that infamous accusation ever been excelled or even equalled? and to what benevolent construction of motives is a public man now entitled who made such a charge, at the very time when he was smoothing down the 'anger' of Egan's 'friends' for denouncing them as murderers in Parliament?

"To the country at large Mr Parnell, Mr Dillon, and Mr Davitt addressed on the day after the murder the following manifesto :—

"'TO THE PEOPLE OF IRELAND.—On the eve of what seemed a bright future for our country, that evil destiny which has apparently pursued us for centuries has struck another blow at our hopes, which cannot be exaggerated in its disastrous consequences. In this hour of sorrowful gloom we venture to give an expression of our profoundest sympathy with the people of Ireland in the calamity that has befallen our cause, through a horrible deed, and to those who had determined at the last hour that a policy of conciliation should supplant that of terrorism and national distrust. We earnestly hope that the attitude and action of the whole Irish people will show the world that assassination, such as has startled us almost to the abandonment of hope for our country's future, is deeply and religiously abhorrent to their every feeling and instinct. We appeal to you to show by every manner of expression that almost universal feeling of horror which this assassination has excited. No people feels so intense a detestation of its atrocity, or so deep a sympathy for those whose hearts must be seared by it, as the nation upon whose prospects and reviving hopes it may entail consequences more ruinous than have fallen to the lot of unhappy Ireland during the present generation. We feel that no act has ever been perpetrated in our country during the exciting struggles for social and political rights of the past fifty years that has so stained the name of hospitable Ireland as this cowardly and unprovoked assassination of a friendly stranger; and that until the murderers of Lord Frederick Cavendish and Mr Burke are brought to justice, that stain will sully our country's name.

"'(Signed) { CHARLES S. PARNELL.
JOHN DILLON.
MICHAEL DAVITT.'

"Here, again, the peculiar language employed will be noted. It is 'the evil destiny which has apparently pursued us for centuries,' which 'has struck another blow at our hopes,' etc.

"Only a fortnight ago, on the first reading of the Crimes Bill, Mr Parnell took occasion to refer to this manifesto in the House of Commons in the following remarkable terms :—

"'I do not believe you would ever have broken up that' [the Invincible] 'conspiracy if it had not been for the denunciation of Mr Michael Davitt, the Member for East Mayo, and myself, issued after the crime in Phœnix Park. It was the denunication that shook that conspiracy and enabled the officers of the law in Ireland, by means of their secret inquiries and other agencies, to get under it, and finally break it up.'

"An interval of more than half a year elapsed between the Phœnix Park murders and the discovery of the perpetrators. In that interval, while the 'stain on the name of hospitable Ireland,' in spite of 'the appeal' made in the manifesto, still adhered to it, Ireland's uncrowned king[1] actually addressed to his trusted subordinate, the Treasurer of the Land League, the following extraordinary letter, which tells it own tale.

"In the *facsimile*, which we place before our readers, the paper ies open, the first page being to the right and the fourth to the left."

---

[1] Mr Parnell, by the way, was not the only Irishman invested with the title of "The Uncrowned King." It had been borne by Daniel O'Connell.

Subjoined is *The Times*' leader in the same issue of the paper :—
"We place before our readers to-day a document, the grave importance of which it would be difficult to over-estimate. It is a *facsimile* of a letter from Mr PARNELL, written a week after the Phœnix Park murders, excusing his public condemnation of the crime, and distinctly condoning, if not approving, the murder of Mr BURKE. It needs no further words to recommend this document to the serious consideration of the public, and especially of Members of the House of Commons. At the close of to-night's sitting—if the arrangements made by the Whips hold good—the division will be taken in the House on the second reading of the Crimes Bill. That the amendment moved at Mr GLADSTONE'S instance, and in the interests of his Parnellite allies, will be defeated by a great majority is beyond doubt. There is, however, a preliminary question of great significance to be settled. No greater danger has ever threatened public life in England than the 'demoralisation in politics,' against which Mr GOSCHEN in his speech on Saturday, at Edinburgh, abjured all honest men to make a stand. The disgraceful scene, for which COLONEL SAUNDERSON's statements on Friday might furnish a pretext, cannot be allowed to pass without further explanation. It is bad enough that the House of Commons should be degraded by the use of language which would not be permitted in any decently conducted music-hall, but that is a matter which must be left in the hands of Members themselves until the time comes when the country will have to pass judgment upon the offenders, and those who instigate and encourage them. Something more serious than a question of Parliamentary manners is involved in the charges brought by COLONEL SAUNDERSON against the principal members of Mr PARNELL'S party, and met by Mr HEALY and Mr SEXTON, not with any attempt at disproof, but with the lie direct. Mr HEALY'S breach of orders was punished by suspension from the service of the House, but the decision will be challenged to-day on the motion of his fellow-offender, Mr SEXTON. As for Mr SEXTON himself, he escaped punishment because COLONEL SAUNDERSON had placed himself—technically at least—in the wrong by one or two inaccuracies in his citations from the evidence collected in our articles on 'Parnellism and Crime.' Those inaccuracies, however, do not in the smallest degree affect the cumulative force of the evidence in question. Mr

HEALY and Mr SEXTON fastened upon the possibly indiscreet statement that members of Mr PARNELL'S party 'had been associating with men they knew to be murderers.' It is impossible to prove that the Parliamentary Members of the Executive Committee of the Land League, in the historic days when Mr GLADSTONE denounced the crime that dogged its footsteps, and when Mr PARNELL and Mr SEXTON sat in secret council with EGAN, BRENNAN, BOYTON, and SHERIDAN, were aware of the character of their associates. As Mr ARNOLD-FORSTER in his letter to us to-day observes, 'There is no proof; there is only presumption.' On this point every man must form his opinion for himself, giving such weight as he may think proper to Mr SEXTON'S 'passionate' denials, and arriving at a judgment according to the reasonable probabilities of the case. It is not wise to state a probability, however overwhelming its strength may appear, as a fact. But, after all, the allegation, which COLONEL SAUNDERSON withdrew as far as the proceedings of the Executive Committee of the League were concerned, remains strictly true with respect to the subsequent conduct of Mr PARNELL'S party as a body, and of the principal members of it individually.

"We have publicly stated, and we repeat the statement, that the present allies of the Gladstonians—the men whom Mr GLADSTONE and his colleagues are assisting to paralyse law and to render government impossible in Ireland—have been, and are, associated closely and continuously with the worst of criminals, with the agents and instruments of murder-conspiracies, with the planners and paymasters of cowardly and inhuman outrage, with the preachers of the 'Gospel of Dynamite,' who are at the same time the financiers that furnish the funds on which the 'Parliamentary Party' subsist. These charges have been for weeks before the country. They are protected by no privilege of Parliament or other artificial shelter, and it is open to those persons who are so indignant at their repetition in the House of Commons that they cannot observe the common decencies of civilised speech, to refute them if they can, and recover damages in a Court of Law. Yet neither Mr PARNELL himself, nor any one of his subordinates, has taken a single step to prove that they have been maligned in the extracts we have published from *The Irish World*. While Mr HEALY, speaking to a Sheffield audience, demands to be placed on his trial at the Old Bailey for a crime of which he has never been accused, he and his colleagues in the House of Commons leave the real, the crushing charge against them unanswered, or answered only with brutal insult, unsupported by any evidence except that of their word. In the whole body of testimony we have published, only one insignificant error has been detected, turning upon a mistaken identification of Mr T. P. O'CONNOR, M.P., with another person bearing the same surname and having the same initials. The rest of the story is told, as far as the facts are concerned, in the columns of FORD'S newspaper—the organ of the dynamite party, and the channel through which, as DAVITT has gratefully testified, enormous sums of money have passed into the hands of the League. From this trustworthy source we learn that Mr PARNELL'S party have been associated, not only before, but since the detection of the Phœnix Park murderers and the disclosure of the origin of the 'Invincible' conspiracy with FORD himself, who 'stands by all he has ever said on this doctrine of dynamite' with EGAN, who hinted to the 'Invincibles' that 'talk' would never get the suspects out of Kilmainham, with SHERIDAN, BRENNAN, WALSH, BOYTON, and BYRNE, all implicated by CASEY'S evidence, all fugitives to the United States, and all conspicuous members up to that time of the staff of Mr PARNELL'S constitutional agitation. These men, together with O'DONOVAN ROSSA, FINNERTY, FEELY, DEVOY, and other advocates of 'physical force' in its various forms, Mr PARNELL has always treated as his allies for American purposes, though he has occasionally disavowed some of them on this side of the Atlantic when he deemed it convenient to conciliate English opinion. He has never rejected their money. He has sent congratulatory telegrams to their conventions; his lieutenants of high and low degree, from Mr T. P. O'CONNOR and Mr JUSTIN M'CARTHY down to Mr REDMOND and Mr O'BRIEN, have been entertained and *chaperoned* by EGAN and the FORDS— by the very persons who presented 'that brave little woman,' Mrs FRANK BYRNE, with a well-filled purse at a banquet commemorative of the victory in the Phœnix Park. Finally, as *The Irish World* shows, the proceedings which led up to the Chicago Convention, and at which the Plan of Campaign was hatched, brought together, both in a secret conclave and on a public platform, FORD and EGAN, Mr REDMOND, and Mr DEASY, BRENNAN, DAVITT, and Mr O'BRIEN, SULLIVAN, KERWIN, FEELY, and DEVOY, of the Clan-na-Gael Murder Club, and FINNERTY, described by Mr PARNELL himself as a 'dynamiter.' This confederacy, the ramifications of which we have laid bare, has now been brought distinctly under the notice of the House of Commons, and the country has a right to know whether the Gladstonian Liberals are going to content themselves with a general denial by Mr HEALY, Mr SEXTON, and Mr PARNELL himself, of facts attested by the impartial evidence of *The Irish World*.

"The remarkable document which we publish to-day has no unimportant bearing upon the value of such contradictions. The letter from Mr PARNELL, apologising for the course which he took, as he explained, under compulsion, when he denounced the Phœnix Park assassination, is produced, for reasons set forth elsewhere, in *facsimile*. Mr PARNELL'S statement that LORD FREDERICK CAVENDISH'S death was 'an accident,' he 'cannot refuse to admit that BURKE got no more than his deserts,' is too significantly in harmony with the language of some of his allies beyond the Atlantic. In 1883, FINNERTY, at a 'Martyrs' Meeting' at Chicago, in which he announced Mr HEALY'S return for Monaghan as 'a piece of good news,' said:—' As regards CAVENDISH, it' [the murder] 'was not premeditated; as regarded BURKE, they said nothing.... He' [Lord F. CAVENDISH] 'died because he was in bad company—was with THOMAS H. BURKE, the FOUCHE of Ireland.' But Mr PARNELL, as we show elsewhere, did not consider it prudent to use this sort of plain speaking in the House of Commons. Not only did he express his detestation for the crime, but he attempted to cast the infamy of it upon the enemies of his 'cause,' and he has never to this hour withdrawn the charge. What, then, is the estimate to be formed of the value of disclaimers and denials, when we have before us proof not to be easily rejected that they represent no more than the convenience of the moment? SIR WILLIAM HARCOURT finds it becoming to treat the grave charges which have been brought against Members of the House of Commons now associated with him in Opposition as 'rubbish,' but the country will not share this newly-acquired indifference to the contamination of crime. Mr PARNELL must understand the gravity of the question raised by the accusations we have formulated and supported with evidence, but he cannot expect that his simple repudiation of the letter we publish this morning will have any weight with public opinion. He must be prepared with some more solid proofs, if he is to annul the effect of a disclosure which reduces the passionate denials with which his party encounter unpleasant truths to even a lower value than Mr ARNOLD-FORSTER assigns to them."

The next day *The Times* returned to the charge in these terms:—

"Mr PARNELL'S speech on the second reading of the Crimes Bill was not delivered till 1 o'clock in the morning—too late for detailed account on the passages referring to the letter we published yesterday. Earlier in the evening, however, Mr PARNELL —though he has not yet made any communication to us—appears to have imparted his views on the subject to certain news agencies. It would be unfair to look at the present stage for a complete statement of Mr PARNELL'S defence—beyond the fact, which might have been anticipated even before Mr SEXTON spoke, that he declares the letter in indignant language to be 'a forgery.' It is, however, somewhat remarkable that he has apparently been in doubt as to the grounds on which he is to impeach the genuineness and authenticity of this document. While repudiating the body of the letter, it was open to him either to deny or to acknowledge the signature. At first he was, as it seems, disposed to acknowledge it, assuming that it was an autograph, or possibly a signature, for the use of his private secretary, which might have fallen in blank into some unscrupulous hands. But a different theory is put forward in the latest version of Mr PARNELL'S views. He now asserts that the signature is not his, and he points out various discrepancies, as they appear to him, between the signature reproduced in our issue of yesterday and his usual signatures. Such discrepancies in small points, if they can be shown to exist, prove extremely little. They constantly occur, even in the case of persons whose handwriting does not materially vary. We have in our possession several undoubted examples of Mr PARNELL'S signature, with which that of the letter has been carefully compared, and we repeat that, in our deliberate judgment, there can be no doubt of the genuineness of the latter. We do not know whether Mr PARNELL has made up his mind to adopt the attitude recommended by Mr SEXTON, and to refuse, even after LORD HARTINGTON'S pointed challenge, to attempt to vindicate his character in a Court of

Law. To denounce this letter as a 'villainous and barefaced forgery,' concocted with the object of influencing the division and of calumniating Mr PARNELL, is easy, but inadequate to the occasion. We pay no attention whatever to Mr PARNELL'S big words; and if he should proceed to apply the only test by which the truth can be plainly brought before the world, we are quite prepared to meet him. Disclaimers, of which the value was discounted in LORD HARTINGTON'S weighty speech, are not strengthened by violence of language, nor is the assumption—that the public will look upon Mr PARNELL'S letter as outrageously improbable—safe ground on which to rest the defence of a party associated with English public men. We deeply regret that Mr GLADSTONE, as the CHIEF SECRETARY observed in his reply, joined in the conspiracy of silence which has at last been practically broken through. The Leader of the Opposition cannot afford to ignore grave accusations affecting politicians whom he has enlisted among his followers, and to whom he would hand over the government of the land. LORD SPENCER'S testimony to a negative which he cannot possibly have had the means of proving, or even of conjecturing, his exculpation, gloried in by Mr SEXTON, of those who for years pursued him with atrocious and abominable slanders, is a pitiable example of the lengths to which party spirit will carry a man of honour. The public will certainly not dismiss the statements affecting Mr PARNELL as incredible when they see that Gladstonians, not wanting in good sense or good feeling, are capable of expressing such sentiments as those of our correspondent, 'NOT A TRANSCENDENTALIST.'[1] From this frame of mind to Mr LABOUCHERE'S, when he appeals to the Secret Societies against the judgment of the House of Commons, the distance is not great."

---

[1] "TO THE EDITOR OF *The Times*.—SIR,—If a man has the power of imprisoning any person whom he suspects of what he may please to call 'treasonable practices'; if, exercising that power, he imprisons the leader of the Opposition and some hundreds of others, and keeps them to plank bed and prison fare for seven months; and if after that time he is murdered, is it a matter of serious wonder or condemnation that one of the men just liberated from prison should admit that the murdered man 'had got no more than his deserts'? Does such an expression of opinion mark the man who uses it in a confidential letter as standing in 'a category apart from any who have ever sat in the House of Commons'? Some

That Mr Parnell did take advantage of the Courts of Law to vindicate his character is a matter of history. Nearly two years afterwards, viz. on 28th February 1889, in the same issue as that which contained the report of the 57th sitting of the Parnell Commission, *The Times* published the following leader :—

"When the special Commission met yesterday, the ATTORNEY-GENERAL made the following statement on behalf of *The Times*, which we feel it right to reproduce in full :—' I need scarcely assure your Lordships that since the adjournment yesterday my learned friends and I have communicated with those whom we represent, and have, in conjunction with them, most carefully and anxiously considered the course which it is our duty to take in relation to that portion of this inquiry which has lately been under your Lordships' consideration. My Lords, it is unnecessary to remind you that the letters put in evidence purporting to be signed by Mr PARNELL, the authenticity of which is disputed, including the letter of the 15th of May 1882—also those which purport to bear the signatures of Mr O'KELLY, Mr DAVITT, and PATRICK EGAN—all came into the hands of the managers of *The Times* from one source, from one man—RICHARD PIGOTT. I desire to say nothing respecting that witness except that I presume everyone will agree that no one ought to attach any weight to any evidence he has given; but, taking the most lenient view of his conduct, he certainly confessed in his statement to Mr SHANNON that he forged some of these letters, with the assistance of the man from whom he received others. I need not say, my Lords, that I had not heard the contents of the statement received this morning until it was read by Mr CUNNINGHAM.' This referred to the text of PIGOTT'S confession to Mr LABOUCHERE, which had been forwarded by post to Mr SHANNON, had been handed, with the envelope unopened, to the Secretary of the Commission, and read by him in Court. The ATTORNEY-GENERAL proceeded :— ' My Lords, under these circumstances, it seems to us that the course we ought to take is clearly defined; and, believing that we are merely doing our duty, I now, on behalf of those whom we repre-

---

people, apparently sane and respectable, say the same sort of things now of Mr Gladstone, and others speak in like manner regarding Mr Balfour. You seem to be up in the clouds.—I am, etc.,
"NOT A TRANSCENDENTALIST."

sent, ask permission to withdraw from your consideration the question of the genuineness of the letters which have been submitted to you, the authenticity of which is denied, with the full acknowledgment that, after the evidence which has been given, we are not entitled to say that they are genuine. My Lords, although it is possible that any expression of regret used by me in making this statement may be misinterpreted, those whom I represent request me to express their sincere regret that these letters were published. That feeling, which most truly exists, will, at the proper time, be more fully expressed by themselves. If I were entitled to do so, I could say much as to the manner in which those whom I represent have been imposed upon, but I desire, in making this statement, to abstain from introducing any controversial matter; but I claim, with your Lordships' permission, to state that some words used by my learned friend SIR CHARLES RUSSELL yesterday did not escape our attention. My learned friend said that behind PIGOTT there had been a foul conspiracy. I desire emphatically to say that, if a foul conspiracy has existed, those whom we represent have had no share whatever in it. That they have been misled and imposed upon is true, but therein lies their fault, and if it be suggested that their error extends beyond this fault, they earnestly ask that your Lordships will make the fullest inquiry into any part they have taken, either in procuring these documents or in placing them before the public.'

"We desire to endorse and to appropriate every word of the foregoing statement. It is our wish, as it is our duty, to give expression to that feeling of sincere regret to which the ATTORNEY-GENERAL referred. It was obvious that, after PIGOTT, on his own showing, had proved himself to be a person utterly unworthy of credit, and after he had made two confessions, varying in detail, but both admitting that the letters which he had produced were tainted with forgery, our duty was unreservedly to withdraw these letters from the consideration of the Judges. Moreover, Mr PARNELL having in the witness-box stated that the letters attributed to him were forgeries, we accept in every respect the truth of that statement. In these circumstances we deem it right to express our regret most fully and sincerely at having been induced to publish the letters in question as Mr PARNELL'S, or to use them in evidence against him. This expression of regret, we need hardly say, includes also the letters falsely attributed to Mr EGAN, Mr

DAVITT, and Mr O'KELLY. It is clear now that PIGOTT was guilty of a gross and disgraceful fraud when he produced the documents which reached our hands. Into the circumstances under which we received and published them it is scarcely fitting we should enter. Nor shall we now refer to the grounds, apart from PIGOTT'S testimony, on which we considered ourselves to be justified in dealing with these letters as genuine documents. To do so would be to touch upon controversial matter which cannot for the present be properly dealt with in these columns. We are bound, however, to point out that though PIGOTT was the source from which the letters came, and though they were thus contaminated by their origin, he was not the person with whom we communicated, and who placed the documents in our hands. Moreover, we must add that we firmly believed the letters to be genuine, until the disclosures made by PIGOTT in the course of his cross-examination.

"We heard on Tuesday of 'a conspiracy behind PIGOTT and HOUSTON,' but it must be evident to all reasonable persons that, if a conspiracy existed, *The Times* was victimised by it and not a party to it. Errors in judgment may have been committed, and for them the penalty must be paid. What we have done, it must be clearly understood, has been done by us in the public interest alone. It has been done, moreover, altogether of our own motion and upon our own responsibility. We regarded the undertaking on which we entered as one of national importance, but we must enter an emphatic protest against attempts to make any statesman or any political party conjointly responsible with us for acts which were exclusively our own. We may point out, further, that it is absurd to take us to task for not having at once abandoned the portion of the case dependent upon the letters at an earlier stage of PIGOTT'S examination. We were responsibly advised that it was not within our right or power to express any opinion on the evidence of a witness still under examination, and could not offer any view of our own until that witness's cross-examination was concluded. As soon as the incidents affecting PIGOTT's flight had been inquired into, our counsel at once asked for an adjournment, for the purpose of considering the most proper form in which to present our withdrawal of the letters from the consideration of the Commission. This withdrawal of course refers exclusively to the letters obtained from PIGOTT, and not to the other portion of the case embraced in the 'charges and allegations,' which still remain the subject of judicial inquiry. Our desire is simply to express deep regret for the error into which we were led, and to withdraw unreservedly those parts of our original statements which we cannot honestly continue to maintain."

How Richard Pigott fled to Madrid, and there shot himself, to escape being taken by the emissaries of the law; and how, in the "last scene of all" in the tedious drama of the Parnell Commission, Mr Parnell was awarded the sum of £5000 damages from the proprietors of *The Times*, are facts known to everyone.

II.

ORIGINAL SOURCES OF THE SPEECHES.

Lord Brougham on Negro Emancipation	*Hansard*
T. B. Macaulay on the People's Charter	,,
W. J. Fox on the Corn Laws	*The Times.*
Daniel O'Connell on Repeal of the Union,	*The Morning Chronicle.*
R. L. Sheil on the Jewish Disabilities Bill	*Hansard.*
Alexander Cockburn on the Greek Difficulty	,,
Sir Edward Bulwer Lytton on the Crimean War	,,
The Earl of Ellenborough on the Polish Insurrection	,,
John Bright on Suspension of the Habeas Corpus Act	,,

The Rt. Hon. Robert Lowe on Parliamentary Reform—
> From "*The Speeches of the Rt. Hon. Robert Lowe*," *by permission of the Viscountess Sherbrooke, and A. Patchett Martin, Esq., Author of "The Life and Letters of Viscount Sherbrooke."*

The Rt. Hon. Gathorne Hardy on the Irish Church	*Hansard.*
Earl Russell on the Ballot	,,
Isaac Butt on Home Rule	,,

A. M. Sullivan on the Irish National Demands—
> From "*Speeches and Addresses by A. M. Sullivan, M.P.*" (*Office of "The Nation"*), *by permission of T.D. Sullivan, Esq., M.P., formerly Editor of "The Nation."*

The Earl of Beaconsfield on the Berlin Congress . . *The Times.*

Joseph Cowen on The Foreign Policy of England—
The Newcastle Daily Chronicle.
<small>Reprinted and Revised Copy kindly supplied by Joseph Cowen, Esq., M.P.</small>

The Rt. Hon. W. E. Gladstone on the Beaconsfield Ministry . . . . *The Times.*

Charles Bradlaugh at the Bar of the House of Commons—
<small>From "The Speeches of Charles Bradlaugh, M.P.," by permission of Mrs Bradlaugh Bonner.</small>

Justin M'Carthy in Defence of his Colleagues . . *Hansard.*

Lord Randolph Churchill on the Egyptian Crisis . . *The Times.*

The Rt. Hon. Joseph Chamberlain on Liberal Aims . ,,

C. S. Parnell on the Coercion Bill . . . . . *Hansard.*

The Rt. Hon. John Morley on Home Rule . . . *The Times.*

Richard Cobden on the Corn Laws . . . . *Hansard.*

September 1896

COMPLETE LIST

OF

HENRY HOLT & CO.'S
EDUCATIONAL PUBLICATIONS.

All prices are NET *except those marked with an asterisk* (*), *which are* RETAIL.
All books bound in cloth, unless otherwise indicated.

SCIENCE.

	CATALOGUE PRICE	PAGE
Allen's Laboratory Physics, *Pupil's Edition*	$ 80	2
The same, *Teacher's Edition*	1 00	2
Arthur, Barnes, and Coulter's Plant Dissection	1 20	3
Barker's Physics, *Advanced Course*	3 50	4
Beal's Grasses of North America. 2 vols.		5
Bessey's Botany, *Advanced Course*	2 20	6
The same, *Briefer Course*	1 12	6
Black and Carter's Natural History Lessons	50	8
Bumpus's Laboratory Manual of Invertebrate Zoology	1 00	8
Cairns's Quantitative Analysis	2 00	9
Crozier's Dictionary of Botanical Terms	2 40	9
Hackel's True Grasses (Scribner)	*1 50	9
Hall and Bergen's Physics (*Key*, 50 cts.)	1 25	10
Hall's First Lessons in Physics	65	11
Hertwig's General Principles of Zoology	1 60	12
Howell's Dissection of the Dog	1 00	12
Jackman's Nature Study	1 20	13
Kerner's Natural History of Plants. With 16 colored plates, 1000 cuts. 4 Pts.	15 00	14
MacDougal's Experimental Plant Physiology	1 00	15
Macloskie's Elementary Botany	1 30	15
McMurrich's Invertebrate Morphology. New Edition	3 00	16
Martin's The Human Body, *Advanced Course*. New Edition	2 50	17
The same, *Briefer Course*	1 20	17
The same, *Elementary Course*	75	19
The Human Body and the Effects of Narcotics	1 20	18
Newcomb and Holden's Astronomy, *Advanced Course*	2 00	20
The same, *Briefer Course*	1 12	20
Noyes's (W. A.) Elements of Qualitative Analysis	80	21
Packard's Zoology, *Advanced Course*	2 40	22
The same, *Briefer Course*	1 12	22
The same, *Elementary Course*	80	23
Entomology for Beginners	1 40	24
Guide to the Study of Insects	*5 00	24
Embryology	*2 50	24
Perkins's Outlines of Electricity and Magnetism		25
Pierce's Problems in Elementary Physics	60	25
Price's Fern Collector's Handbook and Herbarium		
Remsen's Chemistry, *Advanced Course*	2 80	26
The same, *Briefer Course*	1 12	26
The same, *Elementary Course*	80	28
Laboratory Manual (for *Elementary Course*)	40	29
Remsen and Randall's Chemical Experiments (for *Briefer Course*)	50	29
Scudder's Butterflies	*1 50	30
Brief Guide to Commoner Butterflies	*1 25	30
Life of a Butterfly	*1 00	30
Sedgwick and Wilson's General Biology, New Edition	1 75	31
Underwood's Native Ferns	1 00	32

Henry Holt & Co.'s Educational Publications

	CATALOGUE PRICE	PAGE
Williams's (G. H.) Elements of Crystallography	$1 25	32
Williams's (H. S.) Geological Biology	2 80	33
Woodhull's First Course in Science: *Book of Experiments*	50	34
Text-book	65	34
Zimmermann's Botanical Microtechnique	2 50	35

MATHEMATICS.

Gillet's Elementary Algebra	1 35	36
Euclidean Geometry	1 25	37
Keigwin's Class-book of Geometry		37
Newcomb's School Algebra (*Key*, 95 cts.)	95	38
Algebra for Colleges (*Key*, $1.30)	1 30	38
Elements of Geometry	1 20	38
Elements of Trigonometry, Plane and Spherical	1 60	39
Trigonometry, separate	1 20	39
Mathematical Tables	1 10	39
Essentials of Trigonometry	1 00	39
Plane Geometry and Trigonometry	1 10	39
Analytic Geometry	1 20	40
Differential and Integral Calculus	1 50	40
Phillips and Beebe's Graphic Algebra	1 60	40

HISTORY AND POLITICAL SCIENCE.

Doyle's History of the United States	1 00	45
Duruy's Middle Ages	1 60	41
Modern Times to 1798	1 60	42
Fleury's Ancient History told to Children	70	43
Freeman's General Sketch of History	1 10	44
Fyffe's History of Modern Europe: Volume I. 1792-1814	*2 50	46
Volume II. 1814-1848	*2 50	46
Volume III. 1848-1878	*2 50	46
The same. Three volumes in one	2 75	46
Gadet's Manual of International Law	1 30	46
Gardiner's English History for Schools	80	47
Introduction to English History	80	47
Gardiner and Mullinger's English History for Students	1 80	47
Hunt's History of Italy	80	45
Johnston's American Politics	80	51
History of the United States	1 00	48
Shorter History of the United States	95	50
Lacombe's Growth of a People	80	52
MacArthur's History of Scotland	80	45
Porter's Constitutional History of the United States	1 20	52
Roscher's Principles of Political Economy. 2 vols.	*7 00	52
Sime's History of Germany	80	45
Sumner's Problems in Political Economy	1 00	52
Symonds's Renaissance	*1 75	52
Thompson's History of England	88	44
Walker's Political Economy, *Advanced Course*	2 00	53
The same, *Briefer Course*	1 20	54
The same *Elementary Course*	1 00	54
Yonge's History of France	80	45
Landmarks of History: Ancient History	75	56
Mediæval History	80	56
Modern History	1 05	56

PHILOSOPHY.

Baldwin's Psychology. Vol. I. Senses and Intellect	1 80	57
Vol. II. Feeling and Will	2 00	58
Elements of Psychology	1 50	59
Descartes, Philosophy of (Torrey)	1 50	64
Falckenberg's History of Modern Philosophy	3 50	60
Hume, Philosophy of (Aikins)	1 00	65

Henry Holt & Co.'s Educational Publications

	CATALOGUE PRICE	PAGE
Hyde's Practical Ethics	$ 80	61
James's Psychology. *Advanced Course.* 2 vols	4 80	62
The same. *Briefer Course*	1 60	63
Kant, Philosophy of (Watson)	1 75	65
Locke, Philosophy of (Russell)	1 00	65
Paulsen's Introduction to Philosophy (Thilly)	3 50	65
Reid, Philosophy of (Sneath)	- 50	65
Spinoza, Philosophy of (Fullerton)	1 50	65
Zeller's History of Greek Philosophy	1 40	66

MISCELLANEOUS. (In English.)

Banister's Music	80	67
Champlin's Cyclopædia of Common Things. Cloth	*2 50	68
The same. Half Leather	*3 00	68
Cyclopædia of Persons and Places. Cloth	*2 50	69
The same. Half Leather	*3 00	69
Catechism of Common Things	48	70
Young Folks' Astronomy	48	70
Champlin and Bostwick's Cyclopædia of Games and Sports	*2 50	70
Cox's Catechism of Classic Mythology	75	71
Davis, King, and Collie's Governmental Maps	30	71
White's Classic Literature	1 60	71
Witt's Classic Mythology	1 00	71

ENGLISH.

Bain's Brief English Grammar (*Key*, 40 cts.)	40	86
Higher English Grammar	80	86
English Grammar bearing upon Composition	1 10	86
Baker's Specimens of Argumentation. Modern	50	73
Baldwin's Specimens of Prose Description	50	75
Boswell's Life of Dr. Samuel Johnson (abridged)	*1 50	86
Brewster's Specimens of Prose Narration	50	76
Bright's Anglo-Saxon Reader	1 75	87
ten Brink's History of English Literature: Volume I. To Wyclif.	*2 00	88
Volume II	*2 00	88
Browning: Selections. (Mason.)		
Burke: Selections. (Perry.)		77
Clark's Practical Rhetoric	1 00	89
Exercises for Drill. Paper	35	89
Briefer Practical Rhetoric	90	90
Art of Reading Aloud	60	90
Coleridge's Prose Extracts. (Beers.)	50	77
Cook's Extracts from Anglo-Saxon Laws. Paper	40	90
Corson's Anglo-Saxon and Early English	1 60	90
De Quincey's English Mail Coach and Joan of Arc. (Hart.)	50	78
Ford's The Broken Heart. (Scollard.) Buckram	70	78
The same. Cloth	50	78
Hale's Constructive Rhetoric	1 00	91
Hardy's Elementary Composition Exercises	80	90
Johnson's Chief Lives of the Poets. (Arnold.)	1 25	91
Rasselas. (Emerson.) Buckram	70	79
The same. Cloth	50	79
Lamont's Specimens of Exposition. Cloth	50	80
Lounsbury's History of the English Language	1 12	92
Part I, with Appendix of Specimens and Index.	90	92
Lyly's Endymion. (Baker.) Buckram	1 25	81
The same. Cloth	85	81
Macaulay and Carlyle: Croker's Boswell's Johnson (Strunk.) Cloth	50	82
Marlowe's Edward II. (McLaughlin.) Buckram	70	83
The same. Cloth	50	83
McLaughlin's Literary Criticism	1 00	93
Nesbitt's Grammar-Land	*1 00	93
Newman: Selections. (Gates.) Buckram	90	83
The same. Cloth	50	83

iii

Henry Holt & Co.'s Educational Publications

	CATALOGUE PRICE	PAGE
Pancoast's Representative English Literature	$1 60	97
Introduction to English Literature	1 25	94
Sewell's Dictation Exercises	45	100
Shaw's English Composition by Practice	75	99
Siglar's Practical English Grammar	60	100
Smith's Synonyms Discriminated	*2 25	100
Taine's History of English Literature	*1 25	100
The same, *Abridged. Class-room Edition.* (Fiske.)	1 40	100
Tennyson's Princess. (Sherman.)		85

GERMAN.

Andersen's Bilderbuch. *Vocab.* (Simonson.) Boards	$ 30	116
Die Eisjungfrau und andere Geschichten. (Krauss.) Boards	30	116
Ein Besuch bei Charles Dickens. Boards	25	116
Stories, with Grimm's, from Bronson's Easy Prose. *Vocab.*	90	117
Auerbach's Auf Wache with Roquette's Gefrorene Kuss. (Macdonnell.) Boards	35	117
Baumbach's Frau Holde. (Fossler.) *Poem.* Boards	25	101
Benedix's Der Dritte. *Play.* (Whitney.) Boards	20	102
Dr. Wespe. *Play.* Boards	25	102
Eigensinn. *Play.* Boards	25	114
Beresford-Webb's German Historical Reader	90	129
Blackwell's German Prefixes and Suffixes	60	130
Brandt Day's Scientific Reader		130
Bronson's Colloquial German (*Key*, 65 cts.)	65	131
Easy German Prose. See also *Andersen, Grimm, and Hauff*	1 25	132
Carové's Das Märchen ohne Ende. *Vocab.* Boards	20	117
Chamisso's Peter Schlemihl. (Vogel.) Boards	25	117
Claar's Simson und Delila. *Play.* Paper	25	115
Cohn's Über Bakterien. (Seidensticker.) Paper	30	118
Ebers's Eine Frage. Boards	35	118
Eckstein's Preisgekrönt. (Wilson.)	30	118
Eichendorff's Aus dem Leben eines Taugenichts. Boards	30	119
Fischer's Practical Lessons in German	75	134
Elementary Progressive German Reader	70	134
Wildermuth's Der Einsiedler im Walde	65	134
Hillern's Höher als die Kirche	60	134
Fouqué's Sintram und seine Gefährten. Paper	25	119
Undine. *Vocab.* (Jagemann.)	80	119
" Boards	35	119
Francke's German Literature	2 00	135
Freytag's Karl der Grosse. (Nichols.)	75	120
Die Journalisten. *Play.* (Thomas.) Boards	30	102
Friedrich's Gänschen von Buchenau. *Play.* Paper	35	115
Gerstäcker's Irrfahrten. (Whitney.)	30	121
Goethe's Egmont. (Steffen.) *Play.* Boards	40	102
Faust. Part I. *Play.* (Cook.)	48	103
Hermann und Dorothea. *Poem.* (Thomas.) Boards	30	103
Iphigenie auf Tauris. *Play.* (Carter)	48	104
Götz von Berlichingen. (Goodrich)		103
Dichtung und Wahrheit. *Selections.* (von Jagemann.)		120
Görner's Englisch. *Play.* Paper	25	104
Gostwick and Harrison's German Literature	2 00	135
Grimm's Die Venus von Milo; Rafael und Michel-Angelo. Boards	40	121
Grimms' Kinder- und Hausmärchen. *Vocab.* (Otis.)	1 00	121
Boards. (Different selections and notes, *no* Vocab.)	40	121
Selections, with Andersen, from Bronson's Easy Prose. *Vocab.*	90	117
Gutzkow's Zopf und Schwert. *Play.* Paper	40	104
Harris's German Reader	1 00	136
Hauff's Die Karawane. From Bronson's Easy Prose. *Vocab*	75	122
Das kalte Herz. Boards	20	122
Heine's Die Harzreise. (Burnett.) Boards	30	122
Helmholtz's Goethe's Arbeiten. (Seidensticker.) Paper	30	122
Heness's Kinder-Komödien. *Play.*	48	105

	CATALOGUE PRICE	PAGE
Heness's Der neue Leitfaden	$1 20	138
Der Sprechlehrer unter seinen Schülern	1 10	138
Hey's Fabeln für Kinder. *Vocab.* Boards	30	123
Heyse's Anfang und Ende. Boards	25	123
L'Arrabbiata. (Frost.) *Vocab.* Boards	25	123
Die Einsamen. Boards	20	123
Mädchen von Treppi; Marion. (Brusie.) Boards	25	123
Hillebrand's German Thought	*1 75	138
Hillern's Höher als die Kirche. *Vocab.* (Whittlesey.) Boards	25	124
The same. (Fischer.)	60	134
Huss's Conversation in German	1 10	138
Jagemann's German Prose Composition	90	139
Elements of German Syntax	80	140
Joynes-Otto: First Book in German. Boards	30	141
Introductory German Lessons	75	141
Introductory German Reader	95	141
Translating English into German (*Key*, 80 cts.)	80	141
Jungmann's Er sucht einen Vetter. *Play.* Paper	25	115
Kaiser's Erstes Lehrbuch	65	142
Keetels' Oral Method with German	1 30	142
Klemm's Lese- und Sprachbücher. Kreis I. Boards	25	143
" II. Boards	30	143
" " (With Vocab.)	35	143
" III. Boards	35	143
" " (With Vocab.)	40	143
" IV. Boards	40	143
" V. Boards	45	143
" VI. Boards	50	143
" VII. Boards	60	143
Geschichte der deutschen Literatur (Kreis VIII.)	1 00	143
Klenze's Deutsche Gedichte	90	105
Koenigswinter's Sie hat ihr Herz entdeckt. *Play.* Paper	35	115
Lessing's Emilia Galotti. (Super.) *Play.* Boards	30	106
Minna von Barnhelm. *Play.* (Whitney.)	48	107
Nathan der Weise. *Play.* (Brandt.) New Edition	60	107
Meissner's Aus meiner Welt. *Vocab.* (Wenckebach.)	75	124
Moser's Der Schimmel. *Play.* Paper	25	115
Der Bibliothekar. *Play.* (Lange.) Boards	40	107
Mügge's Riukan Voss. Paper	15	124
Signa die Seterin. Paper	20	124
Müller's (E. R.) Elektrischen Maschinen. (Seidensticker.) Paper	30	124
Müller's (Max) Deutsche Liebe. Boards	35	125
Nathusius's Tagebuch eines armen Fräuleins. Paper	25	125
Nichols's Three German Tales: I. Goethe's Die neue Melusine. II. Zschokke's Der tote Gast. III. H. v. Kleist's Die Verlobung in St. Domingo	60	125
Otis's Elementary German	80	144
Introduction to Middle High German	1 00	145
Otto's German Conversation Grammar (*Key*, 60 cts.)	1 30	146
Elementary Grammar of the German Language	80	147
Progressive German Reader. Half roan	1 10	146
Paul's Er muss tanzen. *Play.* Paper	25	115
Petersen's Prinzessin Ilse. Boards	20	126
Putlitz's Was sich der Wald erzählt. Paper	25	126
Vergissmeinnicht. Paper	20	126
Badekuren. *Play.* Paper	25	108
Das Herz vergessen. *Play.* Paper	25	108
Pylodet's New Guide to German Conversation	50	147
Regents' German and French Poems. Boards	20	108
Riehl's Burg Neideck. (Palmer.)	30	126
Der Fluch der Schönheit. (Kendall.)	25	126
Roquette's Der gefrorene Kuss, with Auerbach's Auf Wache. (Macdonnell.) Boards	35	127
Rosen's Ein Knopf. *Play.* Paper	25	115
Scheffel's Ekkehard. (Carruth.)	1 25	127
Trompeter von Säkkingen. *Poem.* (Frost.)	80	108
Schiller's Die Jungfrau von Orleans. *Play.* (Nichols.) Cloth	60	110

Henry Holt & Co.'s Educational Publications

	CATALOGUE PRICE	PAGE
Schiller's Die Jungfrau von Orleans. *Play.* (Nichols.) Boards	$ 40	110
Das Lied von der Glocke. *Poem.* (Otis.) Boards	35	111
Maria Stuart. *Play* (Joynes.)	60	111
Der Neffe als Onkel. *Play.* (Clement.) Boards	40	112
Wallenstein. *Play.* (Carruth.)	1 00	112
Wilhelm Tell. *Play.* (Sachtleben.)	48	113
Schoenfeld's German Historical Prose	80	127
Schrakamp's Sagen und Mythen	75	148
Berühmte Deutsche	85	149
Erzählungen aus der deutschen Geschichte	90	149
Schrakamp and van Daell's Das deutsche Buch	65	148
Simonson's German Ballad-book	1 10	114
Spanhoofd's Das Wesentliche der deutschen Grammatik	60	150
Sprechen Sie Deutsch? Boards	40	150
Stern's Studien und Plaudereien, *First Series.* New Edition	1 10	151
" " " im Vaterland. *Second Series*	1 20	153
Storm's Immensee. *Vocab.* (Burnett.) Boards	25	128
Teusler's Game for German Conversation. Ninety-eight Cards in a Box	80	153
Thomas's Practical German Grammar	1 12	154
Three German Comedies: Elz's Er ist nicht eifersüchtig, Benedix's Der Weiberfeind, and Müller's Im Wartesalon erster Klasse. Boards	30	114
Tieck's Die Elfen and Das Rothkäppchen. Boards	20	129
Vilmar and Richter's German Epic Tales. Boards	35	129
Wenckebach and Schrakamp's Deutsche Grammatik	1 00	156
Wenckebach's Deutsches Lesebuch	80	157
Deutscher Anschauungs-Unterricht	1 10	158
Die schönsten deutschen Lieder	1 20	114
Deutsche Sprachlehre	1 12	158
Whitney's Compendious German Grammar (*Key*, 80 cts.)	1 30	159
Brief German Grammar	60	160
German Reader in Prose and Verse	1 50	162
Introductory German Reader	1 00	161
German and English Dictionary	2 00	163
Whitney-Klemm: German by Practice	90	164
Elementary German Reader	80	164
Wichert's An der Majorsecke. (Harris.)	20	114
Wilhelmi's Einer muss heirathen. *Play.* Boards	25	114
Williams's Introduction to German Conversation	80	164
Witcomb and Otto's German Conversation	50	147
Zschokke's Neujahrsnacht and Der zerbrochene Krug. (Faust.)	25	129

FRENCH.

Achard's Le Clos Pommier. Paper	25	174
The same with De Maistre's Les Prisonniers du Caucase	70	174
Æsop's Fables in French	50	174
Alliot's Les Auteurs Contemporains	1 20	175
Contes et Nouvelles	1 00	191
Aubert's Littérature Française	1 00	175
Colloquial French Drill. Part I	48	191
The same. Part II	65	192
Balzac's Le Curé de Tours, avec autres contes. (Warren.)		175
Eugénie Grandet. (Bergeron.)	80	176
Bayard et Lemoine's La Niaise de Saint-Flour. *Play.* Paper	20	165
Bédollière's Histoire de la Mère Michel. *Vocab.*	60	176
The same. Paper	30	176
Bellows's Dictionary for the Pocket. Roan tuck	2 55	192
The same. Morocco tuck	3 10	192
French and English Dictionary. Larger-type Edition	1 00	192
Bevier's French Grammar		193
Bishop's Choy-Suzanne. Boards	30	177
Borel's Grammaire Française. Half roan	1 30	193
Bronson's Exercises in Everyday French. (*Key*, 60 cts.)	60	194

Henry Holt & Co.'s Educational Publications

	CATALOGUE PRICE	PAGE
Bronson's French Verb Blanks	$ 50	
Carraud's Les Gouters de la Grand'mère. Paper	20	177
With Ségur's *Petites Filles Modèles*	80	177
Chateaubriand's Les Aventures du dernier Abencérage. With extracts from *Atala, Voyage en Amérique*, etc. (Sanderson.) Boards	35	177
Choix de Contes Contemporains. (O'Connor.)	1 00	173
The same. Paper	52	178
Clairville's Petites Misères de la Vie Humaine. *Play.* Paper	20	165
Classic French Plays:		
Vol I. Le Cid, Le Misanthrope, Athalie	1 00	165
Vol. II. Cinna, L'Avare, Esther	1 00	165
Vol. III. Horace, Bourgeois Gentilhomme, Les Plaideurs	1 00	165
College Series of French Plays:		
Vol. I. Joie fait Peur, Bataille de Dames, Maison de Penarvan.	1 00	165
Vol. II. Petits Oiseaux, Mlle. de la Seiglière, Roman d'un Jeune Homme Pauvre, Doigts de Fée	1 00	165
Coppée's On Rend l'Argent. (Bronson.)	60	178
Coppée and De Maupassant: Tales. (Cameron.)	75	178
Corneille's Cid. (Joynes.) *Play.* Boards	20	166
Cinna. (Joynes.) *Play.* Boards	20	166
Horace. (Delbos.) *Play.* Boards	20	166
Curo's La Jeune Savante, with Souvestre's La Loterie de Francfort. *Plays.* Paper	20	173
Daudet's Contes. Including La Belle Nivernaise. (Cameron.)	80	179
La Belle Nivernaise. (Cameron.) Boards	25	179
Delille's Condensed French Instruction	40	194
De Neuville's Trois Comédies pour Jeunes Filles. I. Les Cuisinières. II. Le Petit Tom. III. La Malade Imaginaire. Paper	35	171
Drohojowska's Demoiselle de Saint-Cyr. With Souvestre's Testament de Mme. Patural. *Plays.* Boards	20	173
Erckmann-Chatrian's Le Conscrit de 1813. (Bôcher.)	90	180
The same. Boards	48	180
Le Blocus. (Bôcher.)	90	180
The same. Paper	48	180
Madame Thérèse. (Bôcher.)	90	180
The same. Paper	48	180
Eugène's Students' Grammar of the French Language	1 30	195
Elementary French Lessons	60	195
Fallet's Les Princes de l'Art	1 00	180
The same. Paper	52	180
Feuillet's Le Roman d'un Jeune Homme Pauvre. THE NOVEL. (Owen.)	90	181
The same. Paper	44	181
Le Roman d'un Jeune Homme Pauvre. THE PLAY. Boards.	20	167
Le Village. *Play.* Paper	20	167
Féval's Chouans et Bleus. (Sankey.)	80	181
The same. Paper	40	181
Fisher's Easy French Reading	75	195
Fleury's L'Histoire de France	1 10	195
Ancient History	70	195
Foa's Le Petit Robinson de Paris. *Vocab.*	70	181
The same. Paper	36	181
Contes Biographiques. *Vocab.*	80	181
The same. Paper	40	181
Fortier's Histoire de la Littérature Française	1 00	196
Gasc's Dictionary of the French and English Languages. 8vo	2 25	196
Pocket French and English Dictionary. 18mo	1 00	197
Translator	1 00	197
Girardin's La Joie fait Peur. *Play.* Paper	20	167
Halévy's L'Abbé Constantin. *Vocab.* (Super.) Boards	40	182
Hugo's Selections. (Warren.)	70	182
Ruy Blas. *Play.* (Michaels.) Boards	40	168
Hernani. *Play.* (Harper.)	70	167
Janon's Recueil de Poésies	80	168
Jeu des Auteurs. Ninety-six cards in a box	80	197
Joynes's Minimum French Grammar and Reader	75	198
Joynes-Otto's First Book in French. Boards	30	199

Henry Holt & Co.'s Educational Publications

	CATALOGUE PRICE	PAGE
Joynes-Otto's Introductory French Lessons	$1 00	199
Introductory French Reader	80	199
Labiche et Delacour's La Cagnotte. *Play.* Paper	20	168
Les Petits Oiseaux. *Play.* Paper	20	169
Labiche et Martin's La Poudre aux Yeux. *Play.* Paper	20	169
Lacombe's Petite Histoire du Peuple Français	60	182
La Fontaine's Fables Choisies. (Delbos.) Boards	40	169
Leclerq's Trois Proverbes. *Plays.* Paper	20	169
Macé's Bouchée de Pain. *Vocab.*	1 00	183
The same. *Vocab.* Paper	52	183
Madame de M.'s La Petite Maman. With Mme. de Gaulle's Le Bracelet. Paper	20	169
Matzke's French Pronunciation		
Mazères' Le Collier de Perles. *Play.* Paper	20	169
de Maistre's Voyage autour de ma Chambre. Paper	28	183
Méras's Syntaxe Pratique de la Langue Française	1 00	200
Légendes Françaises: No. 1. Robert le Diable	20	200
No. 2. Le Bon Roi Dagobert	20	200
No. 3. Merlin l'Enchanteur	30	200
Mérimée's Colomba. (Cameron.)	60	184
The same. Boards	36	184
Molière's L'Avare. *Play.* (Joynes.) Boards	20	170
Le Bourgeois Gentilhomme. *Play.* (Delbos.) Paper	20	170
Le Misanthrope. *Play.* (Joynes.) Boards	20	170
Moutonnier's Les Premiers Pas dans l'Étude du Français	75	201
Pour Apprendre à Parler Français	75	201
Musiciens Célèbres	1 00	184
The same. Paper	52	184
Musset's Un Caprice. *Play.* Paper	20	170
Otto's French Conversation-Grammar. Half roan. (*Key*, 60 cts.)	1 30	202
Progressive French Reader	1 10	202
Owen-Paget (The) Annotations		185
Parlez-vous Français? Boards	40	202
Porchat's Trois Mois sous la Neige	70	186
The same. Paper	32	186
Pressensé's Rosa. *Vocab.* (Pylodet.)	1 00	186
The same. Paper	52	186
Pylodet's Gouttes de Rosée	50	171
Leçons de Littérature Française Classique	1 30	204
Théâtre Français Classique. Paper	20	203
La Littérature Française Contemporaine	1 10	186
La Mère l'Oie. Boards	40	171
Beginning French. Boards	45	203
Beginner's French Reader. Boards	45	203
Second French Reader	90	203
Racine's Athalie. *Play.* (Joynes) Boards	20	171
Esther. *Play.* (Joynes.) Boards	20	171
Les Plaideurs. *Play.* (Delbos.)	20	171
Regent's French and German Poems. Boards	20	172
Riodu's Lucie	60	204
Sadler's Translating English into French	1 00	204
St. Germain's Pour une Épingle. *Vocab.*	75	187
The same. Paper	36	187
Sand's La Petite Fadette. (Bôcher.)	1 00	188
The same. Boards	52	188
Marianne. Paper	30	188
La Mare aux Diable. (Joynes.)		188
Sandeau's Mademoiselle de la Seiglière. *Play.* Boards	20	172
La Maison de Penarvan. *Play.* Boards	20	172
Scribe et Legouvé. La Bataille de Dames. *Play.* Boards	20	172
Les Doigts de Fée. *Play.* Boards	20	173
Scribe et Mélesville's Valerie. *Play* Paper	20	173
Segur's Les Petites Filles Modèles. Paper	24	188
Siraudin et Thiboust's Les Femmes qui Pleurent. *Play.* Paper	20	173
Souvestre's Un Philosophe sous les Toits	60	188
The same. Paper	28	188
La Vieille Cousine, with Les Ricochets. *Plays.* Paper	20	173

Henry Holt & Co.'s Educational Publications

	CATALOGUE PRICE	PAGE
Souvestre's La Loterie de Francfort, with Curo's La Jeune Savante. *Plays.* Boards	$ 20	173
Le Testament de Mme. Patural, with Drohojowska's Demoiselle de Saint-Cyr. *Plays.* Boards	20	173
Stern and Méras's Étude Progressive de la Langue Française	1 20	205
Taine's Les Origines de la France Contemporaine. (Edgren.) Boards	50	189
Thiers' Expédition de Bonaparte en Égypte. (Edgren.) Boards	35	189
Toepffer's Bibliothèque de mon Oncle. (Marcou.)		189
Vacquerie's Jean Baudry. *Play.* Paper	20	173
Verconsin's C'Était Gertrude. En Wagon. (Together.) *Plays.* Boards.	30	173
Verne's Michel Strogoff. (Lewis.)	70	190
Walter's Classic French Letters	75	190
Whitney's Practical French Grammar. Half roan. (*Key*, 80 cts.)	1 30	206
Practical French	90	207
Brief French Grammar	65	208
Introductory French Reader	70	209
Witcomb and Bellenger's Guide to French Conversation	50	210

GREEK AND LATIN.

Brooks's Introduction to Attic Greek	1 10	216
Goodell's The Greek in English	60	217
Greek Lessons. Part I. The Greek in English. Part II. The Greek of Xenophon	1 25	217
Judson's The Latin in English	1 00	218
Peck's Gai Suetoni Tranquilli De Vita Cæsarum Libri Duo	1 20	218
Latin Pronunciation	40	220
Preparatory Latin and Greek Texts	1 20	221
Latin part separate	80	221
Greek part separate	60	221
Richardson's Six Months' Preparation for Cæsar	90	221
Scrivener's Greek Testament	2 00	221
Williams's Extracts from Various Greek Authors	1 00	221

ITALIAN AND SPANISH.

ITALIAN.

Amicis' Cuore, abridged. (Kuhns.)		211
Montague's Manual of Italian Grammar. Half roan	1 00	213
Nota's La Fiera. Paper	60	211
Ongaro's Rosa dell' Alpi. Paper	60	211
Parlate Italiano? Boards	40	213
Pellico's Francesca da Rimini. Paper	60	211

SPANISH.

Caballero's La Familia de Alvareda. Paper	75	212
¿ Habla vd. Espanol ? Boards	40	212
¿ Habla v. Ingles ? Boards	40	212
Lope de Vega's Obras Maestras. Burnished buckram	1 00	212
Manning's Practical Spanish Grammar. (*Revised Ed.*)	1 00	212
Ramsey's Text-book of Modern Spanish	1 80	214
Sales's Spanish Hive	1 00	215

www.ingramcontent.com/pod-product-compliance
Lightning Source LLC
Chambersburg PA
CBHW020323240426
43673CB00039B/904